Praise for *Sub-Human*

"*Sub-Human* is the most-needed book for the Animal Freedom movement right now. Emma Hakansson gives us a wide, deep view of oppression that explains the links among speciesism, racism, sexism, and homophobia. Most importantly, she gives us strategic thinking and practical advice on how to make change. This book is the 'new testament' for the movement."—**Jim Mason**, author, *An Unnatural Order*

"This remarkable book opens readers' eyes and hearts to the critical intersections between human and non-human animals. The book's title says it all—humanity has assumed a hierarchical superiority over other animals. Emma Hakansson brings an impressive breadth of knowledge and critical thought to her work as she examines the history of animal exploitation, its deep connections to other forms of oppression, and the forces of change propelling the movement towards compassionate living. The points clearly come across that our survival as a species depends upon a transformation in perceptions of our kindred animals, and that each of us as individuals holds a unique privilege to create positive change."—**Dr. Joanne Kong**, editor of *Vegan Voices: Essays by Inspiring Changemakers*

"*Sub-Human* is an important contribution to the work we must put in to see total liberation for us all—nonhumans and humans. All animal advocates, and anyone interested in social justice and dismantling oppression, should read this book."—**Leah Garcés**, president of Mercy For Animals

"*Sub-Human* is a diligently researched and written book that is both provocative and utterly reasonable. Now more than ever, it's critical we understand that animal rights are a part of a wider movement for total justice, and *Sub-Human* argues this perfectly."—**Chris Delforce**, director of the *Dominion* documentary and executive director of Farm Transparency Project

"The movement for animal rights is inherently political, and *Sub-Human* explores just how the plight of animals, as well as people and the planet, relates to our current political context, and the history that led us here. It is an important read that helps us to better consider how we can best protect the animals exploited today."—**Georgie Purcell MP**, Animal Justice Party member and the youngest woman in the Victorian Parliament, Australia

"It's not enough to simply understand the issues. The importance lies in how you react to that knowledge. In *Sub-Human*, the enormity of the oppression is laid out before you, but so are the stories and philosophies of those who have fought to stop it. By learning about the issues, their interconnectedness, and the struggles to overcome them, the reader isn't simply educated, but passed a torch to carry on the fight."—**Jake Conroy**, activist, The Cranky Vegan

Sub-Human

A 21st-Century Ethic; on Animals, Collective Liberation, and Us All

Emma Hakansson

Lantern Publishing & Media • Woodstock & Brooklyn, NY

2024
Lantern Publishing & Media
PO Box 1350
Woodstock, NY
www.lanternpm.org

Printed in the United States of America

Library of Congress Cataloging-in-Publication Data

Names: Hakansson, Emma, author.
Title: Sub-human : a 21st-century ethic; on animals, collective liberation, and us all / Emma Hakansson.
Description: Woodstock, NY : Lantern Publishing & Media, [2024] | Includes bibliographical references.
Identifiers: LCCN 2023045550 (print) | LCCN 2023045551 (ebook) | ISBN 9781590567241 (paperback) | ISBN 9781590567258 (epub)
Subjects: LCSH: Animal rights. | Animal welfare. | BISAC: NATURE / Animal Rights | HISTORY / Social History
Classification: LCC HV4708 .H35 2024 (print) | LCC HV4708 (ebook) | DDC 179/.3—dc23/eng/20231204
LC record available at https://lccn.loc.gov/2023045550
LC ebook record available at https://lccn.loc.gov/2023045551

To the estimated 170 billion land and 2.4 trillion sea animals who were slaughtered in the time it took me to write this book, and to everyone deemed sub-human.

Thank you to Sebastiano Cossia Castiglioni for supporting the creation of this book.

Author's Note

This book was written in 2020 amid major lockdowns as COVID-19, a virus developed through the exploitation of our fellow animals, spread. Both a lot and very little has changed in the years between writing and publication. While an early 2023 edit served to update *Sub-Human* to ensure reference to legislation was up to date, inevitably, further changes—including positive progress—will have occurred in the global landscape since then. Please keep this in mind when reading.

Content warning: Please note that there are mentions of sexual assault on pages 38–42. Existential derealisation and suicide mentions are also present in the book. Please feel free to skip if these are topics close to you or they distress you. While much of this book is distressing, in many different ways, personal triggers are important to consider and these are themes I know need to be warned of. This book also mentions racism, xenophobia, homophobia, and of course speciesism, amongst a wide range of complex issues that intertwine.

Table of Contents

Acknowledgments

Thank you to everyone I interviewed during the research stage of this book's creation:

Iye Bako Collective liberation educator and activist, expert on veganism and capitalism

Alexandra Clark: Food policy consultant, involved with the United Nations, Humane Society, and EU Parliament

Jake Conroy: Former Stop Huntingdon Animal Cruelty organizer and prisoner, activist, strategic commentator

Sebastiano Cossia Castiglioni: Vegan activist and start-up investor

Chris Darwin: Conservationist, great-great-grandson of Charles Darwin, Darwin Challenge founder

Chris Delforce: Founder and executive director of Farm Transparency Project, creator of *Dominion*

Matthew Dominguez: Lawyer, political advisor at Voters for Animal Rights, chairperson at Barn Sanctuary

Leah Garcés: President of Mercy For Animals, author of *Grilled: Turning Adversaries into Allies*

Dr. Mehr Gupta: Doctor, College of Surgeons Global Health volunteer, Animal Liberation Tasmania founder

Rich Hardy: Undercover investigator, author of *Not as Nature Intended*

Dr. Helen Harwatt: Food and Climate Policy Fellow at Harvard Law School

Dr. Melanie Joy: Social psychologist, author, founder of Beyond Carnism and CEVA

Patty Mark: Founder of the Open Rescue movement and Animal Liberation Victoria

Dr. Ash Nayate: Neuropsychologist, activist

Georgie Purcell: Animal Justice Party MP and former president at Oscar's Law

Christopher Sebastian: Writer, researcher, lecturer

Connie Spence: Founder of the Agricultural Fairness Alliance

Peter Young: Former Animal Liberation Front prisoner, activist, "the one who got away"

The Voiceless Institute

Anonymous investigators

Introduction

Many of us may consider that the only regular contact we have with animals is with our companion dogs and cats, and with birds we see in the sky or on the street. But animals are everywhere. They lay on our plates, rise in our cakes, wrap over our feet, hang in our closets, fill our pillows, bubble in our soaps. They are caged in our countries, killed on our terms, paid for with our money. If we look around, their bodies are hidden in plain sight.

Most of us know to a degree what happens to the animals we farm, eat, and wear, and perhaps, too, what this means for our environment, fellow humans, and ourselves. Yet, most of us do not understand or feel this viscerally—and how could we, when most of our experiences with these animals are with their processed remains? To the majority of us, the lives of animals, beyond those we share our homes with, are invisible. Their rights, lives, and deaths are at most passing thoughts, perhaps ethical arguments to scroll past or discuss over dinner, to briefly consider and downplay. To animals, it is all they have.

Over 73 billion animals are slaughtered every year so that we can eat meat, dairy, and eggs, wear leather, wool, and down.[1] At a minimum, another 96 million animals are slaughtered specifically for their fur.[2] At least one trillion fish are estimated to be killed for our consumption annually.[3]

If we look only at the land animals we know as "farm animals," in the ten or so seconds you've just spent reading about their deaths, about 93 cows were killed. 181 sheep were slaughtered. 470 pigs, dead. 20,715 chickens, dead.

The human brain is not wired to be able to grasp the reality of how many lives lost this really is, or to grasp the enormity of any vast number of somethings. Instead, we can think of just one individual, and what it might be like when next in line at a slaughterhouse. For even one life to be lost. To be stolen.

Every second, every minute, every hour, and every day, more individuals have everything taken from them. As we lie in our beds, sit in our cars, wait for our trains, eat our dinners, and brush our teeth, it's happening. Picture them in our cages, in our sheds, in our paddocks being packed onto our trucks. In our abattoirs with the smell of death filling their noses and its sounds ringing in their ears.

When we justify violence against animals, silently and without conscious awareness each time we eat, wear, test on, exploit, own, and incarcerate them, we also justify violence against other beings, other humans.

When we accept oppression for some, we feed the oppression of others; we make space for domination driven by false ideas of inferiority, of lesser worth. When we discount the inherent preciousness of animals who think and feel, we erase precious parts of ourselves, of those we love, of us all. When we consider living beings as "livestock," it's no wonder we pillage the unthinking yet irreplaceable living Earth.

I get it. It's easier not to think about any of this. It's more comfortable. But here's one more thing we forget about animals and our proximity to them. We are around them all the time because we are them. We are the animals called "homo sapiens." We are just one of 8.7 million unique, known species on the planet, just 0.01 percent of life here.[4] We are a part of the most incredibly beautiful and complex web, one of such mysterious wonder it has inspired poetry, music, art, and our minds for millennia, as it will always continue to do.

Forgetting the relationship of this web and our own animality has allowed us to consider every species outside our own as "other," "less," "sub-human." It has allowed us to deem even some of those within our species as somehow less human, somehow more animal, and so somehow less precious. We offer some safeties and privileges only to those supposedly farthest from the animality innate within us all. But there is another way.

In coming to remember who we are, and who our fellow animals are, we can deconstruct the linear hierarchy of harm that we've built. We can grow in its place an ecosystem of perfect equilibrium.

The ramifications of following a way of life so intimately wrapped around death and hurting are everywhere, but it can be difficult to see these outward-rippling violences when they are all we have ever known. They are hard to confront as harms we contribute to, as they are likely to go against core parts of the beliefs we have carved out for ourselves. We are animal lovers; we are environmentalists; we stand for human rights and compassion, against brutality, corruption, and evil. Perhaps most important for us to know—we are capable of radical systemic change that aligns with these parts of who we are and want to be.

It is tremendously uncomfortable to learn things that grittily sand down the bones of what we were told, what we thought we knew, what we thought we were. It is phenomenally freeing to carve our own way, to align ourselves with our ethics.

We owe it to ourselves and to us all to sit with discomfort so we may have the freedom to know and form a world that is led by connection and compassion—with and for ourselves, and for each other. This book may bring about deep discomfort, but also a deepened relationship with all who make up this Earth that we so admire and cannot live without. By the end of the book, I promise any despondency will move into hope.

Part One

What We Do to Those "Sub-Human,"
Why We Think It's Normal

Chapter 1

This Is What We Know About Animals and How We Justify Their "Use"

Animals are both like and unlike us, but the latter has seen us frame them in a light that allows for their continued exploitation and suffering.

Consciousness and Sentience

Consciousness is the state of being aware and responsive to one's surroundings. Sentience is the capacity to feel, perceive, or experience subjectively. Philosophers often speak of *qualia*, individual instances of subjective, conscious experience. We all live and experience the same world from an utterly unique perspective. The moon I look at is the same moon you look at, but my biology and my experiences—my DNA, my physical capacities, each second of my waking life, my upbringing, my privileges, my pains, my education, my values—mean I experience watching the moon in a way that can never be quite the same as you do. I've broken my elbow, but I can't say I know exactly how someone else who broke their elbow felt. I've been through a breakup, but I don't know exactly what your breakup felt like. I like the taste of soymilk more than most other plant milks, but I don't know that my perception of the taste is the same as yours. Some people love coriander and other people are convinced it's a leaf that tastes of soap, which should stay far away from all food—I personally am not horrified by its existence in culinary work but have rarely chosen to cook with it myself.

Some philosophers question whether they know if anyone but themselves truly exists as a conscious, sentient being. René Descartes, perhaps one of the most famous philosophers, only felt certain he himself existed after meditating on the question for some time. Finally, he concluded that for him to question his existence, there must be a conscious "he" to do so—"I think, therefore I am." Descartes was untrusting of all his senses—perhaps every other person is an automaton, or a figment of his imagination; maybe we really are in the Matrix (at least some seventeenth century–thought version), you get the idea. It's a fascinating and perhaps frightening idea to consider that we don't know if anything other than ourselves is real, that we may indeed be dreaming this whole thing we think of as life. Extending this supposed uncertainty is also incredibly dangerous.

Descartes believed that animals were machines. Not that if you crack open the ribcage of a pigeon you'd find wires and metal, but that only the law of matter, the physical substance, was there. Basically, animals are not conscious or sentient. Their brain is just a lump of flesh that enables movement and engagement with an external world, but not thoughts or feelings. They may as well be intelligent robots that just happen to be, like us, made of flesh and bone, not mechanical pieces. It was with this belief in mind that Descartes threw himself heartily into the world of vivisection, dissecting animals alive as they screamed out in terror, convinced their screams were essentially the same as "Siri" or "Alexa" telling me I hurt her feelings by swearing at her. It's even said that Descartes nailed his wife's beloved dog to a chopping board and cut them open while they were conscious.

Today, with a far better understanding of animal brains—human or otherwise—we tend not to nail dogs to chopping boards. The Cambridge Declaration on Consciousness, written by "a prominent international group of cognitive neuroscientists, neuropharmacologists, neurophysiologists, neuroanatomists, and computational neuroscientists," declared that "humans are not unique in possessing the neurological substrates that generate consciousness."[1] Absurdly, this was considered to many as ground-breaking, released only in 2012. But vivisection is still thriving, beagles are one of the commonly exploited and slaughtered animals used as test subjects, and we kill all sorts of animals because we wish to eat and wear them. It's sort of phenomenal in a completely rubbish way that animal sentience needs to be argued, and even more so, that once we recognize it, often nothing really changes.

Partially, this is because we mistakenly focus far more on nonhuman animal intelligence than sentience. It's absolutely fascinating to know that the limbic system, a combination of multiple structures in the brain that deal with emotions and the formation of memories, in a whale is so intricate and large that it is perhaps more so than in a human. It's extremely intriguing that orcas in the wild have social rules that prohibit real violence. Astounding, that "they seem to have worked out a way to peacefully manage the partitioning of resources among different groups . . . something we humans haven't done yet," as Lori Marino, a neurobiologist who helped co-write The Declaration of Rights for Cetaceans, found.[2] These findings are seriously gripping and force us to consider intelligence beyond our own ways of living and communicating. But surely all we should need to know is that animals can feel physical and emotional pain for us to not inflict it upon them?

Does it matter that in many ways a pig is probably smarter than a dog?[3] No doubt it is interesting, and I don't question that learning about the intelligence of animals has built a human respect for them, but intelligence should not be the "boundary" by which we decide who ought to have freedom from suffering. In *Practical Ethics*, Peter Singer said that "to mark this boundary by some characteristic like intelligence or rationality would be to mark it in an arbitrary way."[4] It is no more defensible to deny someone their right to freedom, safety, and life based on their level of intellect than by race or sex.

We know less about fish than about other animals. We know that they can learn tricks, they have far better memories than we thought, they work as a team, trust and distrust each other, and even hold cultural customs. While compelling, none of these facts hold relevance to their equal right to safety from suffering and slaughter based on their equal capacity to suffer and feel pain.[5] Fish do not have a neocortex in their brain, but the Declaration on Consciousness found that the absence of this does not exclude an organism from "experiencing affective states." Fish are now recognized as, undeniably, able to feel pain. They choose comfort, can't concentrate on tasks well when they are hurt, and avoid what they are fearful of, what has caused them harm in the past. Perhaps their pain is different, but it is pain just the same.

We don't know that any one pain is the same. My opposition to the slaughtering of fish is akin to my opposition to the slaughtering of cows—I don't know exactly how it feels to be killed as a fish or a cow, but I (unsurprisingly) don't know how it feels to be killed as a human either. Because of qualia, I don't know that my being slapped in the face, even at the exact same force by the same hand in as similar conditions as possible, would feel the same as your being slapped in the face. I still promise I won't slap you in the face, because it would hurt you, a conscious and sentient being.

Speciesism and Carnism

We consider ourselves the most evolved animals in the world, to the point we have forgotten we are animals. We are both human and animal, just as someone can be both tiger and animal, chicken and animal, tuna and animal. When we think someone is selfish, we say that they think the world revolves around them. We as humans can quite collectively be so judged. Largely, this is the case because we consider that our coming to be as homo sapiens is the apex of evolution, and certainly the most important aspect, regardless of whether this is true or important.

As life on Earth evolved, it split off into different branches. A lot happened even before this, but 530 million years ago a fish with a backbone came to be. The first land-inhabiting animals entered the scene 500 million years ago—someone between a modern-day insect and crustacean. Approximately 460 million years ago, fish split into two—those with bones (think tuna) and those with cartilage (think sharks). A kind of bony fish eventually evolved into amphibian creatures, then came reptiles, followed by birds, and finally mammals. Over tens of millions of years, primates split off from one another and evolved into all sorts of different creatures—gibbons, orangutans, and gorillas among them. Eventually, 6 million years ago, those we consider "humans" diverged from their closest relatives, chimpanzees and bonobos.[6]

We look at the "great apes" as those closest to the supposed glory of humanness. While we admire their similarities to us, we also patronizingly find humor in their differences—their comfortably open nakedness and sexuality, or their defined "infantile" ways of communicating and throwing tantrums (as though an adult human has never lost it—I did so a few days ago). We seldom look at them and remark at their ability to live in a natural environment without destroying it, or admire how they groom and care for each other as a means of keeping peace, when we often are careless.[7]

Why have we decided that "latest to evolve" is akin to "greatest?" Bella is a Cavapoo I adopted before my awareness of the harmfulness of dog breeding. Right now, she is lying below my feet, mostly relaxing, sometimes looking expectantly up at me in hopes for a treat or walk. Hard to imagine as I look at her now, that she evolved from wolves, far later than I from apes. Is she greater than me? Is she greater than wolves? Are pigeons greater than eagles? Are salmon greater than great whites? Or are we all just different—different world debuts, different lineage, different abilities, different features, different skills, different ways of life?

Anyway, we humans think we're the best and, overall, love ourselves sick. The bee's knees but better—maybe we start saying human's knees? It follows that as a rule of opposable thumb, the less like "us" (with an idea of the "most human," "us" generally centering masculinity, heteronormativity, whiteness, and an able body and mind, not just species) we recognize someone to be, the less we value them, and the worse we treat them. It's true—no one is safe from our callousness no matter how close to human another animal may be, chimpanzee test subjects being the most jarring example of our blanketed insistence of human superiority and sequential right to the bodies of other species. But the rule of proximity as protection generally applies. Plenty of people don't eat pigs because they hear about their intelligence being on some levels akin to a human toddler, but will eat chickens, deemed far "less than" us. For about a year, I said that I didn't eat animals, but I ate fish (revoking their claim to animality because of my inability to connect to their scaley sentience, though it was there all the same).

The Oxford Dictionary defines "speciesism" as the assumption of human superiority leading to the exploitation of animals. But it's not just human and non-human; there's a hierarchy amongst all those below us, the "sorry non-people." It's why people who begin working in laboratories are eased into animal testing through rats before they graduate to dogs and monkeys, and more relatable to most of us, it's where carnism comes in.[8]

A sub-ideology, or specific expression of speciesism, is carnism, relating more specifically to the animals we eat—"carn" meaning "of the flesh." Dr. Melanie Joy, who coined the term and shared it with the world in her book *Why We Love Dogs, Eat Pigs, and Wear Cows*, speaks to the importance of naming an ideology. Veganism is an ideology many have something to say about. Until recently, carnism was an invisible ideology, so little could be said of it. People choose to become vegan based on their ethics, but due to carnism's predominantly invisible existence, people do not realize they also choose to be—and stay—a carnist.[9]

Fed by speciesism, carnism keeps us feeding on flesh through mythmaking. From the moment we are born, most everything in the world is positioned to tell us the story of eating (and wearing) animals—it is natural, it is normal, it is necessary. We've done it forever, everyone else does it, our wellbeing requires it. These three justifications are baseless distractions from the world we could have, forms of moral disengagement used to justify continuing on as per usual.[10] The strong taking from the weak would largely be considered *natural*. What is *normal* changes all the time (think of the many historically accepted human rights violations that are now illegal). The existence of millions of thriving vegans is proof that carnism is generally not *necessary* to our existence—and as we will see, in fact works against our most peaceful and well way of life.

Arguments in favor of carnism often revolve around the idea that there are "food animals," somehow different to who we consider companion or wild animals. One of my favorite absurd arguments is, "If we aren't meant to eat animals, why are they made of meat?"—as though we too are not made of flesh (unless everyone around me is an automaton or figment of my imagination and Descartes was right). But why are some animals food? Why are some animals friends? Why did we all love watching *Finding Nemo* and chant "fish are friends, not food" along with Bruce the no-fish-for-me shark and conveniently forget that as we munched our freezer fish fingers or sushi? There is no sound reason for one animal to be considered food but not another—and this is made clear in our hypocritical shock and disgust at cultures different from ours eating different animals than us. Dogs are eaten by some in Cambodia, kangaroos are eaten by some in Australia, moose are eaten by some in Sweden, cats are eaten by some in China, and lambs are eaten by some in England. Is there any tangible difference between these deaths and meals, or just one perceived through tradition and mythmaking, the persistent whispers in our ears and messages filtered through our eyes that tell us what, or who, is here as food and here for us? The last animal flesh I ate was cut from a moose while living with my Swedish family. Somehow, eating them, an animal I had not previously considered food, was what made me realize something was off about eating animals, and that it was not what I wanted to do anymore.

Animals to "Livestock"

Our ability to disconnect ourselves from the reality of animal eating, wearing, and killing is the most powerful weapon in carnism's arsenal. We disconnect by changing the words we use—dead bodies, carcasses, and butchered flesh become meat. Cow skin becomes leather. Boiled animal tendons, bones, and ligaments become gelatine. We also change what words themselves mean. If I ask if you feel like eating chicken or fish tonight, do you picture what's on your plate, or do you picture animals—a chicken, a fish? The objectification of animals is so deeply defined, rooted in centuries of culture and tradition, that we may sooner picture cooked carcasses than living animals themselves when offered their species name. Animals have become "livestock"—stocks for trade and profit, who just happen to live and breathe, think and feel. When we talk about the potential for fishless oceans, scientists and media often refer to "depleted fish stocks," rather than endangered species or mass killings of trillions of individuals.

Pigs and sheep on farms and rabbits and rats in test facilities are identified by numbers. Reduced to a series of digits, so disposable are these individuals that names would be a waste of time, and perhaps worse, an opportunity for us to connect to who we harm. My favorite antidote to despondency when thinking about this disconnect is the story of a woman called Renee who married Tommy, a fourth-generation cattle rancher in Texas. When Renee moved to the ranch, she began to spend time with the animals. Tommy told her, "Don't name those cows."[11] She didn't listen, and now, years later, that ranch is known as *Rowdy Girl Sanctuary*, that couple is vegan, and they run an advocacy program helping ranchers develop sustainable businesses on the land, without rearing animals. Identity matters to us all, and our revoking of it allows violence.

The root of our linguistic objectification of animals is the word "it." Notice how you use this word around them. The first time I ever considered my own use of the word was at a slaughterhouse vigil. We were bearing witness, showing a little love to chickens who did not know human care, before their throats would be cut. We were stopping trucks from entering so we could document the condition of individual chickens before they inevitably went through the gates to their death. You will not die unremembered, is the point. Crammed into stacked-high pallets on the stopped truck, I noticed a chicken upside down, panting, eyes barely open, blood on their wings. I brought over Lizzi, who was running Melbourne Chicken Save at the time, and offered what was clear to me: "It's upside down and its wing is all bloody." Lizzi, who is a bit older than my Mum, and who has bleached hair and always wears thick, black eyeliner, listened to me empathetically and simply said, "'Their,' love." I looked blank, so she repeated, gently, "We don't call animals 'it.' He, she, and if we don't know, they." I looked at this chicken, feeling a little stunned, and put my finger through a gap in the pallet and stroked them. They calmed a little, their heart and breath slowing steadily in response.

As I hurt for this individual chicken and what came next for them, I realized the incredible power to diminish and deny suffering that my words had. If this chicken really were an "it," none of this would matter. "Its" don't pant, don't bleed, don't panic, don't feel soothed by gentle touch. I don't lie in bed at night thinking of the vegetable crops I've seen growing in paddocks or being chopped up on a cutting board; I think of the animals I have heard cry out or seen be shot in the head. I think of the billions no one will ever see, but who bleed and fall to the floor just the same. That chicken was killed years ago now. They have long been plucked and gutted, they have been eaten, digested, and excreted by someone faceless to me, who saw their meal as faceless, too. The meal won't be remembered, but they have not been forgotten.

Just as it's easier to put "keratin" rather than "animal hoof" moisturizing conditioner in our hair, it's easier to be served minced meat than a spit-roasted pig, less contentious to wear tanned cow skin leather than recognizably once-alive mink fur. Do Western cultures rarely eat animal brains, hearts, and tongues because they don't taste as good, or because recognizing a butchered individual on our plate leaves a bad taste in our mouths? Animals as themselves, rather than as consumable objects, are absent in our feasts on their flesh, of our draping ourselves in parts of their bodies. It's easier that way.

Further, animals are deindividualized. Not only do the stack of woollen sweaters or markets full of sausages not really remind us of animals, farmed animals themselves do not compute as truly "animal" to us. Imagine you saw a pride of lions lazing in the sun, a pack of wolves skulking, a family of deer nibbling on grass. You see a group of individuals, you consider their experience, their feelings. Imagine you see a paddock of grazing sheep, of resting cows. Often, unless we spend some time considering them, they appear to us as a collective, an unthinking mob. They are animals, but they are missing something, not quite animal in the way they would be if they were a clowder of cats and kittens roaming the countryside.

What is missing, though, is not from them but from us. When we take in the world around us, our ears full of "it" animals, our eyes absorbing advertisements for barbecue pork ribs, soft poached eggs, smooth goat's cheeses, fluffy down pillows, and supple leather sofas, we must inevitably let go of a deeper understanding we once had of these animals. Children new to the world see a cow and they are more likely to see an animal the way we might see some enormous dog. They see a life, and perhaps they see a friend.[12] If we weren't to grow out of this view, if we were to truly see a cow for who she is, the vast majority of us likely could not comfortably wear leather, eat beef, drink milk, or lick dairy ice cream like we do. The truths of who animals are and what we do to them are just too confronting when put together, so we dull the former from our minds.

We think that dogs and cats are unique in their way of loving us, but I've snuggled by fireplaces with lambs and eaten lunch as a turkey snoozed on my lap. When animals do not show us love, it is because we give them no reason to. How disjointed a thought to think the uninterested animal as "less than" because they won't engage with the species who sends their sons and daughters to slaughter, who cuts off their tails or the tips off their beaks, who pierces plastic tags with numbers through their ears sooner than names them. As a species other than human, it is mostly safest to stay away from us.

Humane Myth

The world is waking up to the pivotal ways in which our fellow animals are just like us. By and large, even if we disregard it, even if we feed on the myths, we mostly all have felt a knot in our stomach at some time. We've had a prickly thought piercing out from our subconscious that the animals we kill share the same emotional, thoughtful lives as the animals we love. It's a deeply unpleasant thought because if any of us were to see our dog or cat go through the same slaughterhouse the animals who became our lunch or shoes did, we would be traumatized. So why do we think that same end is acceptable for sheep, chickens, ducks, pigs, or cows? We tell ourselves that since it is *normal* to kill these particular animals, it must be *humane.*

What is humane? To be humane is defined as having and showing compassion or benevolence—it is a quality of kindness. Kindness is not in well wishes or good intentions; it is seen in tangible action in how we relate to and treat others. In 1958, the United States created the Humane Methods of Slaughter Act, intended to prevent the "needless suffering" of farmed animals we kill—except for farmed birds like chickens and turkeys, who to this day are not included in the act—they're thought of as not "animal" enough.[13] The Royal Society for the Prevention of Cruelty to Animals (RSPCA) defines humane slaughter as "when an animal is either killed instantly or rendered insensible until death ensues, without pain, suffering, or distress."[14] I recognize that yes, I would rather be killed quickly, shot in the head, my throat slit so I would bleed out and die, than be cut at the throat, have my skin ripped off, and my body sawn apart while conscious. Obviously. Absolutely, for me, and for anyone, that would mean less suffering and less distress. But if I, my dog Bella, or a protected species were killed in this more efficient and "humane" manner, we would not consider the perpetrator humane.

My killer, who would be legally defined as a murderer, would be seen as sick, not humane. Maybe some would even call him an animal in an attempt to detach him from his humanity entirely—so wrongly can it be thought that kindness or morality are exclusive to humans. If he (and I use "he" and "his" because most women are killed by men, and particularly men they have had a relationship with[15]) were to justify his actions by claiming the way he slaughtered me was painless and that I didn't suffer long, people would be mortified. The means simply do not justify the end, not even a little bit. I know the ways I'd prefer to be killed if I had to choose one, but I still certainly want to live. I know at this point you might think I'm losing you, how ridiculous for me to compare a man slaughtering me with a man slaughtering a cow, a duck, or a fish, but that's the point. This is speciesism, this is carnism. Humane slaughter is always a fiction when the individual wants to live. Animals do not go willingly to their deaths.

When we talk about humane animal farming, we think not only of a humane killing, but a humane life. We picture an illustration in a children's book where, unlike most real farms, a chicken lays her egg in a rustic wooden box laid with hay before roaming a meadow. We don't think of this hen sitting in the same wire cage or crammed shed, out of sunlight, for all or at least most of her life. We picture a fantasy, or at best, a rare exception from the norm.

In Australia, about 90 percent of pigs and broiler chickens are factory-farmed.[16] In the United States, 99 percent of all farmed animals live in factory farms, including 70.4 percent of "beef and dairy" cows and 98.2 percent of chickens raised for eggs.[17] Meanwhile, 70 percent of all animals in the United Kingdom live in factory-farms, too.[18] Despite the grass and sunshine, the rarer animals kept in free-range systems are still overwhelmingly victims of agonizing but legal mutilations like dehorning, tail docking, and castration without pain relief. The case is the same across much of the world.

Regardless of the life an animal lived, to forget that they were bred purely to be slaughtered is a mistake. Farmed animals are forced to exist in whichever conditions we choose, often through artificial insemination, always through controlled breeding, and only for the short amount of time we need to make the most profit from them until or when we decide to kill them.

Bob Comis was a pig farmer featured in the documentary *The Last Pig*. He raised "happy pigs" and felt he had an obligation to give them the best lives he could. The pigs were free to roam in nature, to sleep in warm, deep, straw-laid barns on cold nights, to play in puddles as Bob laughed with them. He recalls: "Their various expressions of contentment, of happiness, are infectious." This is exactly the life sold by adverts of humane meat, ethically sourced leather, wool, dairy, or eggs. A happy life traded in for what a butcher described to me once as "one bad day." But it is not so simple. When speaking of the pigs he raised and the good lives he gave them, Bob said: "What they don't know is that this communion is a lie. I am not their herd-mate. I am a pig farmer . . . and sometime soon, I am going to have them killed." Bob is no longer a pig farmer, but is now a vegan, growing vegetables and writing.[19]

There is no mutual agreement, there is no consent. We recognize the innocence of animals that comes with their, in some ways, lesser understanding of the world and their engagement with us. We cannot claim partnership in this linear kill system. It is the most spectacular form of victim-blaming to suggest someone's enjoying the small comforts we give them in life somehow means their lives are shortly owed to us in return. We lie to ourselves, and we collectively feed off that lie when we claim the dead animals in our fridges and wardrobes came to be that way through compassion and benevolence. We decimate our own humanity when we put the word "humane" anywhere close to the needless slaughter of living beings.

All these animals are killed at a fraction of their natural lifespan. If we believe animals deserve good lives, the way they are slaughtered is perhaps not even the part of their life to focus on. We should focus on what they lost, what we deny them. The years in the sunshine, the nuzzles with family members, the thirst-quenching slurp of fresh water, the curious excitement of something new, the contentment of a good meal. The right to grow old. When we see advertisements for touted-humane products made from their bodies, we must not see just the short life she lived, but the life that was stolen from her. A life made only to be shortly taken away because you are considered more "product" than "person" is not a life anyone would wish to live, let alone describe as compassionate. Our fellow animals are certainly more person than they are product. Philanthropist Philip Wollen once said, "In their capacity to feel pain and fear, a pig is a dog is a bear is a boy." We cannot rationalize killing someone who does not want to die any better because of their species.

Chapter 2

This Is What We Do to Animals

An insight into the treatment of animals who are exploited under our will.

Animals Used for Food

How many farmed animals have you met? Chickens, sheep, pigs, ducks, fish, cows, rabbits, turkeys? How many have you felt—their soft fur or feathers against your fingers, their slimy scales gliding by you? How many of their eyes have you looked into, how many of their hearts have you felt beating? Most significant of all, how many of these animals have you tasted?

My favorite meat used to be lamb, specifically lamb shanks. Slow-cooked for hours, it was the special meal I'd ask my mum to cook for my birthday. Shank meat comes from the upper legs of lambs. I didn't know that until a few minutes before I wrote this, and I feel quite squeamish now. I've fostered rescued lambs, and I've massaged their little legs affectionately, particularly with Foggy, who had difficulty walking in his first days of life. If you have a companion animal—a dog, a cat—run your hands over their bodies. Pet them. Feel their rib bones under their fur-covered skin, feel their heart beating beneath it all. Feel their warmth. The same love and tenderness you feel for them, I feel for Foggy, for Willow, for Claude, and for every lamb I have had the pleasure to know. The tenderness of flesh like theirs is something I am sorry to know, sorry to have ground my teeth over.

Here is a glimpse into the lives and deaths of just two animals considered food and food-makers.

Killed for Their Flesh

Some 66 billion chickens are slaughtered and eaten every year.[1] The chickens we eat are called broilers, and mostly they have white feathers, red combs, and yellow feet. They have been selectively bred and genetically altered to grow 300 percent faster than they did in the 1960s.[2] Google what a "meat chicken" looked like then—they look like the small, gawky cousins of today's supposedly most delicious birds. A current-day broiler can reach a weight of 4.8 lbs (2.2kg) in just over a month.[3] Farmed chickens are not raised to live more than a couple weeks beyond that at absolute most. If a human baby grew that fast, a two-month-old would weigh 661 lbs (300kg).[4] It's all a little bit Frankenstein's monster, and it's this way because if baby chicks grow to slaughter weight faster, they can be killed faster. Less time alive is fewer days to feed someone. More money, less time. By and large, mainly four international poultry genetics companies sell breeder chickens with "improved genetics" across the world so that everywhere, chickens may continue to be killed younger for the same if not more profit as before.[5]

All this speed is not something the chickens have benefitted from. Aside from the obvious downfall of being bred only to be killed as a month-old-if-that baby, their short lives are literally crippling. Growing to such mutant size so quickly means lameness, leg injuries, and difficulty walking.[6]

Sudden death syndrome is a common metabolic disorder in fast-growing broilers. Casually referred to in the industry as "flip-over," birds convulse and are found dead, stuck on their backs, legs up as they become too weak to turn over again. Another reason broilers commonly die on farms is from heart failure. Despite their enormous mass of muscle and flesh, their heart is still only able to pump blood to the same capacity as if they were not an utterly deformed breed. Their hearts simply cannot keep up.[7]

Whether crammed by the many tens of thousands in sheds for their entire lives, even in many "humane"-approved systems, or one of the incredibly small percentage of chickens that is farmed free-range, they're all trucked to the same abattoirs. Outside slaughterhouses, I've often watched wistfully as trucks pick up neatly packaged bodies—some with proud "organic" and "free-range" labels on them, others with none of the sort. Some with imagery of grass and sky, those often owned by companies that don't farm free-range anyway. With their lives lasting in some cases as little as twenty-one days, and at "best" short of two months, which truck we buy from ultimately makes little difference to the birds who want to live. Taken off one truck coming into such a place came Isaac, who lived happily for four full years despite his chronic health issues.[8]

In the abattoir, the method of slaughter we consider to be our absolute global best is as follows: chickens are shackled by their feet and hung upside-down on a moving chained line. Flapping their wings, their heads are dunked into electrified water, stunning them. Shortly after, a mechanical blade slices across their throats, spraying blood onto feathers. A meat worker stands by to kill anyone who has survived the ordeal. All a chicken need do to be cut open fully conscious is raise their head above the water. This has been seen in hidden camera footage—though it's not hard to imagine.[9]

Killed for Their Secretion

It's not only those whose flesh we eat that die for our food, but those in the egg and dairy industries. For now, let's look at dairy. Animals raised for dairy are treated essentially the same. Let's look at goats, because we hear about them less despite the breadth of their exploitation. Their milk is drunk, turned into cheese, yogurt, and baby formula (as well as skincare products).

Like every other mammal on Earth—cats, cows, and humans included—female goats only produce milk after they have been pregnant and given birth to their offspring. Humans only need to drink milk when we are breastfeeding, and human milk is nutritionally perfect for us. Only baby goats (kids) need to drink goat's milk (note the apostrophe, even language tells us the milk is theirs), which is different and nutritionally perfect for them.

The female babies are taken from their mothers to grow into milkers themselves. Their mothers' only perceived value is monetary, so as their milk production slows, they are "culled." Their daughters are their replacements, and the cycle continues.

Some male kids are raised and killed for meat, though most are killed within a few days, many within the first twenty-four hours of their lives. In 2019, while working for Animal Liberation Victoria, for the first time in the world we exposed what is completely legal in Australia, the United States, the United Kingdom, New Zealand, and most other countries—newborn male goat kids being killed with blunt force.[10]

At this particular farm, it was a metal pipe. I still remember seeing it all for the first time. The huge pile of tiny, stiff, and lifeless bodies. Their eyes popped out of their sockets. Their coagulated blood on their pure white coats. In the footage, one goat is picked up by their "scruff" and thrown to the ground. Letting out a cry, he gathers himself and runs for a second before being clubbed to death. The sound of metal on bone reverberates. He never stood a chance. He convulses on the ground and is hit again. That part isn't legal—they're supposed to be killed in one blow, but there is nothing measured or scientific about a man with a metal pole killing kids while their mothers watch.

I fostered Atlas and Mercury, near-newborn goats who were rescued from that farm. Mercury didn't survive more than a month, nor did a few other of the kids who were rescued, because they were in such poor health from day one. Atlas is one of my favorite beings. He is cheeky, thinks he deserves the world, and is incredibly cuddly. When I sit with him, I feel both complete joy that he is safe and alive and utter despair that he is the exception. The farm he comes from continues to kill every dairy season, as all farms do, across the globe.

Animals Used for Fashion

The animals who are used and killed for fashion often live and always are killed violently and without grace. Skins ripped from carcasses, bloody mutilations, caged existences, and terror transform behind closed doors into the sleekest purses, the most elegant coats, the cosiest sweaters, and the sexiest stilettos.

Joshua Katcher dedicated his book, *Fashion Animals*, to "every animal whose body has vanished into a silent fashion object." Leo Tolstoy—a historical vegetarian—said "how complete is the delusion that beauty is goodness."[11]

Though sometimes we may prefer for it to be so, most of us do not truly consider beauty to be enough. Is the dress still beautiful if the woman who made it is impoverished by her poor treatment? Is the shoe still perfect if the baby cow who died for it bled hot red onto the cold of the abattoir kill floor? What suffering can we happily pay for, and whose lives can we live with ourselves for taking?

Killed for Their Fur

While we see less floor-length mink fur coats parading down the street than we used to, the fur industry is very much alive (profit-wise anyway; otherwise, it's very much full of dead animals). Just as fur coats were once commonly and acceptably made of dogs we consider "pets," the way we now wear fur has changed, too.[12]

A "rich-looking" fox fur coat, though still certainly produced and considered a luxury that some demand is their right, is shunned by many. Certainly, most people don't tend to drape foxes around their necks—head, tail, and all—anymore. But a parka with a far less identifiably "animal" trim made of a dead coyote? Still cool to some. A fluffy white-fur bobble on a key ring or beanie? That's cute. Even a soft draped vest, light sections of rabbit's fur knitted delicately into it, is deconstructed enough to make the rabbit more "fluff" than "friend."

While the furs may be presented differently, dyed into unnatural colors that help us forget who they once were, the "who" is very much the same. Minks are the most killed "fur animals." Foxes, raccoon dogs, chinchillas, coyotes, and rabbits are "pelted," too. "Pelting" is the industry term that means slaughtering and skinning, though that sounds less clean, luxurious, or victimless.

Two common ways animals who are factory-farmed for their fur are slaughtered are with gas-chamber boxes and by anal probe electrocution. The industry thought themselves clever to develop these methods, protecting "their" furs from profit-damaging blood and cuts.[13]

Before their death, these animals—except free-living animals like coyotes who are caught in painful steel traps, known to prefer to gnaw their own trapped limb off than to remain caught—live their lives in cages. Minks and foxes are both territorial species who would naturally roam wide, and, in the case of minks, enjoy swimming. But when kept in close confines, they often resort to cannibalism. Maddened by their incarceration, they pace their tiny cages, spending hours repetitively circling and nodding their heads, over and over again.[14]

Killed for Their Skin

Over 371 million bovine animal skins are produced each year. "Produced" means cattle- and buffalo-bred, mutilated, slaughtered, and skinned. In the case of mutilation, their budding horns are often cut or burned off their heads without pain relief. These animals stand on often cleared land that is rid of wildlife, and are normally just a few years old when it's deemed time for them to be skinned, becoming wallets, belts, shoes, and bags. Contrary to misguided popular belief, leather is not a worthless by-product of the meat industry, but a valuable co-product. When skins don't sell as leather becomes less popular, slaughterhouses make significantly less profit. The idea that skins are used purely for waste reduction is naive and forgets that we live in a supposedly "free-market" capitalist world where money comes first. Why would anyone bother fleshing and processing skins into leather unless it turned a profit?[15]

The most valuable cow skin is the youngest cow skin. This is where the dairy industry comes in. Newborn male bobby calves killed in the dairy industry, and those raised for veal, have skin that is soft, supple, and unmarked by a life that may include bug bites, branding, and barbed wire. "Animal welfare" organization the RSPCA (much to say on this later), which endorses "humane" veal, states that "valuable hides" can be produced from the dairy industry. They claim that raising calves for young, pink meat and soft skin offers a "real opportunity" to give these animals a "life worth living." Yes, letting baby cows live for some weeks rather than some days is doing them a favor, even "improving" their "welfare."[16]

The leather industry states, too, that as the veal-eating population declines, in some countries there are not enough cows to produce the quality hides luxury brands demand. So, calves are raised in pens, never to go outside until they're trucked to their slaughter, filling the gap. It's just supply and demand. As total ethical alternatives to leather—free from animals and plastic alike—become the new norm, as is expected, the cattle industry as a whole will be forced to shrink.[17]

The first time I really recognized leather as skin, I'd already stopped buying it. Continuing to wear my most trusted vintage Dr. Martens, I rescued two cows, Malayla and Elira. Learning to trust me, Elira would lean forward from as far back as possible to take treats from my hand, her big tongue slobbering on me. A piece of her snack dropped out of my hand, landing on my shoe, amongst the grass. She licked that shoe, and so she licked another cow's skin. No amount of chemical processing has made me able to forget leather's origin since. I never wore them again.

Killed for Their "Fiber"

Animals exploited and killed for fiber, reduced to material, include geese and ducks for down, goats for cashmere, as well as alpacas and sheep for wool. "Okay you've lost me now, sheep aren't killed for wool, it's just like a haircut" I hear you respond. You're technically correct, but it's also more complicated.

If you are a domesticated sheep, your lineage goes back to the mouflon, an animal who still exists today and who, unlike you, has a thin wool layer covered by hair that is shed in the summer to avoid overheating. You have been selectively bred to have as much wool as possible because humans like to wear it. If you're a merino, like 70 percent of the sheep in Australia, the largest wool-producing country, you've also been selectively bred. Today, you grow more, finer wool, on more folds of skin—increasing your chance of flies feeding on your skin. So, the "sheep need to be shorn" thing is an issue we created. If we stop breeding sheep so we can eat and wear them, this problem is solved.[18]

Anyway, back to death. Kept quiet by the wool industry is that sheep are considered "dual-purpose," raised for both wool and meat. Essentially, every sheep will be slaughtered, it's just a matter of when. Whether a farm's primary focus is meat or wool, farms that raise woolly sheep deal in both, and so of course kill animals. Many are slaughtered for meat as lambs at about nine months of age, if not younger. Whether the lambs are shorn for wool prior or kept with long wool for slaughter is dependent on if farmers will make more money from the wool or the skin at the time—and often, shorn then slaughtered is more profitable.[19] While sheep who don't have wool of a quality worth keeping them alive for are slaughtered younger, those selected for "wool-growing" live to be only about five or six years old, half their natural lifespan. The industry has named this being "cast for age," and these slaughters occur because a sheep's wool quality decreases, becoming more brittle while aging, as our hair does.[20]

The eventual slaughter of sheep in the wool industry is only one aspect. There's also the 10–15 million lambs who die every Australian winter lambing season in the first forty-eight hours of their lives. There's the near-globally legal standard practice of unmedicated tail docking, most commonly performed with a sharp or hot knife, as well as tight rubber rings. There's the cruel shearing practices, the battering of animals that is seen time and time again by undercover investigators across the world. The truth about wool is complex, brutal, and successfully hidden.[21]

Animals Used for Scientific Testing

The argument for and against animal testing, or vivisection (performing operations and experiments on live animals for research), is often dominated by a rhetoric that follows along these lines: "No, animals shouldn't be tested on for our vanity, cosmetics, and such. But for medicine and the health of humans, it is a necessary evil, and to argue against animal testing is to argue that hundreds or thousands of rats, dogs, or chimps are more important than the potential saved lives of millions of humans." But even with ethics aside, the data lies in favor of protecting these animals, as it also protects us humans.

The failure rate of preclinical testing of medications today, in an animal testing–centric medical world, is 96 percent. This means that only 4 percent of drugs, ingredients, and products that seem safe for some non-human animals are actually safe for humans and go to market. In no other field would such a low rate be considered something safe or worth continuing with. According to John Ioannidis, professor of health research and policy at Stanford, in *The Collaborative Approach to Meta-Analysis and Review of Animal Data from Experimental Studies*, which has been at the forefront of conducting systematic reviews of animal studies, found that it is "nearly impossible to rely on most animal data."[22]

The funding given to vivisection—something that began in ancient times and frankly hasn't evolved tremendously since—should be diverted elsewhere. There are scientists working with ethically sourced, donated human cell culture and isolated tissue, 3D-printed human living tissue, human computer models and tests, and a plethora of other modern medical practices already in use today. These methods are relevant to our physiology, unlike testing, say, how a human heart may respond to something by looking at the heart of a rat or a dog.

Despite all of this, in your (nearest) city, it is likely there is a university basement filled with caged animals who will be tested on until their "purpose" has been fulfilled and they are killed. Millions of animal test subjects are vivisected for needless basic research, when not required by regulators and when there are so often valid alternatives.[23]

In Alex Lockwood's *Test Subjects*, three doctors share their experience in having tested on animals and come to the conclusion that it is simply "not good science" to do so. Dr. Frances Cheng kept a tally of all the animals she killed to collect data that ultimately did not translate to humans, as is so often the case. Now, working to help large companies agree to switch over and put policy in place stating that they will not "conduct, fund, or commission animal testing," Cheng is in the "net positive," having saved more animals than she has killed. Dr. Emily Trunnell, who has a rat tattoo on her arm, works in science and at a policy level, helping to leave animal testing in the past: "I feel like I'm going to be on the right side of history."[24]

Killed for Medical Testing

They All Had Eyes: Confessions of a Vivisector, written by Michael Slusher, begins with a dedication: "To the many animals whom I tortured and killed in the name of science. If there is a hell, I will spend it forever looking into their eyes." It can be hard to imagine how someone becomes a vivisector, seeing animals as tools, comfortable with the disposability of animal life inherent to vivisection. Slusher began working in research labs first by weighing rats, then by piercing their ears for identification tagging, next injecting them, then gassing them to death, removing and studying their organs, throwing them away. From mice and rats, he moved to dogs, and eventually, to primates. When we value the lives of some animals more than others, and when violence against them creeps up on us, it is normalized. It is frighteningly easy for people to come to do terrible things. It's not so different from how we come to accept eating or wearing animals, we're just farther removed.

Slusher recalls tests (which never resulted in a cure or treatment), where he pierced glass into the eyes of rats, and where they were force-fed liquids that burnt their stomachs, forming ulcers in them until they were "rotting from the inside out," their intestines "twisted into tight, dense masses." He remembers puppy-farmed medical testing beagles, who are "bred for an amazing amount of docility and trust." He recalls betraying their trust as they wagged their tails, "so happy to be held" when taken out of their cages on the final day of their testing lives, of their entire lives—killed because they were no longer useful.

Philosopher Charles Magel said, "Ask the experimenters why they experiment on animals, and the answer is, 'Because the animals are like us.' Ask the experimenters why it is morally okay to experiment on animals, and the answer is, 'Because the animals are not like us.'"[25] True for all animal test subjects, this is especially confronting when considering primate testing. Slusher's experience with our closest relatives, a little monkey, was "the beginning of the end of [his] career as a monster." "Tiny fingers and fingernails, much like a newborn infant, grasped onto my index finger as if asking for just a moment of love. . . . [The monkey] maintained as much contact with me as possible, pressing his little body up against the bars of the cage in hopes that I would stroke him and never leave his side."

While this particular monkey looked at Slusher meekly, the older monkeys glared with hatred. Working the latches of their cages and escaping, grabbing syringes out of his hands and throwing them, speaking up for themselves, monkeys fought back. "Loud, cacophonous noise nearly made me jump out of my skin. The screeching, the crashing of metal on metal . . . helpless prisoners who made it clear in every movement, grimace, and screech that they didn't want to be there and they wanted me to know it."[26]

Killed for Cosmetic (and Other) Testing

Needless bad science experiments exist not only in the medical world, but also for cosmetics—lipstick, mascara, bronzer, toothpaste, deodorant, shampoo, moisturizer. While, fortunately, cosmetics bans do exist in parts of the world, wide loopholes exist in them. Despite proof that animal testing for household and other products, as well as general chemical and ingredient testing, is often needless and ineffective, it is not prohibited.

Median lethal dose tests kill perhaps more test-subject animals than any other test—in fact, their purpose is death. How much of a substance must be inhaled or force-fed to animals for half of them to die? Not just medicine, but anything that is inevitably licked: lip balm, soda, soap, you name it. Rats do not have the ability to throw up, and so are considered perfect for this, though other animals are used, too. Rats have a phenomenal olfactory sense, able to smell when those around them are bleeding or stressed—a smell all too common in testing labs, and which induces anxiety in rats who sense it.[27]

The Draize test exposes rabbits to toxins, chemicals, and ingredients dropped into their eyes to see how much it irritates and pains them. Their eyes weep and burn as they are "lined up in rows of small boxes in which they were confined so that the animals couldn't rub their eyes." Slusher also wrote: "Some days, walking past that room, I would notice people removing the rabbit's eyeballs for study. The biohazard bags filled with the corpses of rabbits were always much larger and heavier than my mouse or rat bags." Rabbits, like all rodents, are gregarious, naturally preferring to live in large familiar groups. Instead, these animals are often confined alone in sterile cages, in pain and with no one to comfort them.[28]

Animals Used for "Fun"

Perhaps the most widely condemned forms of animal cruelty are those that are not shrouded in the myth of necessity. We do not need orcas and dolphins to perform for us at SeaWorld, and whether a fishy claim (how witty) of conservation is put forward by aquariums or not, most fish never feel the currents of a real ocean, instead living trapped in a building claiming to protect them while serving fried fish and chips in the cafeteria.

The animals forced to race as we cheer and drink, to balance balls on their heads, be ridden, jump through rings of fire, and sit drugged so we can pose for a selfie are all our unwilling entertainers. They are snatched from their natural habitats, or bred into our control, imprisoned under the guise of care all the while cheered on as sporting and performing stars, marveled at by spectators. We so broadly claim to love these creatures while their freedoms, safety, and sanity are stolen from them.

Exploited (and Killed) for Companionship

The animals we open our homes to are the animals we treat best. That's quite frightening. Not just because there are people who neglect and abuse their "pets," but because the pet industry is hardly different from other farming. Puppy farms, or factories and mills, are the factory farms of dog breeding. Picture them through the words of a friend who has investigated puppy farms:

> Whoever first claimed dog is "human's best friend" had clearly never been inside a puppy farm. Let me paint you a picture—imagine the cutest beagle, inside a concrete pen with a rag for a bed and surrounded by their own excrement. Imagine the smell of this, multiplied by 20 or 30 for each dog inside this shed, and imagine how much worse it would be for the dogs themselves with the sharp sense of smell they evolved before humans domesticated and commodified them. And then there is the noise—imagine 30 dogs barking at you inside an enclosed space, a mixture of fear and curiosity in their tone, for though some have (rightly) learnt to beware humans, others approach you from behind the bars of their pens, still seeking and offering affection even after all your kind has done to theirs. Imagine this, and tell me again, who it is we claim is our best friend?

These puppies are sold through stores, online, and via brokers, often alongside a falsely reassuring "registered breeder" claim that means very little. Investigators and police who have raided puppy farms with horrendously neglectful conditions have often come to find they are registered with supposedly quality councils. Puppy farms selling online often use houses as shop fronts that hide the true living conditions of breeding dogs. I can't help but wonder where Bill, the Jack Russell–Maltese I grew up with, only four years younger than me, really came from.[29]

Purebred dogs exist because we breed what we think is cute. Meanwhile, one in three bulldog breed individuals has a severe breathing problem. Miniature and toy breeds (poodles, schnauzers) often experience persistent kneecap dislocation. Some breeds can no longer mate or give birth naturally due to severely manipulative selective breeding. When breeding mothers are no longer producing, it is common and even often legal for breeders to kill these dogs should a suitable home not be found, even under tighter legislation. We might love how cute dogs are, or how they make us feel, but we do not treat them with love by supporting a system that farms them as stock just like any other farming system, though perhaps less blatantly because the product is a companion, not a meal.[30]

An industry that commodifies motherhood and sees female dogs as beings whose primary function is to be impregnated for profit is very *Handmaid's Tale*–esque. Reducing a male dog's value to the success of his sperm and making money by selling living beings is deeply unsettling with consideration. Dog mothers and pups recognize each other, even on scent alone, years after their separation.[31] "Are puppies sad when they leave their mum?" has hundreds of millions of hits on Google. Deep, primal, familiar bonds are far from exclusive to humans, and clearly many of us, rightly, worry we are tearing them apart. Rescue shelters across the world are full of millions of dogs who need homes, love, and comfort, who have been churned through and spat out of the dog industry. Every dog who is bought from the system means another dog left in a shelter, too often with the green needle inching closer to them each day.

Exploited (and Killed) for Races and Rides

For horses to learn to accept someone sitting on their back, they are "broken in." Whether subtly or grossly, a "no" is pushed at until out of discomfort, fear, or exhaustion, it becomes a "yes." While a horse may not be bucking someone off their back, we (should) understand in human terms that there are many ways someone subtly says "no," and that resigning to someone's will is not truly giving consent. Horse and human do not come to a mutually beneficial agreement; their relationship is dampened when the horse's autonomy is taken. Alexander Nevzorov, once revered as a prominent figure in horsemanship, let go of riding horses to form a deeper, leveled bond with them. His organization, Nevzorov Haute École, shares that a "horse saying 'no' may be disconcerting to a loving human as it may be perceived as a sign of rejection. In reality it needs to be celebrated as the starting point of a relationship worth having."[32] The utter core of this message is something that hit me quite profoundly in my thinking about all relationships.

Ren Hurst's *Riding on the Power of Others* shares this reverberating message of releasing control and expectation in relationships, too. Animal domestication makes for an inherently unequal dynamic; horses rely on their carers to provide their basic needs. As guardians of these animals, Hurst says we have a "fundamental responsibility not to take advantage" while domestication continues. Whether or not a horse "allows" themselves to be ridden, it is not in their best interest. Hurst describes a learned helplessness developed by horses who come to accept their domination.[33]

Physically too, horses are not "meant" for riding. Back problems and pain are very common in horses who are ridden. And it's not so surprising—imagine if we carried individuals who were smaller though still of substantial weight on our backs all the time. Ridden horses come to accept low-level pain in their lives, and for many, even chronic pain. Horses simply are not built physiologically to bear a human's weight—they exist here in their own right, not for us.[34]

An entitled relationship with horses is pushed to the extreme in the racing industry. They are whipped into running faster, their tongues are tied so they may be more easily controlled, they are pushed to absolute exhaustion. Research found that due to exercise-induced pulmonary haemorrhage (EIPH), 43–75 percent of thoroughbred racehorses have blood in their windpipe or lung after a single race. In horses that race two or three times consecutively, 80 percent have evidence of EIPH on at least one post-race examination. The same horse who is covered in the most "luxurious" animal leather saddlery, their mane combed to perfection, bleeds onto a kill floor just like a cow or a pig, their hair caked red. We call the horses who are broken in, ridden, and whipped "equine athletes," until we call them "pet food." Horses who have won their owners tens if not hundreds of thousands of dollars of prize money end up at a knackery or staring down a rifle. No longer of monetary value alive, with their care "too costly," or finding them a home "too much effort," they are defined as "wastage" when they are sent to be killed. These animals are not beloved by the industry.[35]

Exploited (and Killed) in Captivity on Land

When a Danish zoo openly killed Marius, a giraffe in their "care," outrage spread globally. But this was not a unique occurrence. Zoos cannot maintain a continually mating and growing population of "display" animals, and there is generally no capacity for animal release—no endangered tiger in an American zoo makes their way back to the wild in Asia. So, animal populations are totally controlled by zoo institutions, either through birth control or killing. In the practice coined "zoothanasia" by Dr. Marc Bekoff, animal "surplus," or "unneeded" healthy animals, are culled regularly in zoos across the world, despite claims of being safe spaces for animals. No individual is unneeded, as animals do not exist for our needs. Many claim that zoos exist for the purpose of conservation, but culling the incarcerated species you claim to conserve is surely oxymoronic.

Similarly, against the true interest of animals, many zoos play the conservation card while locking up bred and shipped-in animals on land that once, before its clearing, was home to native species. In his essay *Zoos Revisited*, philosopher Dale Jamieson condemns the intense moral discordance of "a culture that drives a species to the edge of extinction and then romanticises the remnants."[36]

Zoos began as barren, concrete cages holding animal (and not so long ago, that included human) beings so that the wealthy could gawk at them before walking freely back to the comfort of their homes. We hold animals captive, prisoners for entertainment, because they captivate our interest—we think they are "exotic," awesomely powerful, curious, incomprehensible. So many animals across the world are maddened by their confinement that the psychological stress of animals in zoos has its own word: "zoochosis." Animals pace their enclosures, turn circles, rock and sway, even mutilate themselves—gnawing at their skin or bashing their heads over and over. Dangerously bored, it cannot be claimed that animals live these wretched existences for the sake of conservation. Their lives are little, if anything, like that of their habitats, they are nearly never released. Steep captive animal populations do not equal environmental sustainability or animal care. Exhibiting animals as though they were ornaments grows fascination, but not any true respect or learning of animals as precious individuals or wild species.[37]

I remember being at a zoo far "better" than most, advertised as "open-range," when I was twelve. In the fairly large and quite lush environment three gorillas lived in, one sat by the glass, looking out at the humans watching him, beyond us, but mostly, down into his lap. I read that his coloring meant he was the silverback, Motaba. He lived with two of his sons, though his sperm had been used to inseminate gorillas internationally, and he had five others. The glass between us was incredibly thick, more so than any other enclosures. I wondered why. An older teenage boy began incessantly knocking on the thick glass by Motaba's face. Motaba abruptly rose, pounding furiously on the glass with his great fists, then pacing back and forth before sitting again, head hanging. The boy laughed with his friends and did it again, the whole process replaying a few times as I watched, distressed but unsure what to do. Why wasn't there an adult to tell him off to protect Motaba? Maybe three glass pummellings later, when the boy's banging began again, Motaba ignored him for far longer than he had before. Watching, I could almost feel his heart rate in mine, his trying to keep cool. When he finally snapped, he bared his teeth, bashing the glass so hard I was frightened by his strength. Finally, I yelled at the smirking boy, something incoherent and nervous but defensive of Motoba all the same. The boy looked back at me, slightly surprised I had opened my mouth. "Shut up," he said, and knocked on the glass, again. When he was bored, he left. Motaba never will.

Exploited (and Killed) in Captivity Under Water

Aquariums are wet zoos with many of the same farce conservation claims, confinements, and killings. Water parks like SeaWorld are the most exceptional slap in the face to genuine marine animal conservation—that which goes on in the open ocean or shortly leads back to it. Whatever small tokens of rescue and rehabilitation come out of such places are given only to mask blatant disregard for the wellbeing of animals. In *Blackfish*, former SeaWorld trainer Carol Ray describes the agony mother orca Catina expressed when her baby, Kalina, was taken from her. Placed with different orcas, "she stayed in the corner of the pool . . . just shaking and screaming, screeching, crying like I'd never seen her . . . the other females in the pool maybe once or twice during the night, they come out and check on her. And she just screeches and cries and they would just run back. There is nothing that you could call that watching it besides grief."[38]

Water parks like SeaWorld claim cetaceans have the company of their "families," but they are human-constructed groups, not families. Relentlessly social creatures, just like humans, orcas and dolphins alike do not feel as at ease with a random group of individuals as with their kin. In fact, both orcas and dolphins speak in socially transmitted dialects. So, when Kalina was placed with stranger orcas from different cultures and locations, or when a dolphin is placed with who the dolphin trainers decide is "best suited" for performance, their connection is hindered by their ability to communicate. It is similar to if I were put into an arranged family of people who spoke German and Mandarin, but I could not speak either—forming a meaningful bond, let alone resolving the tensions of our captivity, would be difficult.[39]

Living in small pools rather than a vast ocean without their families or wide social networks, and with little to keep them from despair, marine animals live far shorter lives in captivity. Female orcas can live to be over 100 years old, but die at around 25 years old in captivity. Bottlenose dolphins die on average at just over 12 years old in captivity, but can live to be 30 to 50 years old in the wild. Not only their quality of life, but also years of life itself, is stolen from these animals.[40]

What we do to animals, when we look closely, is so far from what most anyone is willing to accept. What would we do if we saw any of the horrors that occur behind closed doors laid out in front of us? Would we intervene? Or would we turn a blind eye? The treatment of animals we are willing to accept, whether we see it directly or not, must say something about who we are as individuals and as a society. More, it speaks to what we will accept for others we "dehumanize."

Chapter 3

This Is What Else We Justify

Our justification for treating animals as we do is rooted in a wider system of oppression that "others" those we consider "unlike" us and so "less" than us.

The Intertwining of Oppressions

The system that oppresses animals, incarcerating, killing, and commodifying them as we've seen, does not exist in a vacuum. All oppressions are linked because the social structures and hierarchies that exist today are entirely made up by humans. There is no concrete basis for a belief that one sex, gender, race, or species is superior, because "superior" is a created idea itself. In *Beasts of Burden: Disability and Animal Liberation*, Sunaura Taylor argues that an ideology of disability is the basis of all oppression.[1] Different oppressed groups have been falsely labeled with impairments (as though impairment is reason to oppress)—women have less intellectual capacity, transgender people are mentally ill, queer men are infected, other animals are simply not human, and that is considered a kind of disability in itself. Through fallacy, marginalized groups become synonymous with their "lackings" or "diseases." But there is nothing inherently better or worse about one human or another, one animal or another—humans included in the animalia branch of life. Biological differences between humans or species are hijacked by our constructed social determinations of them. An equal line of beings with excitingly unique features and abilities is tipped sideways, turned into a ladder we all must cling to from least to most deserving of the goods and freedoms of the world.

Christopher Sebastian, a Black writer and liberation activist, says: "Everyone probably understands 'human' as a biological classification, but it was actually white supremacy that set up 'human' as a political identity." People fear being dehumanized, because they fear being animalized. There is a constructed hierarchy among humans. We do awful things to those classified as less than. Those considered "human" (even if to varying degrees) sit at the top end of the ladder, looking down upon the rest of the animal kingdom—our food and clothing, our test subjects and entertainers. They live on "our" planet. A human belief of superiority, of "most evolved," exists through a white (patriarchal, cis-heteronormative) lens, in which white people have and often still claim whiteness as the pinnacle of evolution, with other humans supposedly resembling missing links between non-human animals and white male humans. Those deemed "sub-human" are pushed farther down the ladder, denied personhood, and still today are denied equal rights. The dangerous idea of a "master race" lays its foundations on the belief of a "master species," with all aspects of this fictionalized premise requiring dismantlement.

From our made-up hierarchies, we offer made-up rights—nature does not owe us any safeties. There is no biologically inherent reason I should not be able to kill you because you take my food, because you annoy me, or because I'm just bored. There are no rules by which the world turns that promise we ought to be free from harm and suffering. Having said that, I'm certainly glad that we've created a world in which you have the right to live and I do not have the right to take that from you. Such rights do not yet apply to most other animals, as my right to eat a cow for dinner and wear her on my feet legally trumps her right to freedom and to life.

Animals may be less intelligent, and they may not all communicate in a way so nuanced and complex as we do. They don't build skyscrapers, sell goods, or trade stocks, but why should this have any relation to their rights? Why would this negate our leaving them in peace? Perhaps in a productivity- and profit-orientated world, animals have little to offer us, so by and large they are given little in return. It is for a similar reason that many people with disabilities are not duly considered, accessibility being considered a "cost," not a right for individuals we wrongly demoralize as less "useful" in our rigid and exhaustive framework of exponential financial growth. It could be for this reason, too, that indigenous communities across the world, who live in greater harmony with their environment, are condemned as "less intelligent" or, even again, "unevolved" and "sub-human," in our commodity-centric, capitalistic, and materialistic framework.

Nothing changed about Aboriginal people when they were given their legal claim to "humanity." Nothing changed about African Americans when they were given the right to vote. Nothing changed about Namibian, Greek, or Finnish women when marital rape was outlawed. All that has ever changed the rights of the masses is the perceptions of those in legal power, or, more likely, their hands being forced by the people. Following suit, nothing will change about animals when we decide we have no right to kill or own them, other than our perception of them.

If the rights we offer ourselves and others are made up, all forms of oppression intersect and in fact are the same in that they exist only because of dominant human greed, superior treatment gained through mythmaking, force, and violence. If the rights we offer ourselves and others are entirely made up, it also means that it should be quite easy to imagine what rights others should have. If we were them, what would we want? Knowing we are all fundamentally the same in the ways that matter most—our capacity to feel joy, sadness, fear, suffering—what would we hope for ourselves, should we trade places? Here we will consider some of the ways in which the oppression of our fellow animals entangles with and entrenches the oppression of other marginalized groups.

Feminism

If we can justify that someone is deserving of fewer rights than we have, we can justify anyone else is, too. If a hen is only valuable as someone with a female reproductive system to exploit for the profitable production of eggs, a woman is only valuable as someone who can offer (or be forced into) sex, as a carrier of offspring, as eye candy.

Women today in such countries as Saudi Arabia are still forced into marriage, legally controlled by their male partners and relatives.[2] Women in Western countries, where we are afforded these rights, are no different from those without them—the constructed hierarchies we live in are. Outside of such an overtly oppressive hierarchy, it's easy for us to consider it a baselessly discriminatory nightmare, that women are obviously thinking, feeling individuals who deserve autonomy, freedom, and safety. We think of the inhumanity of those oppressing these women and we consider our own maltreatment, in our own sexist environments.

We speak of the global rape culture that denies us our bodily autonomy. And we do so as we put on our lipstick and eat our low-fat dairy yogurt, one which saw a rabbit painfully tested on, the other a female cow forcibly impregnated and killed. We forget that so much of the everyday choices we freely make shackle others.

Years of cultural conditioning have been and continue to be unpicked in our minds so that we may see women are not inferior to men, just because we are different. I walk to the train and I subconsciously assume the woman coming home in scrubs is a nurse, not a doctor. Despite being friends with a woman who's a doctor, whom I hate to think of knowing I thought so. Years of cultural conditioning must be unpicked in our minds so that we may see some species are not inferior to others just because they are different. I drive past a field of sheep and somehow forget each one of them is an individual, just like all those people packed in the train. Female farmed animals are exploited in a way that is specific to their sexual organs, and this reality undoubtedly makes space for the exploitation of human females and women.

Imagine you are forcibly and "artificially" impregnated. Semen is put into your vagina with an instrument forced inside of you. You are most likely restrained. It's the kind of distress that leaves you only to fight, freeze, or attempt to break free.

This is the first step in the "working life" of a female dairy cow. She is forcibly impregnated, the calf she has grown inside of her for many months will either be slaughtered or stolen into the same oppressive cycle, depending on their sex. The mother cow will be killed when her body cannot cope with the stress anymore, when her udder hangs as low and heavy as her outlook.

Exploitation based on sex, human or other, is a hard truth to bear. In this instance, this is the truth of the purposeful, greed-driven exploitation of the sexual organs, anatomy, and being of a cow. No matter who is the victim, this is a lack of consent. This is the truth of animal sexual exploitation.

This is not to equate the experiences of any two beings. I was sexually abused as a child. I do not pretend to completely understand the emotional trauma and anguish that comes from being attacked and raped by a stranger as a grown woman. These instances are different. The emotional burdens that come from them, unique. I extend my empathy all the same. I know the gut-wrenching trauma, anxiety, depression, complication, and deep-rooted pains that come from my experience. I do not know the exact pains, cognitions, or emotions of another survivor. I don't need to. I don't need to know if their pain is "less" or "worse" than mine. All I know is there was inflicted, undeserved pain. All I need to do is empathize with them.

Cows may not be able to put their pain into words we recognize. They likely do not understand their exploitation in the way I do mine. They do not know of the scale and commercialization of their and other cows' suffering. But they feel it. I know the deep, primal howls of pain I made as a child. I know the torment I felt, even when I did not understand what had been done to me. When I hear the crying of a cow, wailing for the newborn ripped from her teat, the roots sound the same. When I see the panic in her eyes, the frozen horror that paralyzes her, the attempts to kick herself free as something is forced inside of her, I get it. I feel it. I could not ever wish her that pain, so I do not ever consume dairy. I extend the same empathy to hens. Just like cows, their sexual organs, their anatomy as females, is twisted, manipulated, and used against them.

An egg, like the egg that comes from my ovaries and falls out of me in my monthly period, is the reason for her exploitation. Over many decades and generations, hens have been selectively bred so that they now ovulate almost every day of the year, about 300 times. In nature, chickens, like their red jungle fowl ancestors, lay between 10 and 15 eggs a year—not so different to the 12 menstrual cycles I have annually. I imagine my life, my exhaustion, if I had been selectively bred to ovulate so constantly.[3]

I imagine that I was to take a one-way trip to the slaughterhouse after my body had been exploited for so long that it could not keep going. I cannot fathom such a reality, but I try. I try to imagine myself as someone, as a hen, who is killed at only 18 months old when the strain of living in my fatigued, mutated body means I can no longer continue to "produce" in a way that is "financially viable." I think of this as I remember a hen's natural lifespan, once ranging up to ten years.[4]

It is estimated that around the world, there are around six billion hens exploited in the egg industry. I see a hen who gasped for air, flapping increasingly hopelessly, as she was gassed to death during "egg-layer depopulation." She was killed because she was no longer seen as profitable. Her life not treated with the value it deserved. Her body perceived as something to exploit and discard.[5]

I mourn for her, six billion times over.

It is estimated that around the world, currently 264 million cows are exploited in the dairy industry. I see a cow whose panicked eyes dart past me, her head sticking out of the truck packed with bodies as it turned down the road to the slaughterhouse. She, too, was killed when she no longer served a financial purpose alive. She, too, was seen as a body to exploit and discard. A cow like her is often killed at about five years old, not allowed to live out her natural lifespan of 15 to 20 years.[6]

I mourn for her, 264 million times over.

It is estimated that around the world, 35 percent of women have experienced physical and sexual violence by a non-partner, with countless more experiencing this violence within relationships. This 35 percent alone would equal to around 3.86 billion women. I think of a woman, a friend who every day feels as though she is without a little part of herself, which was robbed from her. I think of the women like me who clutch their keys sticking out from their fists as we walk home at night. I think of our bodies on high alert. We, too, are often seen as a body to exploit and discard.[7]

I mourn for us, more than 3.86 billion times over.

There is no comparing trauma. There is no competition. There is no equating pain when it is something so uniquely personal and awful. There is no discounting or undermining of suffering that does any good. But there is empathy. There is an extension of compassion, and the non-human females in our world desperately need that from us. Whatever differences they may have in the way, they understand their pain, do not discount that it is there, that it is burning and raw inside of them. We need only look into the eyes of a female animal in these exploitative industries to see her suffering, her hopelessness. I know that we are different, but the same.

It does not matter what form discrimination takes. There is always an "othering" involved. A way to construct an "us" and "them." For our world to be one of peace, one without violence against women, against anyone, we must feel our pain in unison. Feel their pain as ours. Audre Lorde, who did not feast on flesh herself, said it best: "I am not free while any woman is unfree, even when her shackles look very different to my own."[8]

But how did we get here? Why is it completely normal for a female dairy cow to be forcibly impregnated, and why are so many women—including trans women—sexually abused by men? How did this ever become our normal? While this is an exceptionally big question, one element of the interconnectedness of this oppression, of this objectification of individuals, is expressed in Carol Adams' *The Sexual Politics of Meat.* Here, animals are described as "absent referents" in their own consumption, who in turn take on metaphorical meaning.

Animals and their objectified, butchered bodies come to represent the height of denied agency and of disenfranchisement. In turn, they become the reference for women made to feel the same way by men. We march, we advocate for ourselves, we demand respect and safety, arguing that we are not just "pieces of meat." We forget there is no piece of meat that is "just" that, only bodies stripped of life, dominated by might, brute power, and force. The visceral moments of terror before an animal's slaughter are lost in a woman's feeling like a piece of meat, because meat has become devoid of connection to life. This diminishment of "being" to "object" is the exact reason for our comparison—we are made into sexual objects, as they are made into breeding objects, fashion objects, edible objects.[9] The hen, sow, cow, and woman are beings in their own rights, not to be grabbed at or devoured by unwelcome chewing or kissing mouths, lingering eyes, grabbing hands, or demeaning words. We are not to be dismembered with butchers' knives or by the greedy male gaze of those who just want a "piece of ass," unconcerned for the woman attached to it. We are not consumable.

This overlapping of objectification and sequential violence is most clear when we look at the intersections of "meat work"—killing and butchering work—and domestic violence. Data collected over a number of years across 500 U.S. counties found that communities surrounding slaughterhouses fall victim to disproportionately higher incidences of violent offenses, including sexual assault and rape. It is "theorized that the reason for this increase [in crime] was 'spillover' in the psyches of the slaughterhouse workers, an explanation that is backed up by sociological theory and anecdotal evidence."

"This is seen in one worker's testimony about how working a long shift slaughtering livestock affected how he viewed and treated his co-workers: 'I've had ideas of hanging my foreman upside down on the line and sticking him. I remember going into the office and telling the personnel man I have no problem pulling the trigger on a person—if you get in my face, I'll blow you away.'" Slaughterhouse work is carried out by a largely male workforce. Domestic violence is predominately perpetrated by men and against women. We especially endanger and victimize those we consider less than, and systematically, women and animals are considered less than men.[10]

A friend who chose to only be interviewed by her first name, Charlize, worked undercover in an abattoir. One night while texting, she casually remarked: "[Male] slaughterhouse workers flirt with you by wiping blood down your arms." The text ended with an upside-down smiley face emoji, perhaps her attempt to soften the blow of what she wished to pass as somewhat light-hearted but knew was sinister. If you could gasp in your own head, I did. When I thought about it more, what she experienced really was an extension of the male teacher in the schoolground telling you the little boy is only being mean to you, pushing you over, because he has a crush on you—How exciting! How sweet of him! Except, this ugly interlocking of violence and attraction has far more time to mutate out of control than it has in an eight-year-old boy. There is death and carcasses, blood and guts, and a conditioned commodification of bodies different to his own. I went to bed that night feeling unnerved on behalf of women working in slaughterhouses, living around them, and living with those who work inside them. The killing industry is not one that fosters a respect for the autonomy of others, particularly those considered less than.

Mental Health Issues

It can be easy to vilify slaughterhouse workers. Someone who kills every day, who is statistically more likely to go home and hurt others more. To cast them as the enemy, though, is a mistake. The system is the enemy, not the people working under it. These are lowly paid positions, fulfilled in unusual hours for long stretches, often by vulnerable groups of people—this is not a job anyone really chooses, but one taken out of necessity.

To the vast majority of us, killing does not come naturally. In World War II, as little as 15 percent of soldiers actually shot at people, more willing to die than kill for their cause. David Grossman, author of *On Killing: The Psychological Cost of Learning to Kill in War and Society*, wrote that "when the military became aware of that, they systematically went about the process of trying to fix this 'problem'. . . . And fix it the military did. By the Korean War, around 55 percent of the soldiers were willing to fire to kill. And by Vietnam, the rate rose to over 90 percent." Through role modeling, Pavlovian and operant conditioning, violence was normalized.[11]

People were manipulated and changed. The same desensitization occurs in slaughterhouses, and it makes way for not only animal harm, but also harm unto oneself. Ed Van Winkle, hog sticker (the person who cuts a pig's blood vessels so they bleed out) at a Morrell slaughterhouse plant in Iowa, explained:

> The worst thing, worse than the physical danger, is the emotional toll. If you work in the stick pit [where the hogs are killed] for any period of time, you develop an attitude that lets you kill . . . but doesn't let you care. You may look a hog in the eye that's walking around down in the blood pit with you and think, God, that really isn't a bad-looking animal. You may want to pet it. Pigs down on the kill floor have come up and nuzzled me like a puppy. Two minutes later I had to kill them—beat them to death with a pipe. I can't care.[12]

If a kill-floor worker, a farmer, a vivisector, a fisherman, a shearer, or anyone else grows indifferent to animals, convinced that animals don't feel anything, it is easier to cope, and it is more likely that animals will be treated worse. "I have to switch my love of animals a bit off. You have to if you work here." These are the words of a cattle-farm worker speaking (unknowingly) to an undercover investigator, who later exposed painful, bloody mutilations and mass graves of suffering cattle who were shot with rifles on site at a free-range farm. Severing your compassion and empathy, switching a loving part of yourself off, is damaging.[13]

Perpetration-induced traumatic stress is similar to post-traumatic stress disorder (PTSD), with a fundamental difference: The trauma and stress come not from being a victim, but from being "the direct reason for another being's trauma." Suffered by soldiers and slaughterhouse workers alike, symptoms comorbid with PTSD include "drug and alcohol abuse, anxiety, panic, depression, increased paranoia, a sense of disintegration, dissociation, or amnesia, which are incorporated into the 'psychological consequences' of the act of killing." As someone who has suffered with diagnosed PTSD, I would not wish this on anyone. For a long time and every now and then still, I exist but am hollowed out. One man working in a slaughterhouse said he became "emotionally dead" in his work, and those two words give me a lump in my throat.[14]

Perhaps the most confronting part of these traumatic stress disorders, because it is the most inescapable, are the nightmares. I remember a couple of years ago, I was involved in street outreach—we offered two dollars to anyone who wanted to watch a video showing the farming and slaughter of animals (*Thousand Eyes*, from Farm Transparency Project)—when a tall, slightly agitated-looking man with slicked hair and ragged clothes came up to me. Although nervous of his skittishness, I said hello and asked how he was. He told me that he was okay, but that this sort of footage got him really shaken up. He said to me that he "used to do that stuff" we were showing.

I'd never had a conversation with someone who had worked on a kill floor before and wasn't sure what he thought about me or what we were doing yet. I engaged tentatively, asked him how long he'd worked in a slaughterhouse. He told me he had worked in them for years, but that he'd had to quit. I asked him why. He told me that he had started having nightmares every night. He would see himself killing animals, like he did all day. Except in his nightmares when the animals let out screams and cries, the sounds were of human children and babies screaming and crying. He couldn't look at the animals, or children, the same way again in the day. As he told me, I felt a part of him glaze over, a protective barrier coming down. I felt a part of me break for him, want to hug him.

At that time, I had spent almost every night for the past few years having nightmares that played out my abuse. In mine, I would try to scream out, but no one could hear me, or they'd hear, see, and do nothing. I woke up every night in a cold sweat. I hated going to sleep because I knew what was coming for me. Life was exhausting. I couldn't imagine what all that would feel like, with a thick layer of guilt weighing heavy on top of you, and a part of your nightmare still being a part of your day, too. After a little while, the conversation tapered off, I sensed that sharing had exhausted him and he didn't want to speak much anymore. He told me what work he was doing now, and that it was better not working "with animals." I told him I was really glad he'd been able to find something else, and I wished him well. That night I had a nightmare; I wondered if he did too.

Michael Slusher, on his medical testing on beagles, wrote: "Barely able to stand up, he still tried wobbling to the front of the cage to greet me but fell onto his face instead. Lying there with his eyes never leaving mine, he was still rapidly wagging his tail at the sight of me. I was purposefully killing him slowly and painfully and yet he was so very happy to see me." Slusher called himself a monster: "As soon as I'd try to imagine what they must have felt, my brain wanted to shut down." Slusher, too, had nightmares where he woke soaked in sweat. He dreamt of sterile corridors and the eyes of countless rats whom he killed.[15]

Former pig farmer Bob Comis once wrote: "It is death that is our aim, our purpose. Death is the end. Life is the means. Money the reward."[16] No matter how hard a farmer may work to give "their animals" a good life, an emotional burden comes with knowing those animals will be killed. Jay Wilde, like many farmers, became a cattle farmer by taking on what was once his father's role. After working on the farm for a few years, Jay couldn't bring himself to eat the animals he had known and cared for but didn't know how to move away from farming animals himself. "You couldn't help thinking 'do they know what you really have in store for them?' and wondering if they knew that you would betray their trust in you." Jay felt he had to "steel himself" to send cows to slaughter, feeling like a "criminal playing a dirty horrible trick" on those animals. "It is soul-destroying."

One day someone asked Jay if he had heard of veganic farming, offering a number to *The Vegan Society*, which offers agricultural transition assistance. "I think it was because I felt secretly ashamed of what I was doing and therefore defensive, it took me more than a year to actually call. I also felt bound to carry on my father's work, trying to bury my own feelings." Jay and his wife Katja's story is shared in Alex Lockwood's film, *73 Cows*, which sees 73 cows gain safe haven at Hillside Animal Sanctuary as Jay and Katja begin the process of transforming their farm into a veganic one. Though the money from selling his remaining cows for slaughter would have helped their transition, Jay said it "wouldn't be a good way to start vegan farming." Every time I have watched the short film, I've teared up when Katja shares that no longer farming animals changed Jay: "I think the biggest change is, I think that he talks more . . . that is just so beautiful to see."[17]

Racism

Keith Thomas, who wrote *Man and the Natural World: A History of Modern Sensibility*, said: "Once perceived as beasts, people were liable to be treated accordingly. The ethic of human domination removed animals from the sphere of human concern. But it also legitimized the ill-treatment of those humans who were in a supposedly animal condition."[18] Rooted in a denial of personhood, racism is built upon the idea that to be animal is to be less than, and to be white is to be exclusively above animality. White supremacy has created a world in which people of color are made to do the "dirty work" of white people, including the traumatic work of close proximity and participation in the exploitation, slaughter, and "deconstruction" of our fellow animals.

More bovines are slaughtered and skinned in China and India than anywhere else, and about 1.5 billion square feet of hides are tanned in the latter annually. The Indian city of Kanpur, home to 300 tanneries, exports

90 percent of their leather products to Europe and the United States.[19] Most skins around the globe are tanned with carcinogenic chemicals, including formaldehyde, chromium, and arsenic. These chemicals cause chronic coughing, skin ailments, and other diseases. Exposure to these chemicals, recorded in Kanpur, resulted in a doubled likelihood of morbidity.[20] Toxified water spills across cropland and through the river Ganges, which is the most important Indian waterway for both urban and rural communities and their wellbeing. Sean Gallagher's *The Toxic Price of Leather* sees children in Kanpur working unprotected in tanneries, suffering from illness, blindness, and permanent skin damage.[21] Across the globe, tannery workers suffer cancer at high rates. In another top tanning country, China, the leather industry, among other polluting industries, has been identified as one of the main causes of illness in communities now referred to as "cancer villages."[22]

Racism interweaves with abattoirs, too. Slaughtering work is not only mentally damaging, but also physically dangerous. An average of two UK abattoir workers are injured every week in the United Kingdom over the past six years, 800 workers suffered serious injuries, 78 required amputations, and four people died at work, labeling the industry one of top concern by the Health and Safety Executive.[23] Upwards of 62 percent of that workforce is made up of migrants.[24] Following the same theme, a large portion of US slaughterhouse workers are migrants—often undocumented and so less able to stand up for themselves. So, too, are the refugees Hispanic and Black people. Almost one-quarter of these people are ill or injured at any one time.[25] Their plight has seen their factory job called the most dangerous in the country by Human Rights Watch.[26] Late in 2019 in Australia, Lê Tuấn Nhã, a 45-year-old migrant father, was crushed and killed at work in an abattoir. He had been manually pulling goat carcasses into a machine using force and speed to remove a goat's hair from their body, because a conveyor belt stopped working and was not tended to.[27] This story is not as unique as it should be.

Slaughtering facilities across the world struggle to fill positions in these brutal jobs, with people "[walking] away after a couple of hours" due to the mental and physical exhaustion that comes with butchering our earthly kin.[28] In Canada, Syrian refugees were encouraged to fill this role by the Canadian Meat Council that offered express entry to the country. Essentially, "we will help you flee brutal war and persecution if you, traumatized, work in this physically and mentally destructive job no one here wants."[29] Teys Australia, one of the largest slaughtering companies in the country, touts a tale of "multiculturalism at its best" due to their disproportionate number of migrant and refugee employees. However, union investigations report allegedly underpaid work, forced strenuous labor unmatched by physical build, overcharged rent, and overcrowded accommodation for these vulnerable people.[30] It's not difficult to see that an industry committing atrocious violence against vulnerable animals does not extend great care to the vulnerable humans they employ, either.

Further removed from animal death itself, interconnected human oppression continues. Of Asian communities, 90 percent are lactose intolerant, and yet the FAO describes Asia as the strongest-growing region for dairy consumption.[31] Meanwhile, 75 percent of African Americans are lactose intolerant, yet current US Dietary Guidelines encourage this community to consume dairy regularly.[32] Dr. Milton Mills, a Black physician who has addressed the advisory committee in charge of these guidelines and reported on racial bias in nutrition policy, states that said guidelines are "an egregious form of institutional racism."[33] Animal agricultural lobbies with financial power in dietary guideline decision making choose profit over the health of already oppressed groups. "To intentionally harm the health of a large swath of our population so that industry operatives can profit from it," Dr. Mills says, is "reprehensible."[34] Food is not a cure-all, but Dr. Mills finds many of his patients feel new life breathed into them on a plant-based diet, even in some cases no longer requiring insulin for since-reversed diabetes.

Sister authors of *Aphro-ism,* Aph and Syl Ko, are decolonization theorists. In their work, they speak to the importance of undoing the narrative and system in which European settler-colonialism has "displaced beings from their original dwellings; ended or shredded important social ties and traditions; and restricted moral, legal, and social rules such that they advantage one group while disadvantaging and casting out 'inferior' others as mere resources."[35] Essentially, the colonially rooted system in which we all (human and our fellows) live is centred around whiteness, with people of color and our fellow animals transformed into commodities used to strengthen this system. Animals shall be our food and clothing, people who aren't white shall be our poorly or unpaid laborers, neither shall keep what was theirs either in physicality or in spirit. The ways in which the financial success of the animal–industrial complex is built on the backs of not only oppressed other-than-human animals, but also oppressed humans, are countless.

A white, "West is best" attitude informed by racism and speciesism also attempts to justify claims that people of color are immoral in their killing of animals, despite white, Western, and industrialized killing being not only accepted but also defended. The COVID-19 pandemic was thought to have likely originated from an animal in a wet market in Wuhan, China.[36] At this and other similar markets, animals including but not exclusive to dogs, cats, bats, pangolins, lizards, and snakes are held live, slaughtered at sale for freshness. Such wet markets also exist in New York City and across the world, particularly for marine animals. However, as (mostly white) people in Western countries became increasingly aware of the realities of these markets and the animal species slaughtered there, many had a lot to say about it. Globally, people openly expressed outrage, disgust, and total disdain for not only the markets, but also Chinese people as a whole. Bolstered up by thoughtless and dangerous statements by news media outlets and politicians (think Donald Trump calling COVID-19 "the Chinese virus"), racially motivated violence and assault was spewed over Asian communities worldwide.[37] An online reporting forum received 650 reports of discrimination against Asian Americans in one week.[38] A 23-year-old Asian man was shouted at, "I don't want your coronavirus in my country," beaten, and left with a black eye in the United Kingdom.[39]

That hatred being directed at Chinese and, more broadly, Asian people is spurred on by flagrant racism. It's pushed by an uncritiqued idea that because some Chinese people eat, prepare, and sell certain animals unlike the way we do, they are more cruel and less clean. The first thing to note is that not every Chinese person eats wild animals or dogs. Many do not. In April of 2020, the Chinese agricultural minister stated that dogs should be treated as companions, not "livestock," perhaps signaling a move toward the end of the meat trade for such animals.[40] Many Chinese people don't eat animals at all. The second point to consider is that a wet market is not necessarily less hygienic or more brutal than a Western slaughterhouse; it is simply more transparent.

The vast majority of meat, eggs, and dairy come from feedlots and factory farms, where animals are packed in tightly, living against their natural instinct and will, in their own filth. COVID-19 is also not the first animal-origin virus to infect humans. The avian bird flu came from factory-farmed chickens, and the swine flu came from factory-farmed pigs; both have killed thousands of people. Both species live horrendous lives of confinement in appalling and poorly regulated systems. Systems in which they are not legally protected and are slaughtered at a tiny fraction of their natural lifespan. Globally, we slaughter and eat billions of chickens and pigs every year. There is no paralleled condemnation or blame placed on the people farming and eating these animals, despite the flu-tied human loss historically and statistically being far more devastating. The 1918 influenza pandemic, for example, infected a third of the world and killed a total of 50 million people, and it likely originated from farming and hosting live markets of birds.[41]

In much of the global West, it is legal for piglets too small to be profitable to be "thumped," their heads smashed against concrete, their surviving siblings eventually gassed to death. Hidden camera footage has shown fish being sliced open as they gasp and thrash, calves crying out in pain as their budding horns are cut bloodily off their heads, and freshly decapitated sheep's heads being kicked like footballs.[42] Abattoirs are filled with the bodies of dead animals, carcasses ripped off their skins, guts scooped out, bloody floors and gumboots hosed down throughout the day. These facilities are far from sterile, quiet, or compassionate. Images from Chinese wet markets are certainly confronting to animal lovers, but only so much as images from any abattoir should be.

Racial condemnation becomes poorly justified by species-based discrimination. Believing that Chinese people are evil for killing dogs, cats, bats, or pangolins is inconsistent if you sit down for a meal and eat cows, chickens, fish, or any other animal, and it only very thinly veils a kind of racism. In their capacity to suffer, these animals are not different. They all feel pain, they all fight to live. The fundamental difference between a dog, a bat, and a chicken is our perception. They are all made of "meat" in that they all have flesh, just as humans do, just as all animals do. If you want to get self-righteous over some Chinese people eating endangered species, let's also talk about the reported potential reality of near fishless oceans as soon as 2048.[43]

Welfarism—where it's thought, basically, that animals should have good lives but not necessarily the right to keep that life—comes into the mix when we consider the denunciation of live export. People are not upset that animals are slaughtered, but by where they are slaughtered, by who, and how. Australian live export has made global headlines many times. The Asian and Middle Eastern countries Australian animals are exported to often do not have animal protection laws on par with Australia's. The significant difference, animals are not required to be "effectively stunned" before they are cut at the jugular and bled out. Australian citizens, and a global community of proclaimed animal lovers, were disgusted when it was exposed that Australian sheep were clubbed to death in Pakistan, and yet newborn lambs are legally clubbed to death by some sheep farmers in Australia if they are orphaned and it is not practical for them to be given care.[44]

Here are some online comments (which may distress Muslim and Islamic readers) on live export investigations. Note the common use of the word "barbaric":

"I definitely agree with you. Muslims are crazy!!! Those sheep were treated so poorly;"

"Save them from these barbarians;"

"Well people . . . welcome to Islam!!!!!"

"Sick, sadistic, barbaric, EVIL bastards. What do you expect from these people who worship the Devil;"

"Barbaric, we must stop the live export of these poor animals;"

"I support farmers, but NOT this or any live animals going to barbaric cultures. Their fate is doomed. . . ."

Certainly, as investigators have told me, the journeys and deaths that take place in live-export industries are more horrific than anything they have seen before. However, as these comments show, rather than focusing on the acts of cruelty themselves, too often there is a tendency for a Western audience to make false and unnecessary connections between cruelty and ethnicity. What we really ought to consider is our wider human ability to be violent.

The racist comments above often refer to non-white people's being "barbaric." To be barbaric is to be savagely cruel, primitive, and unsophisticated. When we refer to the actions of people, and to those people themselves, from different places as barbaric, we are implying that we are more civilized and that they are less evolved. We dehumanize, which, as we've covered, in a deeply speciesist world is incredibly dangerous. It's also a simple way to avoid considering what cruelty we inflict on animals in our own cultures.

The horrors of live export are often more to do with the foundations of speciesist systems than the human individuals doing the killing. Investigators have told me that what makes the experiences within live export so much worse are the awful conditions these animals endure for so long on the ships themselves. This has less to do with the local people that receive and slaughter cattle and sheep, and more to do with our own authorities and communities that allow this to happen. It is us who send off the ships, though the political tide is turning on the permissibility of this.

In being so quick to blame a specific ethnicity or culture for cruelty, rather than identifying the true culprits, we allow ourselves to racistly shift blame. The gruesome slaughter of animals killed in live-export systems is certainly of great concern, but so are the animals' journeys there. So are the systems of exploitation and slaughter we have in our own backyard, which send our less "valuable" animals overseas. Without concern for all of these issues too, perhaps we are more xenophobic than we are genuinely and widely concerned with the safety of animals.

Chapter 4

This Is How We Got Here

We started killing and eating animals a long time ago, and the way we've done so has transformed a lot since then.

Gathering and Hunting

Today, wearing and eating animals is so normal that if you don't, you're generally required to explain yourself to those around you. Why? We've been doing it for a long time. We haven't, however, been doing it the way we are now for very long. Billions of animals slaughtered annually, factory farms, excessive consumption of both food and fashion generally. Where did it all start and how did we get here?

In what we often think of as caveman times, times I am glad not to live in but that people opposed to veganism can seem oddly obsessed with replicating, yes, we killed, ate, and wore animals. We collectively used to do a lot of things generally frowned upon in a modern society. We often killed our elders or sickly young if they were slowing our travels (and yet "sub-human" animals like elephants, orcas, and chimps have been seen doing the opposite).[1] Rape was not even understood as problematic (to say the least). You know, just "caveman" things.

If you'd like to justify eating animals by noting that our historical ancestors did it, you're welcome to. But if you'd like to be consistent in your argument, you should also take off your underwear, your T-shirt, your jeans, and anything with a zipper on it. You should throw away your mobile phone and any books you have, forget about a mattress forever, and stop paying your rent so you can live the nomadic life and find that nice temporary cave home you seem so nostalgic for. While nomadic peoples certainly still exist, hunt, and live off the land, how anyone near a supermarket eats animals is utterly unrelated to that way of life.

Prehistoric homo species (we being homo sapiens, though there have been many other "homo" breeds, some living in the same time periods) ate varied diets, depending on where they lived, just like we do today. Most ate plenty of veggies.[2] There's no point questioning if our ancestors ate meat and wore animal skins too—they did. But there are misconceptions about how central it was to their wellbeing and development, and so, too, about how important it is for us now. There's a whole lot of history between then and now, and I'm pretty sure most of us like to think we've advanced in a plethora of ways since then, one being morally.

A common claim that's made is that eating meat made us smart. It seems far more likely, though, that our ability to control fire and use it to cook was what helped our brains grow. With the domestication of fire many hundreds of thousands of years ago, food became more accessible, as we could digest foods we otherwise could not, like wheat, rice, and potatoes—which quickly became staples (I couldn't be more glad). Chimpanzees spend up to seven hours a day chewing raw food, whereas humans spend only one hour a day eating cooked food. Cooked food is softer and so is easier to chew and digest, not only for grains and starchy plants but also for fruits, nuts, insects, and flesh. With cooking, our teeth became smaller and our intestines became shorter. The culmination of all this meant that less energy was spent fuelling our bodies, so more energy was available to go to our brains, leading to their growth.[3] We also had more time to think, communicate, and create—culture, tools, new ways of living and performing tasks. It's worth noting, too, that human inventions like oil lamps, needles for sewing warm clothing, and boats came well after any dramatic changes in our diet. Most researchers think the only reason for the cognitive revolution that occurred at that time—thirty thousand to seventy thousand years ago—is genetic mutation. Yuval Noah Harari's fascinating *Sapiens* looks deeply into all of this and several elements of the following history.[4]

Even if meat isn't responsible for our big and juicy brains, didn't our ancestors eat big, juicy steaks? So, shouldn't we too? Followers of the carnivore diet, who would sooner suck on bone marrow than eat a carrot, think so, convinced that anything other than flesh should stay out of your mouth. While today many of us are fortunate to eat not only for survival but also for pleasure and socialization, when we were hunter-gatherers, eating was surviving, so anything that could be eaten was. As far back as the Stone Age, this included ground grains, fruits, vegetables, and animal flesh.[5]

Eating will forever be central to our survival, but how we live today means that what we eat is far more up to us individually than it has been ever before. We can eat the diverse abundance of plant-based foods that millions of people thrive on, or we can eat animals, their eggs, and their milk. Health benefits of a plant-based diet and detrimental impacts of animal consumption aside (there are plenty, but that's not the book I'm writing), you probably can get your food and clothing in a store, not out in the wilderness. Even if you're a hunter, I'm betting you likely buy food from a store too, choosing to hunt animals rather than buy something else. For many, it's no longer about what we must do to survive, but about what we choose to do.

While on the topic of hunting, there is a false idea that ancient civilizations always hunted sustainably, keeping populations intact. It is perhaps an argument that fuels the head on the wall, skin as a rug, "Daddy's little hunter" bumper sticker–donning hunters' justifications today. In many ways, just like us (though we've massively ramped it up), some research suggests our ancestors did not always live in perfect harmony with nature or the animals living as part of it. On lands now called Fiji, New Caledonia, Australia, Canada, and the United States, when sapiens arrived, many species swiftly went extinct, perhaps unable to breed faster than they were being killed. That included a whopping 90 percent of Australia's large mammals, and 75 percent of America's who all saw extinction. Megafauna, such as mammoths, wombats the size of golf carts, giant rodents, and "oversized" lions who had flourished for millions of years were wiped out in a comparative blink of an eye. It seems mass animal bloodshed has been our thing for some time, even if we've only recently excelled at it through colonial captialism.[6]

Looking deeper into ancient animal use, beyond that which was done for food, our choice to use animals in fashion is one that for many tens of thousands of years has been, in some instances, exactly that—a choice. It's interesting to consider why we ever became modest and embarrassed to show certain parts of ourselves at all, why we decided to weave plants into fabrics and slice fat from animals' skins and drape them over us. While some of our prehistoric ancestors began wearing animal skins because of the cold, many lived in climates where this was unnecessary—with some Indigenous people today still choosing to be minimally clothed. So why did we start wearing clothes? Just as some communities of people today, and way back in time, decorate themselves with natural pigments (even perhaps the Neanderthals[7]), and as Cleopatra wore blue eyeshadow and I wear brown-toned lip liner, how we adorn our bodies is symbolic. Clothing tells others about us, and we often hope it portrays us in a positive light. Clothing can make us seem more attractive, more creative, more intelligent. It can show us to be a part of a certain group of thought or people, and can be a symbol of status and wealth. Even those who are uninterested in fashion express something about themselves through dress. Body decoration and jewelry likely existed before clothing in many places, and their symbolism was then extended to clothing.[8]

Prehistoric jewelry was made of all sorts of things, including bone. Archaeologists have shown that some were made from the bones of animals not commonly eaten, so likely killed specifically for decoration and dress.[9] This again suggests that animals have been killed throughout human history, not despite a natural desire to protect them from harm, but regardless of it. If our ancestors felt killing animals was wrong, they wouldn't have done it for anything other than survival. Perhaps in a different way, prehistoric people had some opportunities to make the same choice we have, to kill or not to kill. Like most of us, they often chose killing. With all current rules and rights being human-created, it's interesting to consider what we have kept purely because it's "how it's always been." Perhaps it is time we progress.

The Invention of Farming

After 2.5 million years, humans stopped feeding themselves by gathering and hunting alone. It wasn't necessarily intentional, but ten thousand years ago, instead of eating a phenomenally wide range of plants, people started to focus on cultivating just a handful. They also started herding animals they felt were "suitable" to being farmed—herbivores that are gentle and easy to manipulate, as compared to carnivorous animals that would bite a chunk out of you should you try to bend them to your will.

Barley and lentils. Sheep and goats. Some of the first farmed "foods." While plants didn't know the difference, animals certainly did. Both were suddenly much greater in populace, but only animals could look around and see their herd was suddenly living close by humans. Humans began protecting some animals like sheep from predators—but only so sheep could be exclusively theirs to prey on. The animals who got to live longer and continued to mate were only allowed this freedom if it benefited their new overlords. Animals who were considered too aggressive, too curious, too skinny, too loud had their lives taken first. Most male animals, more likely to rebel against their capturers, filled with testosterone, were castrated. We were playing God, whether we believed in one or not. Unfree to procreate naturally, those whose traits and behaviors would be killed off were now entirely up to our ancestors. Other animals were no longer individuals but things for humans to control, manipulate, and dominate. Anyone who rose against this new world order was to be killed sooner.[10]

While the picture of our first farming ancestors may still be more "wholesome" than the factory farm–filled animal agricultural machine we see today, a belief that our fellow animals are human belongings to exploit for speciesist gain has never been pretty. Some of the first farmers sliced parts of the "their" pigs' snouts off, so it would hurt them when they sniffed for food, forcing them to stay with the hand that fed (and mutilated) them.[11] Nowadays in some modern farms, pigs often have metal rings punctured through their snouts to stop them from digging up the soil as they naturally would (should they ever be outside; most pigs are not), and parts of their ears are cut out as a form of "identification."[12] The Nuer tribe in Sudan would tie a ring of thorns around calves' mouths so that, should they try to drink their mothers' milk, they would hurt them both and be unable to suckle.[13] In the Western world, at most country veterinary clinics, you can buy sharp-pointed "nose tags" that are fitted to a calves' nose—essentially a modern-day plastic ring of thorns. Modern "anti-suckling devices" are used on farms because the sooner a baby is weaned, the sooner his mother can be pregnant with another calf to slaughter and eat.[14] In many ways animal farming has changed, but brutality has always been central to it.

We know people talk about "breaking in" horses. I always find it such an uncomfortable phrase, perhaps because it's painfully accurate. Such originally wild animals as horses, chickens, cattle, sheep, pigs, and goats were to lose as much of their wildness as possible. Made void of their individuality, their instincts, their freedom of movement and expression, they were convenient for humans to reign over. While animals are more widely exploited and slaughtered today than ever before, they have also been selectively bred to be more docile and accepting of whatever horrific circumstances they are placed in.[15] Wild horses are no longer rounded up and "bucked out" until their spirit is broken. Instead, they're born and bred part of the way there. For animals, human and beyond, trauma is thought widely to be carried generationally, not just through a shared environment, but even genetics.[16] While farmed animals still fight for their lives and for their safety, for a number of reasons, a domesticated animal simply does not turn on their "master" the way a free-living one would, should someone treat them the same way.

Not every animal has been "broken." When the British invaded the land they called Australia, they brought with them their animal captives—sheep. They burned down stolen native land to allow space for the sheep to graze before slaughter. In the documentary *Kangaroo*, Uncle Max Dulumunmun Harrison, a Yuin Elder, says: "Kangaroos have been here for millions of years. This is their land, they are the first Australians." But Australia, a land still named by those who pillaged it and all those on it, was built "on the sheep's back."[17] The British wanted their sheep to grow fat on the same grasses kangaroos were eating, and so they shot the kangaroos. But the magnificent animals are hard to dominate. Kangaroos move in a way that is amazing, both because it is unique and because it is energetically efficient. This means they are almost impossible to farm and more difficult to entrap in regular fencing. Unable to be controlled, instead they have been vilified.[18]

A colonialist, conquering mindset, one insistent on one's right to all they see and superiority to all those different to them, is a frightening one.

This is clear in the genocide of Indigenous people, which still continues today in a modernized and so more covert way. It is perhaps this mindset, too, that resulted in kangaroos, being labeled as a pest and plague to be culled. How dare a native animal evade the whim of invaders? The existence of indigenous kangaroos damaged the economic success of sheep farming and slaughtering. So, kangaroos are now victims of the largest land-based wildlife slaughter in the world, and a hugely profitable one at that.[19] This vilification of a wild animal purely for existing outside the will of people continues today and is representative of an insidious and widespread disdain for those we cannot control, who do not exist under our will. This is an ideology that, in a broadly supremacist and anthropocentric world, exists to different extents within us all. It is one that ultimately, as humans, we can choose to uproot or water.

The side of us who marvels at a deer roaming free is one I like far more than the one who thinks she is beautiful only insofar as that her head would look great mounted on the wall. It is the side of us that smiles at the gleeful song of a free bird as opposed to the one that craves to cage the singer, listening to them as they roast another bird for dinner.

The Invention of Factory Farming

A factory farm, or concentrated animal feeding operation (CAFO), confines a large number of animals in utterly unnatural and controlled conditions. An unfathomably many cages are filled, and sheds are each stuffed with thousands of turkeys, ducks, and chickens. Hundreds of rows of pens and crates trap pigs, dairy cows, and, rarely, even some sheep bred for ultra-fine wool. Most farmed animals live their lives incarcerated within these prison-like systems. About two-thirds worldwide for land-dwelling animals, and 90 percent when you consider farmed fish, too.[20] In contrast, an astonishing amount of people claim to only ever eat free-range meat, eggs, and the rest, sharing that they know most meat comes from animals that are "cared for and loved," just like on their uncle's brother-in-law's farm that they've heard of.

Just like with farming itself, the concept of factory farming was really discovered by accident. Though never really free when you're bred to be killed, the first animals to lose the freedoms of fresh air, green grass, and sun were chickens. In 1923, a time when chickens were primarily commercially raised to lay eggs,[21] Cecile Steele ordered 50 hatchling chickens from a breeder. An accidental "0" on her order form meant she got 500. Unable to return the mail-order birds, she stuffed them into small wooden sheds. Because she had so many chickens, the most profitable thing for her to do was slaughter and sell them all for a lower price, rather than feed and house so many for a longer period of time. The economy of scale worked in her favor, so next she ordered 1,000 chickens, and the year after that, she ordered 10,000. As her profits rose, the living conditions of the chickens inevitably worsened. No one can ensure the health and happiness of 10,000 individuals crammed into sheds. But Steele wasn't worried, and neither were people who started noticing how much money Steele was making and followed suit. In less than 50 years, the previously non-existent chicken meat industry grew so large that by 1973, three billion chickens were slaughtered in 12 months.[22]

As people's obsession with eating chickens grew, so did a generally intensified love of meat. This craving was propelled forward by clever advertising and a booming animal agricultural industry, which spent a fortune embedding their "product" even deeper into the psyche of global culture. In the last 50 years, meat production has quadrupled.[23] Now, across the world, factory farming is the standard. It is this way because of our demand for meat and animal secretions, and also because corporations gave many farmers little choice. As demand for cheap meat, leather, dairy, eggs, and everything else grew, some farmers were aggressively encouraged by large corporations to sign rapacious contracts. For many, this meant being bought out to raise animals for slaughter exclusively for specific companies, rather than to saleyards where they chose the buyer and price. These big businesses were and are able to have a constant supply of dead animals, and in many cases have created a near-monopoly for themselves in which they can control how much they'd buy them for, too.[24]

Just the same as for Steele, these companies make more money because they can sell more dead animals for a lower cost. Except now, we're talking the likes of a single egg farm in the United Kingdom confining a million (yes, you read it right, a million) hens for egg laying, never to see the sun, peck through grass, or dust-bathe in dirt as they so love.[25] We're talking a single pig farm in Australia trapping 170 animals, both mother pigs in farrowing crates they cannot turn around in, and many of their piglets, who are raised in concrete pens.[26] Meanwhile, fifteen thousand cows stand on concrete, milked by machines in one US farm—Fair Oaks, exposed in 2019 by Animal Recovery Mission for horrific cruelty and outright lies about their treatment and killing of calves.[27]

A similar story exists in every country—there are fewer and fewer farms, but there are more animals being killed within massive operations. Broadly, the familyrun farm is either as dead as the animals they raised, or now a factory farm, generally owned by a huge company. The farmers themselves usually aren't making more money, even making less, locked into contracts without autonomy and paying more and more money to keep their farm running. Factory farms are expensive to operate—they use enormous amounts of energy with a constant cyclical air, temperature, and light pattern running. The urine and fecal matter animals relieve themselves of have to be disposed of, too. It's pumped into waterways or sprayed over fields, polluting the natural environment and creating oceanic dead zones.[28] It harms the health of the generally lower-income, marginalized communities surrounding them.[29] But at least we're free to eat animals, who often live in their own waste, even drowning in it until it's all cleared.[30] At least the big-ag conglomerates are profiting.

When an animal is injured or sick on a factory farm, they generally go unnoticed. After all, if you're going to look after animals, you'll need to be able to check in on their individual wellbeing. *Poultry Hub* states that a typical new farmhouse has at least three and up to about ten sheds, containing in total approximately 320,000 broiler chickens.[31] In a 24-hour day, to check up on everyone you'd need to attend to over 220 chickens per minute and do literally nothing else all day. Even with a reasonably-sized team of attendants (who don't exist, that would be too expensive), many would not receive due attention.

Animals who are crammed in together and not provided any kind of life enrichment—things to do, look at, play with, explore—unsurprisingly get bored out of their mind. They bite at the bars of their cage until their gums bleed, they rip out their feathers, and they take it out on each other. Stir-crazy, some pigs bite and eat each other alive. Turkeys scratch, peck, and attack each other. Such fighting is particularly prevalent because in such terrible conditions, and when so many animals are trapped together, they aren't able to function socially as they otherwise would. They have no space to create—like humans do—a social hierarchy where they know who is the leader and who fits in with who. The skewed sociology of it makes me think of *Lord of the Flies* but in a dank, dark shed instead of an island way.

Weaker animals have nowhere to run, animals who are feeling agitated and aggressive have no space and lash out. Imagine one turkey is feeling frustrated by their absolutely rubbish life, and a turkey next to him is pushed into him by the turkey next to them. The first turkey is further aggravated by their personal space being breached and attacks the second bird. The second bird tries to flee in fear, and knocks into the third bird, who is similarly frustrated by the situation. You see what I'm getting at. The solution that industries use to "improve the welfare" of these animals? Mutilate them. Instead of a pig biting off another pig's tail, pigs have their teeth cut out and their tails cut off when they are newly born.[32] No pain relief, just pliers and scissors.[33] Turkeys have their beaks and toes burned and cut down to blunt stumps.[34] Problem solved, apparently.

Factory farming is everywhere, even when advertising is used to deceive us. Eggs marketed as cage-free can come from chickens who live their entire life inside a glorified metal box—a shed crammed full of birds is factory-farming just as much as a shed full of individual cages, it's just one big cage.[35] Pork listed as "bred free-range" comes from pigs who were born with access to the outdoors, but who spend the rest of their lives inside dull pens, sometimes green-washed as "eco-shelters."[36] Even words that have nothing to do with how animals are treated mislead us, like the word "natural." I think natural, I think green grass, blue skies, imagery displayed in the logos, packaging, and truck sides of many meat companies. Investigator Rich Hardy, in his book *Not as Nature Intended*, shares his experience at a chicken farm that confined 25,000 chickens who were slaughtered and packaged up for US supermarkets, recalling a remark made by the farmer, Chip:

> "Yep, they're all natural, animal-protein free, no antibiotics. You can't buy them locally—only in the big town stores." I struggled to see how these chickens, which were essentially confined in a huge warehouse and unable to stand without great difficulty, could ever be seen as "natural" to most consumers, yet it seemed they were being sold as a premium product.

On this farm, which pumped out chickens labeled "proudly raised by a family farm," all the chickens grew fat on gravity feeders and only had contact with Chip when he killed them, if they had become totally immobile. Rich described Chip swinging a crippled chicken around by the head in "large circles like a cowboy would swing a lasso."[37] We've come far from the roots of animal agriculture, but this is not what I'd call progress.

A Greedy Intensification

As with the wider perils of a speciesist world, the cruel mess of animal agriculture is far from confined to the factory farming of "food" animals on land. According to the Food and Agriculture Organization of the United Nations, almost half of all fish eaten today are farmed.[38] No, our fishy and oceanic friends did not escape our greedy will. We decided we wanted to eat more fish, and that aquaculture was a good way to do that since we're desecrating the oceans anyway—something I'll come back to. We also decided we wanted to eat more pigs and birds, like chickens and turkeys, so we feed them fish, too. This was an inefficient decision, considering that about one-fifth of all wild-caught fish is fed to farmed mammals, birds, and fish. For us to kill and eat 2.6 lbs (1.2 kilograms) of farmed salmon, 2.2 lbs (1 kilogram) of small fish are also killed, used as feed.[39] This system also results in seriously terrible lives for those farmed.

Salmon are one of the more commonly farmed fish species. In the wild, they enjoy the freedom to follow their instinct to swim thousands of kilometres over their lives (if they are not caught, beheaded, gutted), but today they are often confined to marine cages. With minimal if any laws protecting fish and their rights as individuals across countries, these pens can be really any size, filled with as many fish as a business thinks will be best for their profits. A welfare-approved "humane" fish farm in Australia uses sea pens (cages, but don't pens sound a bit better) that are 240 metres (~787 ft) in circumference and at least 5 metres (~16 ft) deep. They are considered the biggest in the world. Fish can be "stocked" at 15 kg/m^3 (~13 lbs/ft^3), which near the time of their slaughter means about three distressed, large fish sharing one square metre (~3 ft^3).[40] The world of a salmon just got a whole lot smaller. Some other fish spend their entire lives in indoor farm tanks before they're eaten.

Farmed fish, as many as 1 in 4, have been found to exhibit behaviors and brain chemistry nearly identical to that found in humans who are severely stressed and depressed. Unsurprising, if we imagine ourselves in their place; surprising, if we're yet to have extended empathy to fish. In their depressed state, fish eat less and have stunted growth, their suffering manifesting in the physical world.[41]

All farmed fish are generally bred indoors, with brood (breeder) fish either being "massaged" until their eggs or semen spray out of them or sliced open for easy access to them. Picture a single salmon fish. This fish is born out of one such egg and is made to live first in an indoor tank. Not even glass to look out of. This is a boring, empty life. The first half of his life is spent here. Day in, day out, nothing stimulating ever happens. Until, to his distress, he is pulled from his tank, pumped into a truck full of water, sucked up again, and spurted out into ocean cages through water-filled pipes. Here, he swims amongst many fish, jostling for space. Eating less as the stress of his confinement and inability to perform natural behaviors wears him down, he becomes somewhat emaciated. Soon, he and everyone else here will be slaughtered. Some fish farms claim they are more ethical or humane because they club fish like him over the head when slaughtering, whereas, largely, fish caught from the wild and unruly ocean slowly asphyxiate.[42] Yes, this death is faster, but considering the construction of an intensive farming and slaughtering system for previously wild animals, a welfare improvement is more than a stretch.

Like with fish, our need to totally control the lives of animals, how they're born, how many of them shall live, how long they'll live, and under what conditions, continued beyond those we normally consider farm animals. We have somewhat recently begun to factory-farm crocodiles and snakes so we may more easily obtain their skins, sold as wallets, shoes, and bags worth tens, even hundreds of thousands of dollars. These reptiles are (sometimes illegally) turned into these expensive products to flaunt power and wealth—the rarer the animal slain, the greater the wearer. As animal populations in the past became deeply threatened by their being hunted—saltwater crocodiles nearly became extinct in Australia in the 1970s—a "solution" appeared: capture these ancient reptiles from the wild and breed them in captivity for commercialized slaughter.[43]

The idea behind this "solution" is essentially that if you can commodify and monetize animals, their population will be "cared for." Not out of any actual care, but because it makes financial sense to keep their numbers up, so they can continue to be skinned for the rich to wear. It's doubtful any of these crocodile individuals feel fortunate to be alive for the sake of their "thriving" populations, though, so calling this slaughter industry a "conservation effort" truly misses the mark. Especially so because today more saltwater crocodiles live in factory-farm cages and concrete-floored pens than in their natural habitat. Conservation is not killing animals who have an average lifespan of 70 years at just a few, it is not keeping reptiles in deprivation, it is not shooting a captive bolt gun through their heads and claiming the species is lucky to have been "saved." Conservation ought to show compassion for the animals it claims to help protect, it should be habitat protection, education, but it is being hijacked for a money grab at the expense of animal lives.[44]

Symbolic of a far wider issue, this is an example of our insistent need for more all the time, in turn excusing exploitation. More puppy farms so we can both cuddle and perform tests on dogs. More chickens so we can eat more of them. More boiled-alive silkworms so we can feel soft fabric against our own skin. More introduced and exploited bee species so we can eat their honey, despite the threat to critically important native bee species this industry may pose. A hunger for perpetual growth comes at a great cost for humans, our fellow animals, and the planet.[45]

We're a long way from where farming began. Mega–factory farms continue to open, hideously cruel "innovative" new ideas continue to come out of animal agriculture and out of industries that want more and more money at the expense of everything and everyone around them. We're so clearly divergent from our gathering and hunting ancestors, even from our grandparents and great grandparents and the system in which they lived. Just as we decided to change, evolve, and "improve" our past agricultural and other production systems, we can change the ones we have now, and we must. I'm far from the first person to think this way, and fortunately will not be the last.

Part Two

The Fight For and Against Animal Rights

People have advocated and fought for the rights of animals long before many of us realize, but understanding the history of this movement is important to its future and progress.

Chapter 5

How We Began to Fight the System

Ancient and Historical Liberationists

> "All tremble at violence, life is dear to all. Putting oneself in the place of another, one should not kill nor cause another to kill."
> —The Buddha, around 2,500 years ago[1]

> "India is a strange country. People do not kill any living creatures, do not keep pigs and fowl, and do not sell live cattle."
> —From the travelogue of Faxian, a Chinese Buddhist monk and translator who traveled by foot across Asia between late fourth and early fifth century CE[2]

While no entire country has ever abstained from the killing of animals, Faxian's writings tell us that people have stood against suffering and for the rights of animals for well over a thousand years, long before people threw paint on fur coats, or even before the word "vegan" existed. Veganism is often painted as a "white thing," animal rights as a fairly young and so somehow less significant liberation movement. Neither is the case.

Even earlier, in ancient India, the Buddhist emperor Ashoka (304–232 BCE) lived without eating animals, advocating for nonviolence to them. Compassionate and revolutionary laws were put forward in his edicts, inscribed on sandstone pillars in bustling public spaces: "No living beings are to be slaughtered or offered in sacrifice." These edicts were written in his own words, personal in tone rather than in the pompous royal terminology that had predated him. In the time following his coronation, over two dozen animal species were protected from huntsmen, forest and wildlife reserves were created, and what may perhaps be the first prohibitions of cruelty toward animals, both wild and domesticated, were put in place. All people were encouraged (even if imperfectly) to practice morality and to extend kindness and respect to those around them: "Proper behavior towards servants and employees, respect for mother and father, generosity to friends, companions, relations . . . and not killing living beings."[3]

Ahimsa aims to be the ethical principle of nonviolence for all—humans and our fellow animals—which proliferates so many ancient and modern Indian writings first shared in Vedic texts as early as 1500 BCE and onward from then. "Without doing injury to living things, flesh cannot be had . . . hence eating of flesh should be avoided." "Do not injure the beings living on the earth, in the air, and in the water." "May all beings look at me with a friendly eye. May I do likewise, and may we all look at each other with the eyes of a friend." Such simply kind ideas have existed for so long, and so I cannot help but wonder why it is that not all people came to these conclusions so long ago. How absurd it is that, in contrast, white colonists like the British targeted and killed so many humans and other animals they viewed as without value, and passed their first act against cruelty to non-human animals in only 1835 CE.[4]

The protection of our fellow animals against suffering and slaughter is seen throughout history across all different parts of the world. Take Greek mathematician and philosopher Pythagoras, king of right-angle triangles and the first to suggest that Earth is indeed round, not flat, who lived until around 497 BCE. Pythagoras believed all beings had souls, and described meat as the "sad flesh of the murdered beast," as is recorded in Ovid's *Metamorphoses*.[5] In fact, a diet free of all animals was called a "Pythagorean diet" until the modern vegetarian movement began in the mid-1800s (CE).[6]

In 675 CE, Emperor Tenmu of Japan placed bans on some animal consumption and made all eating of flesh taboo.[7] Many prominent historical figures kept animals in their hearts and off their plates. Leonardo Da Vinci, Italian renaissance architect, engineer, painter of the Mona Lisa, and basically man of many talents, is one of these figures. In *Codice Atlantico 76*, da Vinci condemns the immorality of animal eating, people having made their bodies "a tomb for other animals, a haven for the dead, giving life by the death of others, a coffer full of corruption."[8] Both he and Pythagoras referenced aforementioned Indian ideology as the grounding of their ethics.

Vegetarianism rose strongly during the Romantic Era of the nineteenth century.[9] It's worth noting here that what we now consider veganism once was strict vegetarianism. Those whom we now call vegetarian, who do not eat animals but eat milk and eggs derived from slaughtering, exploitative systems, were called lacto-ovo-vegetarians. Anyway. In Mary Shelley's classic Romantic-era novel, *Frankenstein,* the Doctor's Creature expresses his true benevolence through his choice of food: "I do not destroy the lamb and the kid, to glut my appetite; acorns and berries afford me sufficient nourishment. . . . The picture I present to you is peaceful and human."[10]

In this Romantic period, vegetarian theory began to more clearly intersect with other social justice movements and oppressions, including ideas of hierarchical class oppression. Flesh eating was defined by writer and abolitionist Thomas Day as a means to "gratify a guilty sensuality."[11] Animal agriculture is inherently wasteful, requiring more land and more plant matter to be used and consumed by other animals than if humans ate plants directly. So, animal eating was considered a greedy vice of the wealthy, who could afford it regularly. With animal consumption being directly linked (and still so today) to lessened food accessibility, environmental destruction, and inequality, eating flesh became symbolic of oppression and consumerism. Arguments that combined issues of class and animal oppression continued on, and in Victorian England, it brought vegetarianism and feminism together, too. Feminist writers like Charlotte Perkins Gilman and Margaret Fuller advocated for the end of animal consumption. They considered that the liberation of women would, in turn, transform society away from the toxified ideas of masculinity that promote violence, inevitably leading to a predominantly veg(etari)an world.[12]

Veganism—not killing animals, and the idea that the lives of animals (humans included) matter—is simply not new or revolutionary, just something we have continued to push aside for too long.

Exposing Words and Their Tangible Power

The animal liberation movement has a rich history of written theory and argument of animal sentience, soul, and right. A pivotal step forward for animals was when the written word became journalistic, sharing real-world happenings and leading to action and change.

In 1902, a time in which "humanitarian fashion" boasted substitutes for animal skins,[13] vivisection was perhaps most broadly considered the greatest animal rights issue. So, Swedish feminists Lizzy Lind af Hageby and Leisa Schartau, who founded the Anti-Vivisection Society of Sweden, used their familial wealth and intelligence to enroll in medical studies in London, gaining medical training that would legitimize and inform their campaigning for animals. Attending lectures at the University of London, the women took detailed notes of "educational" vivisections in a diary. Of a grey rabbit they wrote: "[Their] throat has been opened, the jugular vein exposed, and a cannula inserted . . . the rabbit begins to struggle . . . thrown into tetanic convulsions for about a minute, the eyes become bloodshot and start from their sockets, and the animal falls back—dead." Of students who watched a black and white cat be cut open, kidney pulled out of their body for the purpose of show and tell and blood-pressure testing, they wrote: "Right or wrong, success or failure, an experiment upon a living animal is always interesting, and they reward the zealous demonstrator by applause and laughter." It seemed it did not matter that the killings did nothing for the progress of science and everything for the retrogression of ethics, back to Descartes' absurd "animal machine" premise. It mattered that it was theatrical and easy to make a blooming doctor feel important, no matter the life lost.[14]

What would become most historically significant about these women would be their records of a brown dog who had his abdominal cavity cut open and his pancreatic duct tied so it would not function. The dog was kept in a cage for two months, howling and whining, until he was cut open again for inspection, clamped shut and cut open at the neck for another demonstration. Finally, the dog was killed. It was this dog who came to represent every animal who had been vivisected, cut open, prodded, and discarded. The diary was handed over to the British National Anti-Vivisection Society, who published their findings in a book entitled *Shambles of Science: Extracts from the Diary of Two Students of Physiology.* The book has since been extracted and republished multiple times.[15]

Printed in 1903, the book was birthed in a time when women in the country could not vote and when prominent medical scientists proclaimed that women who educated themselves risked damaging their uterus and ability to have children (their most important role). The book plunged vivisection into the forefront of global Western public debate and led to a libel trial, which the lecturer, William Bayliss of the Department of Physiology, won. The Lord Chief Justice called the book "hysterical," a word too often tacked to women who have a point, who are passionate, who ought to be shut up should they upset the imbalanced way things are.[16]

Despite this, the controversy continued to gain public attention when in 1906, Anna Louisa Woodward, founder of the World League Against Vivisection, raised money for a mighty bronze statue of the dog. Erected with an inscription for him and 232 other animals who had been tortured and killed that same year in campus lectures, outrage ensued. Wealthy male medical students attacked the statue with crowbar and sledgehammer and vandalized it regularly. In 1907, a string of riots saw hundreds of these medical students working to destroy the monument, invading suffragette meetings, yelling, marching with effigies of the brown dog, fighting up to 300 police officers, shouting down Lizzy Lind af Hageby every time she spoke, tearing clothes, and smashing furniture. Lizzy stated: "This had been a battle between the sexes and, more particularly, between machismo and feminism." The statue had become symbolic of victimhood and of those oppressed by what was considered a cruel and greedy establishment. The unionizing working class and the women's suffrage movement came to stand together against vivisection, against the self-righteous and aggressive male students, against cruelty, classist elitism, and sexism, and for the bronze (once brown) dog. It was about the rights of animals, and it was about a lot more, too.[17]

Great uproar brings great press coverage and, eventually, results. Amongst this unprecedented public contention, The Second Royal Commission on Vivisection took place in 1906 and heard from both scientists and anti-vivisection groups. A 139-page report put in place restrictions on curare, a poison used to immobilize animals during experiments, referenced in the book. It was decided that animals must be adequately anaesthetized, and that experiments should not be performed simply as "an illustration of lectures." It was recommended that detailed vivisection records be kept, and a committee to advise the Secretary of State on matters related to the Cruelty to Animals Act would be established. While these decisions did not save animals from their bitter end, or give them the rights they are due, it was real progress. Granted, minimal progress, as exemptions could remove restrictions if they would "frustrate the object of the experiment," but it was something.[18]

This was one of the first times so much public attention had come to the plight of animals in this society, and it showed the power of investigative writings and people outraged by injustice. It was not the last work of investigative writing that led to policy change for animals, either. Queue Ruth Harrison. In 1961, Harrison received a confronting leaflet about factory farming from Crusade Against All Cruelty to Animals in the mail. Harrison was a vegetarian at the time and decided she wanted to do more for animals. She began investigating factory farms and the spaces and practices within them, which were little understood or known by the general public. In a time in which animal agriculture was shrouded by ignorance and a far thinner veil of secrecy—no gag laws, no violence against activists, no suspicion of those interested in learning about animal farming (it's coming)—Harrison visited different farms all across Britain. She asked questions, was invited in to learn more, and wrote meticulous notes on everything she saw. In 1964, Harrison published *Animal Machines: The New Factory Farming System.* While photos, taken by her husband, Dex, were included, the majority of information was text-based.[19]

"If one person is unkind to an animal it is considered to be cruelty, but where a lot of people are unkind to animals, especially in the name of commerce, the cruelty is condoned and, once large sums of money are at stake, will be defended to the last by otherwise intelligent people."[20] Sharing supposed legal protections of animals alongside recounts of the reality that played out before her, the public was shocked by the disparity between the happy, loving farm they pictured and the dimly lit, cage-filled sheds that really held who would become their food. The true scale and sadism of common farming, now factory farming, had been exposed. People were horrified.

Having revealed the continuous striving for greater production and greater profit at the expense of greater suffering, the public and government realized something needed to be done. The British government ordered an investigation into factory-farming practices, and Harrison was invited to be a part of these efforts.[21] In 1965, following this investigation, the Five Freedoms, which underpin most animal welfare laws today, were born. The Five Freedoms are pretty basic: Freedom from hunger and thirst, from discomfort, from pain, from injury and disease, from fear and distress, and to express normal behavior.[22] But this legislation was revolutionary. It was then perhaps the most historically significant legal recognition in the global West that animals not only felt fear and pain, but that they deserved to be free of both.

I'd love to end the book here with a happily ever after, but despite Harrison's powerful work that led to this and all that followed, the Five Freedoms do not exist in practice, and cannot, should the animal–industrial complex exist. Too, while perhaps the freedoms improve the "welfare" of animals to an extent, they in some ways act as a protective shield against scrutiny for an industry powered by needless slaughter and a denied freedom to life itself. Pigs may not legally have their throats sliced open while fully conscious, they just painfully burn from the inside out in gas chambers instead.[23] Higher welfare, right?

One of the texts considered canonical to the animal liberation movement came about a decade later: *Animal Liberation* by Peter Singer. Harrison's book was important to Singer's passage toward the values and moral code set out in his book. Singer bridged a gap in the written arguments for animal rights, delving seriously into the philosophical argument for animal liberation, but exposing, too, in great detail, the depraved realities of animal agriculture, the bleakness of the lives and horrors of the deaths of animals. His language was not as emotive as this—the plain fact of what happens to animals is enough. Bridging theory and practice was powerful because the rights of a chicken aren't so relevant to a person unless it is clear how they themselves deny them, how they are confined, cut open, decapitated, and plucked. "Those who, by their purchases, require animals to be killed do not deserve to be shielded from this or any other aspect of the production of the meat they buy."[24]

The theoretical side of Singer's argument was inspired by a historical, philosophical animal liberationist, Jeremy Bentham. In 1789 he wrote of animals: "The question is not can they reason? Nor, can they talk? But can they suffer?"[25] Singer's utilitarian ideal—to create the greatest good for the greatest number of beings (read, not just humans)—was important because it held animals to, quite simply, deserve to be free from suffering the same as we do. It acknowledged that the animals we eat and wear do not go willingly to their deaths as they saw them coming. And so, he advocated we not eat or wear them. Singer stated: "When we eat plants, food takes on a different quality. We take from the earth food that is ready for us and does not fight against us as we take it."[26] This message reverberated out into the world, garnering *Animal Liberation*—as well as Tom Regan's more totally liberationist book, *The Case for Animal Rights*, which argued our fellow animals had moral rights as "subjects-of-a-life"—great public praise.[27] However, neither received the same government action as *Animal Machines*. After all, not killing animals is getting a little extreme, right?

Direct Action and Animal Liberation

In 1963, The Hunt Saboteurs Association, still running today, was founded by 21-year-old John Prestige. Its purpose: Make it impossible for British hunters to be successful in their blood sport. Saboteurs (sabs) confuse, distract, and ultimately "de-weaponize" the hunter-owned hounds (who are puppy-farmed, often slaughtered if they are of no use[28]) used to catch and kill native animals like foxes and other small mammalian creatures. The dogs, who are trained to pick up the scent of these animals, are thrown off by sabs with a harmless mix of citronella oil and water. Horns are blown, distracting the dogs from the commands of hunters. Everything is legal but incredibly aggravating to those who get a kick out of killing.[29]

For legally sabotaging hunts and filming hunters acting illegally, hunt sabs have been attacked with a pickaxe, beaten until unconscious, lashed, pushed in front of fast-moving vehicles, hit by cars, and even killed. One case saw someone simply wearing a hunt sabs sweatshirt around town be attacked, requiring stitches on their face.[30] Perhaps unsurprising from people killing for fun. Bittersweetly, this violence was likely a sign that hunts were indeed being effectively sabotaged.

Ronnie Lee and Cliff Goodman were hunt sabs who became increasingly displeased with the limits of the purely legal tactics being deployed, thinking it would be better not to sabotage the hunt in progress, but to make it impossible for the hunt to begin at all. The activists renamed themselves the Band of Mercy in 1972, the namesake of a nineteenth-century anti-vivisection educational group. In the spirit of making wildlife slaughter impossible, Ronnie and Cliff and a growing team of sabs began working against the law for animals—slashing tires of hunting vehicles so they couldn't go out for the day being the most deployed hunt disablement. As time went on, the Band of Mercy expanded and worked to oppose violence against farmed animals and animal test subjects. In 1974 the group, made up of less than half a dozen friends, raided eight vivisection suppliers that bred animals for testing. While the primary goal was economic sabotage by property destruction, this was also one of the first recorded animal rescues, with guinea pigs freed from a farm. Activism was gearing up, getting more and more radical, until Ronnie and Cliff were arrested and sentenced to three years of imprisonment.[31]

At Winchester prison, Ronnie was refused vegan food, so began a hunger strike. Calling friends from the inside, media caught on to the story. The attention awarded Ronnie with food he could eat, and led to greater awareness of the issues he stood for. Outside the prison, there was growing support for the cause and his illegal action opposing what was, being frank, the legal torture of animals. When Ronnie was released (early) in 1976, he formed the Animal Liberation Front. Having lived a caged existence himself, though at least with a release date, Lee found strengthened solidarity with animal "inmates." Let the extremism begin.[32]

For the first years up until the 1980s, media generally covered the work of the ALF as extreme but understandable; these were animal lovers in balaclavas who couldn't stand by and let animals be abused. Perhaps it was thought that activists were taking things a little far sometimes, but when the public read of rescued beagles from a facility where they were forced to smoke, masks strapped to their faces, they could hardly see terrorists. But this didn't last, as noted by these activists. "The powers behind the news media began to lean hard on editors, and almost overnight the beagle-rescuing darlings were made over into dangerous fanatics who posed a threat to the very fabric of society." Many a legal battle were to come.[33]

In the broad daylight of 1997, while battling police, activists tore down bricks from the walls protecting Consort Beagle Breeder, which supplied animal testing facilities, until they broke through and stole dogs. After 12 months of campaigning by those who would later become known as SHAC, the breeding facility couldn't handle it and closed. Two hundred beagles were saved from an agonizing life and death, instead given loving homes. Hill Grove Cat Farm pulled the plug after 18 months, and, most successfully, after only seven days, the Regal Rabbits breeding facility closed and surrendered 1,200 rabbits to activists. The land that facility lay on is now a mushroom farm.[34]

You can look at these campaigns as acts of trespass, burglary, intimidation, and a whole lot of other crimes. Or, you can see the buildings no longer full of rabbits, dogs, and cats who would be tested on, tormented, torn open, and eventually trashed. Both outlooks are objectively correct, but what you focus on, whether these actions were justifiable, is based on what you feel deserves most protection—corporate interest or living creatures. An important note, too, is that animal rescue is only considered burglary because our fellow animals are legally considered property. If I stole a computer from a store or a hen from a factory-farm cage, by law it is considered the same. I have committed and aided this kind of burglary, and I have not the slightest doubt that animal rescue, or "theft," is completely morally justifiable, because it is lifesaving. No matter what loss of profit, what strain on business may come from this crime, ensuring someone is no longer suffering, and that they are safe from being killed, is what I wholeheartedly feel is right. What is far more problematic is a legal system that does not consider animal abuse a crime itself.

Returning to the ALF, their action is non-violent, though that statement depends on someone's definition of violence. Right now, I mean action against another living being that causes physical harm. Since the 1980s, the ALF has committed hundreds of millions of dollars worth of property damage and arson. The ALF has also saved countless animals. Both efforts have caused bankruptcy and business closure many times. Arson has never been committed in a building where anyone was inside or at risk. The closest they've gotten to an instance of harm was when a smoke bomb went off in a Seattle office linked to animal testing, or when homes of people connected to animal testing had their windows smashed in the 1990s. There has not been one publicly recorded instance where an animal advocate has caused physical harm to someone. However, mental violence, by way of traumatization and immense stress, was caused in the last cases.[35]

These acts, connected to the Stop Huntingdon Animal Cruelty (SHAC) campaign (which I'll get back to), were supported by some but not all of the Front's spokespeople. But the ALF, as with the SHAC campaign, ran on the idea that anyone could join it. It was everywhere and nowhere, belonging to anyone and no one. This meant that tactics and moral ideas within the group could and did differ. ALF was proudly decentralized all the same, stating from their press office that "that is why the ALF cannot be smashed, it cannot be effectively infiltrated, it cannot be stopped. You, each and every one of you: you are the ALF."[36]

An uncompromising promise to destroy an insidiously vicious part of society is perceived with fear by many, and historically always has been. Dr. Martin Luther King Jr. feared that the actions of more "radical" and violent Black liberationists who rioted and damaged property would only deepen a racial divide. Others like Eldridge Cleaver, who lived to see the assassination of Dr. King and who was a part of the Black Panthers, believed there was simply no other way to get white people to pay attention or make space for Black people and their freedoms. Dr. King's assassination, despite his good faith in those around and even opposing him, could only solidify this belief.[37] Such discussion around the continued fight against oppression exists today in all liberation movements.

While questioning the efficacy of different forms of resistance is critical, it is important these discussions are framed by an understanding of the turmoil behind "radical" actions. In 2020, after yet another innocent Black man, this time George Floyd, was murdered by a police officer, the Minneapolis police station was set alight in a riot. Because of the property damage caused in it, the riot was portrayed as highly violent. Trauma-trained therapist Yolanda Renteria responded to outrage regarding not the murder, but the riot, with: "If it's difficult for you to understand why people resort to violence, it probably means your privilege has protected you from being put in a situation where you feel you have no other choice. . . . Violent protests have consequences. People will die, people will go to jail, people will lose everything they have. How far does someone have to be pushed to risk it all? Sit with that."[38] Flaming police stations of cops who stood with a murderer and burned-down buildings where animals are routinely slaughtered are symptoms of deeply hurtful, violent systems that have ignored peaceful protests. When the proper channels aren't working, other paths are forged. I don't believe they should harm individuals, but they're going to have to harm profits and institutions that cause harm.

Even when there is no violence involved, the unflinching lack of remorse by activists who break the law enrages many. A good example of this is Peter Young, who freed 8,000 mink from fur farms. After being on the run for seven years, he was sentenced to two years in prison (and slapped with a hefty restitution fine). Peter has been described as an "arrogant vigilante," among other things, listed on FBI watch lists.[39] A part of his closing statement at his sentencing, something that gives me chills each time I read it, is something many have described as "unapologetic arrogance":

> This is the customary time when the defendant expresses regret for the crimes they committed, so let me do that because I am not without my regrets. I am here today to be sentenced for my participation in releasing mink from six fur farms. I regret it was only six. I'm also here today to be sentenced for my participation in the freeing of 8,000 mink from those farms. I regret it was only 8,000. It is my understanding of those six farms, only two of them

> have since shut down. I regret it was only two. More than anything, I regret my restraint, because whatever damage we did to those businesses, if those farms were left standing, and if one animal was left behind, then it wasn't enough.

Peter told me that dividing the days and hours of his time in prison between the individuals he released from incarceration helped him feel better about his time inside. Each time he knew enough hours had passed to account for another individual, when he knew he'd been locked inside so someone else could be free, it was worth it. It was Peter's solace, and he said he hoped if the roles were reversed, "someone would do the same" for him. Someone drew a cartoon of Peter sitting in jail, days tallied on the wall, smiling out at mink who had visited him in his cage, looking through the barred window. In reality, those mink were traipsing through long grasses, digging their dens, sipping freshwater. They were never made to see a cage again.

In the late 1970, in Australia, Patty Mark founded the Open Rescue Movement. Patty decided a myth needed dispelling—that activists, animal rescuers, and cruelty investigators were frightening criminals; brazen, entitled people with no respect. To do so, she felt she needed to be totally transparent about breaking the law and why. Patty and her team would go out to farms and slaughterhouse holding pens, and they'd film and expose what they witnessed, filming themselves rescuing animals, too. They did not hide, they committed no property damage, they spoke to camera, they aimed to act as professionally and diligently as any other emergency service—paramedics, firefighters, police arriving at a scene of domestic violence. It was simple and effective in making the public empathize with this form of activism. These were regular people who cared about animals and opposed violence toward them, who saw terrible things happen and who wanted to stop them.

Embracing a principle of non-violence, Patty and those involved in the movement openly break unjust laws under the "moral premise that it is wrong to knowingly let any individual, regardless of their species, be imprisoned, abused, or killed for the profit of another."[40] This is the same premise rescuers hiding their identity follow—these people are not ashamed of their actions but protecting the longevity of their work.

Open rescue worked well to change some public perception and has become a global movement. For some time before industries built on animal exploitation lobbied harder, manipulating public perception again, mainstream media removed the terrorist labels. Patty has, even while facing criminal charges, been publicly perceived as who she is—a mother and grandmother with a deep passion for animals and their safety. A member of Australian Parliament once even joined Patty on an open rescue of factory-farmed piglets to see what it was like. This more positive portrayal hasn't always stuck around, and there has been pushback, but a much more "palatable" representation of anti-speciesist activism has allowed for wider reception and agreement with a liberationist message: What is happening to animals is horrific, they deserve their freedom and they shall get it. Until every cage is empty.

Technological Revolution

An individual animal being saved from a factory farm or slaughterhouse won't change the world, but it totally changes that individual's world. When that rescue is documented, and when the fate that animal is being saved from is too, something with far wider reaching effects can happen.

For too long there was simply no evidence of the many legal, standard, and unjust practices within animal production systems. No one knew that newborn male chicks were ground alive until it was exposed. No one had seen inside live export ships, known what puppy farms were, until they saw it with their own eyes. There are some things that, when read, your imagination can exaggeratingly capture. Animal agricultural enterprises—factory farms, slaughterhouses—are not some of these things. The reality is more confronting than most of our minds can fathom.

Perhaps one of the most famous early examples of video evidence was the liberation and story of Britches. Britches was an infant stump-tailed macaque monkey who was rescued during a 1985 raid of the University of California Riverside. He was one of 260 animals rescued, and his story was shared by PETA, who created a short film from the Animal Liberation Front footage. Britches was found with his eyes stitched shut, his head wrapped up, and an electronic sonar device strapped to his head. Britches was allowed to grow old in a sanctuary, alongside an older female macaque who had cared for other orphans. Meanwhile, the public was horrified by what was completely legal and happening right under their noses.[41]

Without evidence, justifying change is a tough gig. Some of the most significant legal wins for animals have come off the back of photographic evidence, as investigator Rich Hardy told me:

> If I think back to the early 1990s in Europe, almost all commercial hens were in barren battery cages, most sows spent their entire pregnancy confined in gestation crates, and there were no laws that recognised farm animals as sentient creatures able to feel pain and suffer. Fast forward a few decades and the European Union has banned barren battery cages and the use of gestation crates for the majority of a sow's pregnancy. They have also legally recognised animals as sentient. While this doesn't end the suffering of all farm animals, it was a giant step forward, and in my view, makes the next step—an end to animal farming—more achievable. It's noticeable that these legal breakthroughs also came at a time when animal protection organisations began incorporating undercover investigations into their work. For any solution-based campaign to be successful you need to show evidence of the problem. Being able to show decision-makers hard-hitting covert images of hens unable to stretch their wings in cages or sows who can't even turn around in their metal crate, helped turn a "no" into a "yes" with the legislators.

Similar but supposedly "enriched" cages with a stick running through them are still permitted, as is some crate confinement of pigs. But these steps forward contribute to a reduction in suffering while work for more transformative social change persists.

Having grown up with VHS turned DVD turned digital videos of me, taken by my parents, it's hard to imagine a time where documenting cruelty simply wasn't an option, or was a clunkier, more difficult one. Peter Young told me about activists who, in 1998, took a huge, heavy camera into an egg-laying hen factory farm during a rescue, dropping the VHS tape and copies of it into the mailboxes of journalists on following nights.[42]

Footage has become increasingly high in quality, with technological advances allowing almost anyone to capture 4K visuals—even in low-light conditions—of what is happening to animals behind closed doors. It used to be that to capture slaughterhouse footage, an entire cassette recorder had to be complicatedly hidden in the walls of abattoirs, so that equally difficult to hide, bulky cameras could record what happened inside. Few cameras were able to be hidden securely enough, and less footage was captured. Now, cameras the size of fingernails are relatively affordable, more power efficient, and versatile. Optical zoom capacities are phenomenal, and image stabilization for covertly captured handheld footage means the world has seen more than it ever could before. Equally powerful, drone footage now allows us to understand the scale of animal exploitation facilities in a way that was never possible before. It's also allowed people to record things that otherwise go unseen—the slaughter of crocodiles in Australia, dead pits full of animals, the unloading and whacking of animals coming off trucks to their slaughter.

This kind of footage contributes to widespread change. Documentaries like *Earthlings* and *Dominion* have been seen millions of times. Footage has seen farms and testing labs close, and entire industries that were either unknown or wrongly thought of as innocent exposed. Consider the first time male chicks in the egg industry were seen being ground alive in a glorified wood chipper. No one even knew males in the egg industry were considered "wastage," yet now countries like Germany and France are banning maceration altogether.[43] Undercover footage of fur trappers stomping on foxes and watching coyotes whimper while staring down gun barrels has forced change, too. Once using terms like "farm-free" fur to justify and delegitimize cruelty, in 2021, Canada Goose, formerly famous for its use of trapped coyote fur trimmings, announced an end to its use.[44] Footage of tuna fish pierced with hooks and cut at with knives while thrashing to flee has brought oversight to an otherwise totally out-of-view industry operating "as usual."[45]

It's easier to pay for someone to be violated and killed, to undermine the true cost of an animal "product," if you've never seen what that violence looks like for yourself. Improved technology allowed for more of reality to come out from the darkest corners of the world.

Chapter 6

How the System Fought Back

Just as activists began to make serious headway for their cause, corporate and government powers joined forces, working to deconstruct the movement.

Terrorist Label

The Animal Liberation Front, and the similarly named Earth Liberation Front, which is considered to have descended from the former, were picking up pace in the 1990s. This was considered dangerous to those profiting from the slaughter and destruction of millions of animals and millions of square feet of ancient forestry. These groups, and the campaigns they supported, like SHAC, were gaining a massive public support base, causing huge financial backers to cut ties with destructive industry operatives and making people question things they hadn't before. SHAC saw eight companies, including some of the largest investors of an animal testing facility, pull their funding.[1] The ELF made national headlines when they burned down a $12 million ski resort set to expand into a forest habitat, threatening animal species within it. ELF stated if the 885 acres of forest clearcuts for ski mountains and roads were completed, it would result in the loss of one of the last threatened lynx habitats.[2] Even as I research this, I consider types of tourism and the implications on unique and precious eco-systems in a way I haven't before.

The truth cannot do harm to a cause for justice, to a cause based in truth. Since truth couldn't damage the efforts of animal advocates revealing abhorrent cruelty for commercial interest, those ruling animal enterprises instead went with "make something up to distract from the truth." This is how the term "eco-terrorist" came to exist. Out of nowhere, with no basis in what we all understand as "terrorism," adverts began to be published. One advertisement, taking up a page in *The New*

York Times, saw a balaclava-donned person staring down readers with the words "I Control Wall Street" and references to the stock exchange being held hostage by anti-speciesist activists.[3] The justification for the claim was that an animal testing facility was not permitted onto the exchange after its practices had been exposed by activists. Another advertisement, this time by the fur industry of the 1980s, plastered another balaclava-clad person with an axe over newspapers with the statement "Meet the world's newest terrorist. . . . Don't tolerate terrorism in America. Fur is for life." It's funny—I thought the fur industry hinged on ending lives. Anyway, PR companies were hired by industry groups to sprinkle fear-mongering claims about the new "eco-terrorism" concern throughout the media—with even the Center for Consumer Freedom warning parents about *Charlotte's Web*, a sweet children's film with a pig protagonist—or as the industry would say, propogandist.[4] In a freshly post-9/11 world, the "t" word was especially sensitive. This publicly shared fear was manipulated by industries to further insist on the new eco-terrorist enemy to public safety. Industries exploiting animals saw an opportunity to lobby harder to protect their interest against activists. By 2005, the FBI had stated that "one of today's most serious domestic terrorism threats comes from special interest 'extremist movements' such as the Animal Liberation Front, the Earth Liberation Front, and Stop Huntingdon Animal Cruelty campaign."[5] Do you know what SHAC, and more specifically the campaign's organizers, had done to receive this special mention? They protested.

They protested relentlessly. Every day for months on end, wearing people down until they cut ties with the cruel animal testing facilities they were funding. The protesters stood on the street outside the houses of those financially supporting animal testing, day in and out. Huntingdon Life Sciences (HLS, now Envigo), the target of the pressure campaign, could be paid by any company to test on animals for any product—maybe it was a cough syrup, maybe a concealer or mascara, or maybe a mild washing detergent. One by one, SHAC picked off HLS's financial supporters, largely with this tactic as well as with rallies, leafleting, and a media strategy. And it was labeled terrorism. The organizers, who had never been involved in any of the ALF rescues or investigations that coincided with the campaign, or to the earlier-mentioned smoke bomb, were all sent to prison. More wiretaps were used to surveil people involved in this movement than in any other counter-terrorism investigation in US history.[6]

Other, actual terrorist threats addressed by the FBI included white supremacists, who were put farther down the ranks of fear. Despite the FBI's own admission that "most animal rights and eco-extremists have refrained from violence targeting human life," while white supremacists are literally still lynching and murdering people, animal and "eco-terrorists" were considered a greater threat.[7] The supposedly comparable acts of terror were the ALF and ELF being reportedly responsible for "at least twenty-five criminal incidents totalling approximately forty-eight million dollars in damages," compared with a long list of homicides and attacks on innocent Black and Brown people by white supremacists.[8] The unjust reality we must reckon with is that there are still policemen linked to the KKK and alt-right groups, and police brutality is a leading cause of death for young Black men.[9] But this is not the priority of security agencies; this is considered a lesser concern than corporations losing enormous sums of money.

These claims of terrorism frightened those who, of course, imagined actual terroristic violence when they heard and read about the FBI-listed animal rights movement. In retaliation, anti-veganism has practically become its own movement today. Where there are animal advocates, it's likely you'll find anti-vegan or pro-meat types, like the men who were fined for eating dead squirrels in front of children at a vegan food stall despite their parents pleading for the men to stop frightening them.[10] A "Punch a Vegan Day" event went viral on Facebook with thousands claiming they were going to take part.[11] The demonization of animal rights "terrorists" has branched out into hating anyone who doesn't want to eat or wear dead animals. By some, compassion is becoming seen as a threat.

Even vegan products are demonized. If you mention a plant-based alternative, you'll probably hear someone telling you that it's just plastic and you're destroying the planet with your choice (never mind that bio-based alternatives exist and producing synthetic PU leather shoes, while in no way *good* for the environment, results in about seven times less greenhouse gas emissions, compared to also non-biodegradable cow skin leather).[12] The fur industry still creates "what animal activists won't tell you" campaigns, claiming their natural fur is superior to the environmentally destructive faux fur, despite their own commissioned data showing the total opposite is true.[13] Never mind that it's not uncommon for the cattle we wear on our feet to be forced to walk for days to their deaths, chilli rubbed into their eyes, their tails twisted and broken to keep them going. Never mind that the feet of a mink never touch anything but wire cage until they're to be killed.[14] Vegan sausages are decried as terrible for us by the meat industry, even though processed meats are classified by the World Health Organization as Group 1 carcinogens, known to cause cancer, sharing a classification group with asbestos.[15] Never mind neither, that the processed flesh inside them comes from a pig less than a year old. The truth doesn't really matter; calling things fake news and eating bacon is better.

Back to the "terrorists" though. Anti-speciesist activists persisted, despite the labels, because there wasn't and isn't another option. In 2018, Aussie Farms (now Farm Transparency Project [FTP]), the organization that released *Dominion*, held the largest animal rights march in the history of Australia, with a rough estimate of 3,000 people showing up. Yet, almost no media covered it. It seemed no one cared. The next year, they ramped it up. Perhaps the most major intersection in the city of Melbourne—Flinders and Swanston Street—was completely blocked off by activists for half of the working day, and across the country, different slaughterhouses were halted from killing animals as activists locked themselves to the equipment. It made national and international news, even making it to *The New York Times*. Chris Delforce, the founder of FTP, *Dominion* creator, and action co-organizer, alongside everyone else behind the efforts, was called "green-collared criminal" by the then prime minister, Scott Morrison. He showed his and the government's support of any farmer who wanted to sue the group.[16] People said that it was all well and good to peacefully protest, but this was "too much."

Here's the problem. "Peaceful" is not synonymous with "undisruptive." What is a protest if no one is inconvenienced? If the world can go on as though nothing ever happened? No one was harmed, no one swore or fought, even while being pulled off the ground where they sat and put into the backs of police vans. What did happen is the online views of the *Dominion* documentary, which Chris says "had been sitting at around 1,500–2,000 views daily and a total of 400,000—jumped by around 50,000, then 100,000 by the end of the week, before settling into a daily average of around 3,000 for another month or two, and that number has never dropped back to its pre-action low. The total views across platforms have reached over 3 million total."

Chris continued, "The Victorian government launched an inquiry into the impact of animal rights activism on Victorian agriculture, seeking to hear from businesses who felt they had been targeted or otherwise affected by activist actions, but also from activists and animal protection organizations that could voice their concerns. Meanwhile, the federal government passed a Criminal Code Amendment (Animal Protection) Bill, leading to a superficial senate inquiry and ultimately a new law, seeking to punish the organizers of similar actions or the publishers of any kind of material, including footage, that might lead to similar actions occurring. In November, seven months after the anniversary action, the Australian Charities and Not-for-Profits Commission stripped Aussie Farms of its charitable registration, having faced ongoing pressure from the federal government and animal agriculture industry."

Interestingly, this status stripping was celebrated online by the National Farmers Federation and farm-focussed media outlet *The Weekly Times*, even before the organization itself had been officially notified.[17] All this controversy saw animal issues being covered in mainstream media almost constantly, and some small wins for animals came out of the inquiry.

This protest was perhaps a pinnacle of years of heavy pressure, investigations, and actions from advocates. While it might seem that this did more harm than good, wait until you hear the outcome of the parliamentary inquiry.[18] The inquiring committee, which included one Animal Justice Party MP, recommended codifying public interest exemptions in relation to animal exploitation. The government agreed to improve transparency around standard practices inflicted on animals. It supported an update to industry codes of practice and the Prevention of

Cruelty to Animals Act, as a matter of priority. Since then, the government has drafted new legislation that sets new standards for the treatment of animals. Once mere guidance, as recommended by the inquiry, these will become mandatory, with penalties for non-compliance. Government support was also given to examining "world's best"-practice alternatives to blunt-force trauma killing of goats, pigs, and cows, which they'd been shown in footage, and to chick maceration they'd seen, too. Finally, the government supported a recommendation to explore mandatory CCTV recording inside all slaughterhouses.

Disruption works. It's a long game, but it does. Cruel industries clutching their money bags know it, and so they do their best to stamp it out. And so, around this same time, similar concerning labels of extremism and terrorism hit animal and environmental groups all around the world. In the United Kingdom, 24 animal rights symbols and groups were listed alongside neo-Nazis by Counter Terrorism Policing's "anti-radicalisation scheme designed to catch those at risk of committing terrorist violence."[19] Victoria Tauli-Corpuz, UN special rapporteur on the rights of Indigenous peoples, is listed as a terrorist by the government in the Philippines. Human Rights Watch declared the government list a "virtual hit list," as Philippines security forces have a frightening history of assassinating people labeled as supporting the New People's Army, which opposes authoritarian government. In 2020, at least 227 environmental defenders were killed worldwide.[20] In Louisiana, members of the largely Black community who opposed the petrochemical dumping causing them health issues have been charged with "terrorizing," following non-violent action and peaceful protests. They simply held up signs and stood on a burial site for enslaved people, where a plastic production–owned facility was planned to be built.[21] George Christensen, MP from the right-wing Australian political party, the Nationals, previously called on progressive environmentalist then Greens party leader Richard Di Natale to be charged with terrorist offenses, for protesting the build of the Adani coal mine, which Natale stated "would be the seventh largest polluter on earth" if it were a country. Traditional owners of the unceded land of this colonized country continue to protest and sit on their sacred sites, which are continually being demolished for mining, as well as cattle ranching displacing human and other animal communities.[22]

It seems the issue is not terrorism; it's effective activism threatening corporate profit margins. And those activists are now being bombarded and attacked with greater force, backed by more money and power than any animal or Earth advocate has ever had on their side.

Ag-Gag Laws

How did all this talk about eco and animal activists as terrorists actually turn to law? In the United States, The Animal Enterprise Terrorism Act became law in 2006, under the presidency of George Bush, broadening the existing Animal Enterprise Protection Act of 1992.[23] This revised act passed under heavy lobbying by the animal testing, fur, and farming industries. The false advertisements by these industries calling non-violent activists terrorists essentially became law because the industry had money to spend lobbying to ensure it did.[24]

This act, which is still the most significant and first agricultural gag (ag-gag) law in the world, means a few seriously frightening things, but here's the gist. If you damage or interfere with the profit of an animal enterprise, you can be charged and criminalized as a terrorist.[25] This means not only property damage like that which the Animal Liberation Front sometimes took part in, but normally "petty" crimes like trespassing onto a farm, or petty theft—because animals are often worth so little in a monetary sense—also became terrorist acts. What is the worst, though, is that things that are totally legal and protected under American constitutional rights to free speech can be considered terrorism. If you protest in front of a fur store, if you hang a banner out the front of a store selling parts of dead animals, you could be tried as a terrorist in court.

Months out from 9/11, Will Potter was a young reporter when he decided to pass out some pamphlets about animal testing with some local activists. Not long after that, two FBI agents showed up at his door and told him that "if he didn't help them gather information about the animal activists he had helped," he could be put on a terrorism watch list, and the student aid he and his girlfriend had applied for could be pulled.

The charges against Will, simply for handing out leaflets, were dropped, and the FBI's threats were never substantiated. But Will, who has a file on him at the FBI and agents sitting in on his speaking events, has spent the years since dissecting and combating the ways animal activists have not only been labeled as terrorists but also been defined as such in law due to corporate pressure and interest. In the documentary *The Animal People*, Will, who works as an investigative journalist, speaks about these terrorist laws and how they sent non-violent activists to jail following the SHAC campaign. Simply by sharing information and imagery relating to animal cruelty, and for protesting it, they were sent to prison for "animal enterprise terrorism." Essentially, they spoke, and the industry and government didn't like what they had to say.[26]

This is why ag-gag laws are scary and why they implicate everyone. Now, it's animal activists and journalists who report on animal cruelty who are targeted, but these laws set a precedent for every other movement, every other truth that an industry or government hopes to squander.

Today, if you were driving down a country road and you saw someone in a paddock smashing calves' skulls in with a hammer, what would you do? Perhaps you would stop and film, collect evidence. Perhaps you would share it online or send it to a journalist who would publish a story about animal cruelty. This sort of cruelty occurs every day; in fact it is legal, even codified and standard practice across most of the world. However, it's not normally done in plain sight, because that's no good for business. Knowing all that animals suffer through out of the public eye, and the laws that fail to protect them, activists set up cameras inside farms both for those animals, and because it is in the public's interest to know about it. They collect evidence, they share it online as part of advocacy and pressure campaigns, and they give their evidence to journalists. Unlike blunt-force trauma killing, in parts of the United States, Australia, and Canada this advocacy is illegal.

In 2013, a woman was prosecuted for filming a live but deathly cow being dragged by a tractor outside an abattoir in America. She was standing on a public road when she recorded it. After huge public outrage, the case was dropped because the law only makes it illegal to record animal enterprises when standing on their private property.

However, the case raised significant awareness of the extreme nature of ag-gag laws.[27]

Over two dozen American states have attempted to put in place ag-gag laws, which criminalize documenting animal cruelty, not committing it. Multiple states have been successful, though most have either been denied or struck down as unconstitutional, revoking people's right to freedom of speech and equal protection.[28]

In Canada, Ontario's Bill 156 was drafted at the behest of the animal agricultural sector. Now passed but being rallied against, it "criminalizes compassion" and exists solely to cover up cruelty. As a way of attacking people who expose that cruelty, advocates who record or expose animal abuse can be fined up to $25,000. It also targets peaceful advocacy groups like the Animal Save Movement, which holds vigils outside of slaughterhouses.[29]

Regan Russell was a long-time, dedicated, anti-speciesist advocate. Regan spent countless hours at these vigils. She would provide water to pigs (something another activist has been taken to court for[30]), photograph the neglect and state of animals on trucks, and bear witness. Regan was 65 years old when she was struck and killed by a slaughterhouse truck. The driver was charged with careless driving causing death.[31] When I first heard this, I thought of all the abattoir truck drivers I've watched yelling and swearing out their window as they sped up toward my friends, peacefully holding signs on the road. We, like Regan, only wanted to stop the truck for a short five minutes, to document those inside.

Regan's long-term partner, Mark, is fighting against Bill 156, which also allows force by farmers against activists,[32] encouraging violence against those working to uncover it. "I'll fight it the rest of my life. My life ended on Friday [when Regan was killed], so for as long as I'm left here, we have to pick up the torch, and we have to fight things like Bill 156 . . . She died fighting for what she believed in. Whatever it cost, she would pay. Sometimes it's money. Sometimes, it's this." Regan's Law has also been drafted by activists and lawyers seeking to protect farmed animals from violence.[33]

In Australia, the Criminal Code Amendment (Agricultural Protection) Bill and the Right to Farm Bill similarly gag activists and journalists alike. In the state of New South Wales, those who trespass onto farms to record cruelty can be imprisoned for up to three years. Though ignored by ordinary and caring people with social media accounts, these laws can make it illegal not only to record footage of violence against animals, but also to share it.[34] That means that not only the person or organization who uploads footage is in violation of the law, but anyone who, say, shares it on Facebook. Similarly, the Surveillance Devices Act has been used to prohibit not just the publication of such footage, but even news reports relating to the findings of such footage. These laws stop countless important investigations from reaching the media, who don't want to deal with the legal implications.

Uninterested in the wellbeing of communities surrounding animal farms, a "nuisance shield" means that any farm operating in a suburban, urban sprawl area cannot be complained about if their practices are "normal." So, community members could not complain about their children seeing enormous piles of dead animals from their roads, the stink of dead pigs, or the feces of hundreds of them.[35] Similar protections exist for agricultural enterprises in all fifty United States.[36] This means that the largely Black community in North Carolina, for example, cannot complain about the "environmental racism" that sees pig farms expel effluent (feces) over the nearby communities, the farm pollution likely contributing to "higher . . . infant mortality, mortality due to anaemia, kidney disease, tuberculosis, septicaemia along with the lowest life expectancy levels in the state." Environmental racism, because this simply wouldn't be accepted if it were a white community.[37]

These laws, like those in Australia, which protect industry and clearly no one else, are carefully worded and portrayed to seem as though they are not only in the interest of farmers, but animals, too. In the interest of farmers because, without any evidence to prove it, it is claimed and even stated by government officials that farmers are subject to violence and intimidation by politically described "terrorist" activists.[38] In the interest of animals, because claims are made that activists threaten the biosecurity of farms documented to have rat infestations and dead bodies piled and swarmed by flies.[39]

Government and industry often claim that if activists "really cared" about animals, they would report animal cruelty directly to authorities, rather than release investigations, which take time to create. The claim is that by taking this time, violence is able to continue for longer. This is assuming that cruelty is rare and always illegal, and so that authorities have power to stop it. None of this is true much of the time. This industry argument, that the legal route is the most effective for animal protection, only assists the industry in their referencing "bad apples" and one-off cases of cruelty. However, long-term and widespread investigations often prove a pattern of consistent violence. In fact, there is no industry built on commodifying and killing individuals that can exist without violence. Too, reporting violence against animals to authorities would also result in no public awareness, and no action, when the cruelty is totally legalized by animal protection laws that hang farmed animals out to dry.

> In his judgment in the High Court case of *Australian Broadcasting Corporation v Lenah Game Meats Pty Ltd*, Voiceless Patron and former Justice of the High Court of Australia the Hon. Michael Kirby, defended the media's use of surveillance footage obtained by animal activists on public interest grounds: Parliamentary democracies, such as Australia, operate effectively when they are stimulated by debate promoted by community groups. To be successful, such debate often requires media attention. Improvements in the condition of circus animals, in the transport of live sheep for export and in the condition of battery hens followed such community debate.[40]

The industries rendering animals into products are rife with violence; in fact violent acts are irreplaceable cogs in these enterprise machines. Even people interested only in animal "welfare"—the treatment of animals during their lives, but not the needless taking of animal lives—should be deeply concerned by agricultural gag laws. Even people uninterested in animal protection at all should be deeply concerned by governments that allow the interests of industry to come before a society's right to information, debate, health, sustainability, and justice.

"Bad Apples"

When laws haven't stopped people from getting behind closed doors and exposing cruelty that would threaten profit, industries benefiting from secrecy take another approach: Make out like what's been captured is an anomaly, a "once-off." I asked Chris Delforce why he thought collecting so much footage of violence against animals was important, and why he and those he works with have dedicated their lives to sharing it with the world. He said, "Footage grounds in reality the otherwise vague concept of factory farms and slaughterhouses, and disproves commonly held myths like 'that doesn't happen here.'"

It's true that as more illegally obtained footage of animal enterprises in action has been released, it's become increasingly difficult for the industry to seem sincere when they assure the public that all they're seeing is the result of "just a few bad apples." But they try anyway. They assure us this isn't systemic. They assure us the footage of chickens having their heads ripped off is inconsistent with the values of the industry, that the headlines of animals being "punched, hit, kicked and left lame" are devastating surprises to them.[41] But the purpose of animal industries is to make products from bodies. Sliced-up flesh from a fish's body is a snack wrapped in rice. Chemically soaked and dried skin peeled from a cow's body is a belt. There is no real animal welfare, no real health, happiness, or fortune for those born to die. "Cruelty," the antonym to "compassion," is the basis of the system. Workers charged with animal cruelty are treating animals exactly as the industry tells them to—as commodities, as things, as means to ends, to money. They're simply extending upon the culture of violence they're paid to operate in. They swear and whack at animals the way I swear and slam on my laptop when I'm in a foul mood and it doesn't do what it's meant to.

While animals are legal things themselves, in many instances brutality is legally acceptable. Workers may not be following procedure or codes of practice, but often these aren't mandatory to follow anyway. In many countries, including the United States and Australia, farmed animals are specifically exempt from existing animal protection laws in numerous ways.[42] The protections they deserve as animals, written into law, are entirely revoked because they are bred into farms for the sake of commercial production. If this weren't the case, it would be impossible for factory farms or slaughterhouses to exist, for any of the standard farming practices like debeaking, ear clipping, or tail docking to go on.

Animal protection law, which originally provided safety to "all animals" in Connecticut, was amended in a brazenly brutal fashion, representing one of many laws purposely failing animals across countries.[43] This law was amended to add that it is now legal to "maliciously and intentionally maim, mutilate, torture, wound or kill an animal, provided the act is done while following generally accepted agricultural practices."

In other countries, and in the United Kingdom, farmed animals are exempt from safeties because animal protection laws state that harm must not be done unto animals "unnecessarily." Legally, the common commercialization of animal harm and slaughter is considered necessary.[44] The ability to capitalize off of an animal's suffering is an easy way for that animal's legal protections to be revoked. It's exactly how native Australian crocodiles found themselves in factory farms, as did emus, as did endless animals all over the world.

A cruelty conviction and punitive action against an individual worker on a farm, in a shearing shed, or in a slaughterhouse, is seen as a win by many. It might even seem like progress to those who buy what come from these places, and supposedly by those industries themselves. But while these animals certainly deserve justice, this sort of response is replacing one small cog in a machine that continues to function exactly as intended. A system that demands utter disconnect to animals, their wellbeing, and wishes, should you be able to work within it. This is a system that legalizes the cruelty individuals are prosecuted for extrapolating upon.

In the industry's attempts to say footage doesn't really count, doesn't really represent the values of a slaughtering industry, individual workers are thrown under the bus. Individual people like Craig. Craig grew up on a farm, being taught how to castrate newborn calves without pain relief as they screamed. It made him upset, but it was legal, and it was work that "had to be done," said his father. Craig was only nine when he was put into permanent foster care, taken by the state from his parents who were physically abusing him. His foster parents were safer for him, but still had him involved in violence against animals—catching rabbits to use as live bait for the racing greyhounds they trained, and whom they shot. Craig was tasked with digging holes for the slow runners to be buried in. Craig dropped out of school at about 16, and at 19 he started working in a slaughterhouse.

As I write now, I'm watching back on our video interview, and I can't help but continue to go back to the photo he sent of his younger self. Hands up to his elbows coated in blood, white apron splattered with it too. Young Craig stands firm, a fairly thin veneer of stern confidence on his face. A lifeless expression is on the face of an enormous cow hanging upside down in front of him, tongue falling from her mouth as blood pours from the gaping wound in her neck—one that Craig has just made.

Craig worked as a slaughterman for five years, killing roughly 800 animals per day every working day of the week. That's well over one million lives.

Craig's first job was to mop thick-caked blood floors, pick "fallen dead foetuses" from the ground below slaughtered pregnant cows and chuck them into bins, and handle all the guts and body parts no one wants to eat, look at, or think of. "If you can't handle cleaning a floor . . . how are you supposed to handle slaughtering?" This role was one that tested him, to see if he could "hack going up the ladder," if he could shut himself off to what was around him enough to be effective.

He felt "physically sick," but he said, "I needed that job. In a country town, jobs are not really readily available like in the city. . . . So, I stuck with it, I desensitized myself, picked up addictions such as drugs and alcohol to help me cope and go through it. . . . It's very common in the industry." Craig told me that "the most disturbing moment was killing my first animal." When I asked how that moment felt, he paused for a moment and just said, "Traumatic. I didn't like it. I didn't feel comfortable doing it at all."

Thinking back to Charlize and the toxic masculinity she experienced working undercover in a slaughterhouse, I asked Craig if he felt he had to hide his feelings. He agreed, "I had to suppress the emotions because of the ego-factor. I would have been picked on and bullied, and I probably would have lost my job if I looked weak. Or demoted down to a 'shit job,' without that top dollar."

Craig worked in a killing industry, and his friends from the job, including many refugees who had fled incredible violence, went hunting, pig-dogging, on weekends. Violence became the default, it was almost relaxing to do it out in nature, rather than in a monotonous, bloody line of carcasses. One day though, the fast speed of animals-turned-dead bodies churning through the abattoir, their blood flowing down drains, finally caught up to him. Craig quit. "I was over going home in pain, having to get myself drunk or stoned, taking painkillers constantly every day. I wanted to do something different."

Craig started working as a courier driver. It was better. But a little bit down the track, during a relationship breakdown, he started having nightmares. Nightmares of Shadow, a black calf who was almost ready to be born into the world, who was cut from his mother's stomach. Craig watched Shadow blink three times as he lived to shortly die, his throat cut open, a tube in him to collect foetal bovine serum—an expensive pharmaceutical product that would be sold alongside his skin, labeled as "slink leather." "That's burnt into my mind to this day. It turned up when I was having my nightmares of screaming cattle, when I had my breakdown he turned up."

"I just felt this rage. All I knew on how to express it at the time was physical rage, take it out on something. That's how it was modeled to me, in family life, what I witnessed in the meat industry. A life of violence. I didn't know how to ask for help, I didn't know what help was. It was always modeled to me that 'men don't ask for help, I could do this alone, I'm weak if I reach out, I'm weak if I cry,' all those classic stereotypical conditionings. I had a few puppies along with my other two dogs, and one was sick and screaming and I just took my anger out on her. I saw it as I needed to get that rage out and that was the only way I thought at the time to express it."

Craig's breakdown led to him pleading guilty to a 2018 conviction for animal cruelty, after the year before, he beat a Maremma puppy to death and dumped her body off a bridge in a plastic bag.[45] I knew and had spoken to Craig about sharing his story when I found out this had happened not so long ago. I remember not wanting it to be true, messaging and asking him if it was.

It was.

I looked at the media-spread photo of the puppy in the plastic bag. I felt incredibly uncomfortable. I couldn't believe I was speaking to someone who had done this. But who was I to be surprised? And actually, how dare I not see exactly how this could have happened? How could I be more upset by one canine animal being killed than over one million bovine animals? Or by greyhounds buried in the ground? And by what the animal-industrial complex had done to Craig's mental health? Death and violence had been Craig's normal; he had watched his fellow workers partake in "common acts of cruelty, beating cattle that wouldn't move forward, angry laborers kicking them in the head . . . workers making jokes, harassing each other, sexual harassment, racial tension."

It makes me think of what investigator Rich Hardy said to me: "What I've learned from spending time with people in these environments is that we are all capable of becoming immune to cruelties and injustices if we are exposed to them for long enough." Despite working for an animal rights organization at the time, I had to an extent become "immune" to the suffering of those cows Craig had slaughtered, considering their killings somehow less distressing than that of one dog, an animal who happens to not be farmed, eaten, or skinned for fashion here at home. I cannot begin to imagine how this "immunity" would have eaten away at parts of Craig.

When the articles about Craig first came out, he was sent countless messages telling him how disgusting he was, how he should kill himself, how he was evil, mostly from people who were eating the animals he had killed for work. Two days after his sentencing, Craig bought a gun from an old courier customer, drove for hours, and booked into a dingy caravan park. The gun was a dud, or the bullets, he doesn't know. "Two clicks, I had the barrel in my mouth, on the third my phone rang, I answered the phone." A man who worked in men's support circles had called to check in on him. They talked about Craig's feelings, about everything that was happening, that he had done, that he'd experienced. It the first time in his life he'd done that. After this conversation, Craig spent the following hours trying to write down everything he had ever felt, that he had never felt able to express.

The article I saw was from many months later. Craig had become vegan, as the man who called him is, as is another mentor. Craig referred to both as "conscious vegan men" who supported him. Through their compassion, Craig says, he extended that compassion to himself and to the animals he had felt a connection to as a kid, whom he had to harden himself to in order to get by. The second round of articles had come up because Craig had adopted two dogs—something that went against his probation. "I thought it was my repayment to what I had done. I was attempting to give back. These dogs were desperate for a home or they would have gone to a kill shelter and been euthanized."

During his sentencing, Craig recalls the judge recognizing that slaughterhouse work is perfectly legal and "shouldn't affect a person psychologically," saying it was "no excuse" to kill other animals. Similarly, these articles painted Craig to be someone who, instead of unthinkingly breaking his probation to try to do good on his past hurtings, was conniving, calculated, ready to beat another dog. The cruel messages piled up again.

Craig is a complex person. He does not see everything the same way I do, and that's not surprising considering what he has been through. He is passionate about working on himself and on living in greater alignment with his true values. He has begun studying and working on his hopes to make the justice system value rehabilitation above punishment. He goes into jails and just sits, listening to the stories of men who are often marginalized and hurt themselves, who have gone on to hurt others, who have never been listened to. Craig hopes to one day see the judicial system set up mandatory rehabilitation programs for people convicted with animal cruelty charges so they can go into the same support circles that saved him.

Craig's story illustrates that it is the industry, not the individual working within it, that needs to be crushed. Yes, there are some bad apples. The world is certainly not a place of pure goodness (don't I know it). But we cannot keep punching down those who have been made to do monstrous things by an industry that values carcasses with high-profit turnovers above all else. Above all those who suffer for them, who are them. The "bad apple" argument the industry puts forward harms individuals who are often already hurting, who desperately need support, who want out.

Craig, a slaughterhouse worker, was never the "opposition" of animal liberation; he was hurting under an industry that is inherently violent in its entirety. How dare these enterprises throw individuals under the bus to protect themselves, calling them the problem, the outlier, the bad apple? The industry is what needs dismantling, what needs to be left unsupported by us, not the people struggling under it. Wanting better. Wanting liberation for themselves. We can't let them tell us otherwise.

Welfarism

Another way animal industries, and even governments, portray slaughtering industries as "good" and activists as "bad" is by making out that we, especially those living in the city, just don't understand what really goes on in farms (even when we've been inside them). By professing that animal industries deeply care for animals, offering those "in their care" "high animal welfare" laws and protections.[46]

While the total abolition of animal exploitation is not in the foreseeable future, any reduction of suffering that can be offered to those incarcerated individuals, while that greater fight continues to take place, is a start, and is important. The lives of the animals trapped in the system now, which will be taken well before that end goal is reached, matter. If these lives can be any less painful, that matters. Moreover, animal welfare laws, as lawyer and political advisor Matthew Dominguez says, are beneficial in that they "start to elevate the argument and the status of animals." In many ways, animals have essentially no value in the legal system; they are unseen and unheard. Their abuse is not a crime. By winning animals some protections, even if they are small, even if they offer little reprieve to their continued suffering, their status is lifted. The hen who is considered in need of enrichment—even if it means a pathetic perch running through the cage they spend their entire, short life in—is still one step closer to being more broadly recognized as sentient, deserving consideration, rights, and liberation. We're a long way from where we need to be, but welfare laws can be little chips toward carving out genuine protections for animals, which would end their incarceration, exploitation, and slaughter.

However, welfarism is also used insidiously and misleadingly by animal enterprises. "High-welfare" labels are slapped onto carcasses in the supermarket to convince consumers something ethical is happening when animals are butchered. And perhaps worse, welfarism is used as a scapegoat, a false resolution, a distraction from the most serious problem of speciesism, yet another cog replacement in a machine that runs on violence.

A good example of this is mulesing in the wool industry. Mulesing is a hideous practice in which the skin around the buttocks of a lamb is sliced off with shears, extremely sharp, wide-bladed scissors. Blood spurts from these lambs when they're mulesed and tail-docked, and they cry out, but the industry had long claimed this was for the good of the sheep, protecting them from flystrike. Flystrike is a myiasis condition where urine- and feces-soaked wool attracts flies, who lay their eggs in the skin of sheep. The maggots eat away at skin. This would be hideous to experience, but a false dichotomy is made when it's claimed that cutting the skin and tails off of sheep is the solution. Animal sanctuaries around the world protect sheep from this condition by shearing their behinds and tails short regularly, so they're clean. This sort of care is too time- and money-consuming for an industry that uses sheep as a means to make money from.

Mulesing as a practice has been widely criticized by the public, and thanks to a lot of work by animal advocates, many fashion brands now proudly tout their "mulesing-free wool" products. And yes, this is an improvement. It's great for an archaic practice to be more publicly understood and avoided. It's great that more and more often, people are ignoring farming publications and industry claims that a ban on mulesing would "risk sheep," instead seeing the hideous mutilation for what it is.[47]

Here's the problem though. When someone sees a knitted garment in a store with a label that proudly states the wool does not come from mulesed sheep, it's easy for them to think it's therefore a cruelty-free material—especially when brands say things like "our sheep live the good life." It makes it easy to equate the end of mulesing with the end of any problems for sheep.[48] But what about tail docking? What about winter lambing deaths? What about the fact that these good lives are cut short inside slaughterhouses?

Welfarism becomes a serious problem when it is hijacked by an industry that places an animal's ability to make money as a commodity, and as a carcass, above the wellbeing of animals themselves. When symptoms, not root causes, are addressed to save face, it's not really surprising that cruel practices are performed on animals when their deaths are acceptable, is it? Most of us normally consider the taking of life to be the highest height of violence. "Animal welfare" is a buzzword to industries exploiting animals more than a genuine commitment to do good. Animal lives are considered so meaningless and unimportant that their deaths aren't even thought of when their "wellbeing" is. Their lives and rights to them are decidedly unimportant, their slaughter "necessary" for the sake of the enterprise.

Suffering is unnecessary if it is avoidable and if it is brought about purposefully.[49] Mutilating and slaughtering animals is certainly purposeful and can be avoided. Ultimately, though, it's been decided that profit necessitates violence and suffering, profit that comes from consumer demand. Any claims of work toward "higher welfare" for animals by industries and brands that consider some level of profit-driven suffering necessary are deceptive—even when well-intended.

Often, though, these welfare claims aren't well-intended. They're used to make the industry seem rational and compassionate, and animal advocates unreasonable. "What more do you want" fear-mongering is often used to make out that the animal advocates' dream is for animals to be voting in elections,[50] owning houses, doing all that we do. Compassion over commodification is misconstrued into an absurdity. The result of this industry pushed, and polarizing notion is clear when reading the sentiments of people opposed to animal rights online:

"Tree hugging vegans won't be happy until we are all riding bicycles and eating dandelions."
—A hunter on an online bulletin board[51]

"Vegans won't be happy until they are just living off fresh air."
—A farmer on a farming forum[52]

"They're not going to stop until we are all eating grass. That's the reality. . . . Go and take a chill pill, take a lie down and get the hell out of it."
—Hon. David Littleproud, then Agriculture Minister of Australia (now leader of the racist, largely climate-denying Nationals party), following the Dominion Anniversary Action[53]

While these comments are so absurd that they are amusing, it's less funny when politicians are the ones making them. Powerful industries and supportive governments have been able to make very simple opposition to violence against animals into something that seems silly and infantile, yet somehow also terroristic. Equal consideration of interests for animals are about equal right to safety, freedom, and autonomy. There isn't a hidden agenda, and I don't want to live off dandelions, grass, or thin air either.

Chapter 7

Fighting with a "Terrorist" Label

Those protecting animal-derived profits are clear in their messaging of what animal rights "terrorism" looks like. Not driven by any profit, let's be clear on the reality.

What Terrorism Looks Like

The tactics deployed to present compassion as terrorism, to make whistleblowing a crime based on irrationality, and to maintain a misunderstanding of what farming is "really like" are working. So, before we look deeper into the metaphorical fences that need to be broken so we may see real justice and liberation for those harmed by industries built on their suffering, I want to bring you through real barb-wire fencing. I want to remember what is at stake. What's next is a little more flowery than the rest of the book, maybe a little more emotional, but it's at the core of all of this, and it's something that, I think, is worth being emotional about. It's something important to present here. It's a vivid memory of mine.

I'm in a diorama of the natural world, stars are pinpricks of light through navy velvet. Silhouettes of robustly ancient gum trees are black paper cut-outs. I'm not sure if I've seen so many stars before, the Milky Way and the Dark Rift within it truly humbling to absorb. So many millions of stars, such vast space, and here I am, standing quietly in the cold on a floating mass.

The night is cloudless and windless. We are seemingly tucked away from the parts of the world we've paved over, and at this time of night, not a car can be heard. Instead, a gentle melody plays out: a momentary frog ribbiting a beat, the scuttle of a small mammal, insects rubbing their legs together like violinists, and my weight upon soil as I intently listen to the dirt particles shifting in place with each passing millisecond.

The song is disrupted, the peacefulness shattered by a drawn-out, aching groan decimating the delicate sounds. A breathful tone grumbles and lets out a curdled shriek. We are here.

Like a loud clambering of piano keys, reverberant smashing cymbals, a brass section assaulting itself, the wailing engulfs most space available to sound. The grievance and gruelling unrest are palpable. Smothering fertile soil is a series of sheds. Tin, cement slabs, metal bars. Warm light wanders out of it and into the night, but any comfort it may portray is a lie.

I have never been inside a piggery before. The first pig I see is number 7,252, a tag pierced through her mutilated ear, chunks cut out as though she were paper to collage. She looks me in the eyes, her deep brown iris and unflinchingly piercing pupils make me feel naked. My gloved hand slowly reaches out and once she has sniffed at me for a moment, I rub her wiry hair–covered forehead.

I look down the shed. Heat lamps glow warm orange, supposed solace from the cold. The temperature may be a welcome change to the outside, but I have never experienced a more unwelcomingly cold place. Atop the concrete slab of ground are rows of metal cages, farrowing crates mother sows like 7,252 are immured within. All are unable to turn around, to take more than a step forward or back, only free to stand or lie beneath bars on gruff floor. The smell of shit sinks into my pores.

Each mother has at least seven offspring. Some almost new to the world, pink creatures coated with the most gentle dandelion puff–like fuzz. Some perhaps a few weeks old, just as precious, a little more pot-bellied, and with healing scabbed stumped tails. All down the line, every standing sow watches me while others attempt sleep or sing gentle grunts to their feeding children who are crowding their swollen teats. As I walk down the line feeling a strange sense of duty to see them all, my being human feels deeply and unsettlingly convicting.

Some of the sows I move past want nothing to do with me, and fairly so. They are occupied with the torment of incarceration, foaming a little at the mouth, biting at metal bars. Murmurs of madness break into pitched grumbles, and an occasional scream.

Further down the shed, I meet number 24. Laid down next to tiny bodies piled against her, chests rising, breathing in familiar unison, she sees me edging closer. A slight tremble of her trotter tells me she wonders if she should rise. The whites of her eyes communicate fear as she looks from me to her children. I am acutely aware that her human experiences are of being whacked into standing so her muscles don't waste away, of her children being mutilated in front of her, of them being torn away while she does all she is able: watch.

I sit quietly for a little and come to her before her children. I stroke her cheek for a short while, and she eases into what thin layer of mellow one can in her position. As I rub in the crevasses of her ears, her stretching, weary, and lightly pink skin reminds me of an elderly person. She is enormous, but she is fragile.

One of her babies pulls their way over her and scurries excitedly toward me. None of the younger piglets in the shed know about my kind, what their mother does, and he is no exception. With just one finger I pet his tiny head, and with just three he leans against a rusting metal bar as I scratch his warm belly. His siblings squeak with curiosity and a yearning for stimulation, play, companionship. I move a few steps closer to them and they scramble over each other to be near to me. Their eyes look at me with too much trust and I feel a lump in my throat. Perhaps I only don't cry because it's hard to accept as real, or because my spirit has already been cracked by the knowing of animals like them, in cages, in pens, and in blood.

I move into the shed opposite. This is where the weaners are, those just ripped from their mothers' breasts. In boxed off sections of cement they lie in piles, desperate for the comfort of closeness. Hundreds of little eyes note my presence. They aren't to grow as large as their mothers. They're to be trucked to a blood-pooled building within a few months so they may be shackled, dripping red and lifeless, before appearing back in the human world as sausages, deli-sliced flesh, vacuum-sealed rashers, and butchered "whole leg hams."

One cement pen is different from the others, everyone crowded inside is spray-painted with a line of green and purple. Their collective breath is more laboured, some spasm and twitch, one is dead. I can't help but feel the last looks the most peaceful of everyone I have seen tonight. I notice a sign that reads "hospital pen," and for the first time my subtly suppressed dejection is pierced through by a quiet rage. I think of a friend who is a doctor and I feel immensely aggrieved by the disgracing of the word "hospital" this dank, barren, and careless pit offers. Rats scuttle along the sides of the shed as I turn away.

Once I'm outside again, the stars become thousands of tiny sorrows. The beauty of a cold, still sky that offers a glimpse of the universe is dampened by knowing that the night cloaks atrocities. The hurt of knowing this is what we have chosen to do on this Earth lies heavy in my stomach.

I wrote that reflection the morning after my first time inside a piggery, trespassing with friends who needed a lookout while they installed cameras and recorded video footage inside. No one ever knew we were there, but this is what is described as akin to terrorism by the politicians who have created new laws and heavy punishments for such acts.[1] We are not who ought be called terrorists, just as this was not what ought be called a farm.

A farm is rich, dark soil and sprouting green.

This was warm bodies amongst metal bars on cold cement.

This was not a farm.

A farm is fresh, lush with leaves, buzzing with insects. This was thick with a stench of phosphorus-filled feces and neglected pigs.

This was not a farm.

A farm is apples, lettuce, potatoes, barley, hemp, cotton, cashews. A farm is food and is fiber. This was the lives of those awaiting death.

This was not a farm. We should not call this a farm. Sharing the stories of those suffering within these places should not be criminal, should not be considered terroristic. The only terror I saw here was in the eyes of pigs who will only ever truly leave that fear when blood runs down their dead necks. Let us keep them central to what we consider animal rights–related terrorism.

Whistleblowing: The Movement's Core

Whistleblowing is at the absolute heart of this movement. Imagine a world where there was no footage of the animal cruelty, of the industrialized violence against animals that occurs at every passing second. We would not know what there is to oppose. We would be totally reliant upon the industry to understand how it operates. We would likely allow ourselves to believe that gas-chamber killings of pigs really is the most "humane" way to stun a pig before they're slaughtered, that they do just "fall asleep."[2] That everything that happens to animals is mostly pain-free, that inside abattoirs animals meet a quick, even respectful killing. We might let these faux comforts make us feel more at ease when eating the bodies of these animals and wearing their skins. Even if we haven't watched footage ourselves, its existence means that we, animal protection organizations and legislators, know what's really happening and what needs to be changed. Not so long ago, France moved to ban mink fur farming, and Poland put forward a bill to do the same only a month after massive investigations exposed the horrors involved in these countries' industries. The dismantlement of the fur industry in Europe has continued ever since.[3]

> A whistleblower is a person who exposes any kind of information or activity that is deemed illegal, unethical or not correct within an organisation that is either private or public. The information of alleged wrongdoing can be classified in many ways: violation of company policy/rules, law, regulation, or threat to public interest/national security, as well as fraud, and corruption.—Press Freedom Organisation Australia.[4]

Activists who illegally obtain footage from factory farms and slaughterhouses, despite strengthened laws opposing them, are whistleblowers. Not only because often the cruelty that is recorded is illegal, but also because what is legal is deemed by a large portion of the public, whether their actions align with this view or not, as unethical. Recording animal cruelty is whistleblowing because it is in the public's interest to know what is happening to animals that we enjoy watching cute videos of, petting should we get the chance, smiling at as we drive by in our cars. It is a threat to public interest for practices that the general public find abhorrent to be legal, and are so largely because they are hidden. It is a threat to public interest for these violent practices to result in massive environmental racism and degradation, harm to communities burdened with increased crime and psychological distress rates, and growing public health crises, which animal consumption plays a great part in. Industries rooted in such exploitation simply are not in the public interest.

In most cases, like in Australian, US, and British law, whistleblowing can only be considered and protected as such if someone currently or previously employed by or involved with the corporation or industry being exposed is the one revealing what's happening. But why should who is uncovering corruption, cruelty, and illegal acts that threaten public interest matter more than what's being exposed?[5]

Occasionally, animal activists are referred to as "whistleblowers" by those in the public eye. In 2019, one of Australia's most prominent and reputable media reports, the *ABC 7:30 Report*, released "The Final Race." It was a 50-minute exposé, full of illegally obtained footage from knackeries and abattoirs where ex-racehorses were being slaughtered. Not everything that was shown was illegal, though to have shown footage from one Australian state would have been. Illegal or not, the treatment of these horses was shocking and opposed public interest. People love horses, they deserve to know the reality of the racing industry, which is that even the top money-making horses are often slaughtered when they're not money makers anymore. Throughout the report, this mainstream media outlet referred to anti-speciesist animal activists as "whistleblowers."[6]

This report came out around the same time as the government inquiries into animal cruelty laws and the effects of animal activists on agriculture. The inquiries, which led to bills like the Criminal Code Amendment (Agricultural Protection) Bill and the Right to Farm Bill being put into place, also saw heftier on-the-spot fines and jail time for activists put into law. These inquiries painted activists as people who frighten farmers and spread misinformation.[7] Harsher penalties paired with claims that diligently collected video evidence is "misinformation" spells trouble for the truth, and the public's right to it.

There's a powerful investigative video by Animal Liberation that pairs chilling, covertly filmed footage in a slaughterhouse killing newborn calves with promotional audio from the dairy industry. The audio speaks to the "high standards" of "care and attention, to ensure [calves'] health, safety, and comfort." "The mistreatment of calves is just not acceptable" plays out as newborns are dragged by the feet across the floor of a slaughterhouse holding pen, before being thrown onto the belt that will move them to their death.[8]

What was the difference between the activists spoken about in the inquiry, like those who recorded the calf killing, and the activists spoken about in the 7:30 report? The "whistleblowers" were exposing violence against widely appreciated animals, while the "criminals" were exposing violence against animals most of us eat and wear every day. While the racing industry has some lobbying power, finance to support them, and some government support keeping it around, it's incomparable to animal agriculture's power. Animal agriculture has the power of their dispersed myths we are all taught. They have far more money, more government support, and more public endorsement than racing, which is seeing a decreasing crowd of supporters each year.[9] The dichotomies in the way activists behind campaigns for different species are portrayed highlights speciesism, and also why whistleblowers need to exist in the first place. People have a right to see beyond the marketing.

We need whistleblowers. Without them, the work of animal advocates engaging within their communities and legal systems is put into question. It's easier to consider disruptive protests for animal rights as "criminal" and "terroristic" when the true terror behind them isn't understood. It's more easily justified to claim these people "spread misinformation" when no video evidence can prove otherwise or cut through industry claims intended to mislead a public that generally does care about our fellow animals. Not all work for animals is in trespassing and illegally recording animal agricultural enterprises, but a large amount of work trickles down from it.

A Strategic Dismantlement

These are the things we know for sure. One, that violent animal industries are well organized in their sustained fight against truth and justice for the sake of ongoing profits. Two, these industries harm animals first and foremost but harm much of what they touch around them, too.

It is for this reason that, as a community interested in social justice, we must be well organized, too. This is our only opportunity to effectively and strategically move beyond a system built on destruction and oppression.

To delve deeper into collective organized action, I spoke to Jake Conroy. Jake is an activist and a previously imprisoned person, thanks to his work as one of the organizers of the SHAC campaign, which nearly toppled Huntingdon Life Sciences, and which perhaps would have if those behind it weren't jailed. Having been in this movement for far longer than I, he shared, and shares online, lessons he's learned about what is effective and what is perhaps not optimal use of our precious time. What's next is in large part thanks to my mulling over theories and thoughts he has expressed.

Different types of activism work for different kinds of people, and I mean this in two ways. Different people are most effective when they work in different ways, which deploy their unique set of skills, interests, and understandings. Different forms of activism also target different pillars of industries harming animals, which need to crumble to make space for something new and built with justice.[10] There are many people willing to get active for our fellow animals, but we can only go so far on our own. Progress is made when we work together to dismantle and rebuild each of these pillars at once.

Let's say there is an enormous chicken factory farm. If we only advocate for people to stop eating chickens, only the "demand" pillar of this enterprise is being chipped away at, and the whole "building" will never crumble. This is because there are other pillars holding it up too, like their financial backing, insurance, distributors, marketing, and so on. Let's imagine a whole lot of people came together to shut down this chicken factory farm. It might look like this: whistle blowers obtain footage of the horrific conditions from inside both the factory farm and the slaughterhouse where these chickens are sent to death. It's all awful, shocking stuff. For a wider audience of people to see this footage, a stir needs to be made. So, slaughterhouse vigils outside the abattoir take place every day, with a large number of people holding signs with photos from inside. Lots of people similarly protest outside of the supermarkets that distribute the factory-farm "product"—the dead chickens. They invite people walking by to watch the footage from the campaign, they hand out informational leaflets, they collect signatures. Perhaps some people get onto the roof of the store and drop a message-filled banner, creating some controversy for the media to pick up on. The culmination of all of these things likely reaches at least some media outlets who cover the story and even share some of the imagery from inside the factory farm and abattoir.

But what happens once more people know about this? More people are encouraged to join the campaign to seek justice. The informational leaflets that get handed out have, among other things, helpful guidance about alternatives to chicken people can eat, but also, recommendations and encouragement about what else they can do to help with the campaign. The signatures that are collected could be for two separate petitions: One to demand the supermarkets sever their contract with the factory farm or else signatories will shop elsewhere; the other to call for an end to government funding of factory farms like this one. People interested and informed in this more legislative change might draft recommendations and write reports on government factory farm support spending and how else this could be used. These efforts could encourage the government to instead use tax-payer money to support a transition to a more just, sustainable, plant-based agricultural system.

The calls for a more sustainable system are interesting to people who are passionate about environmental justice, and so a dedicated eco-group looks into the environmental impacts of the factory farm: The greenhouse gas emissions related to chicken farming as compared to plant-based protein, the high land use tied to the grain the chickens are fed, and the eutrophication disrupting oxygen levels in waterways near the farm, caused by the heavy presence of phosphorus-rich chicken manure.[11] Some of the community who live near the factory farm, and who are most impacted by this damage, demand more for themselves and their environment, as is deserved. A whole new group of people are now involved in the campaign. They begin making calls, pressuring the banks and businesses that fund and insure the factory farm, demanding better from them. Similar calls and letter-writing efforts go toward local politicians, especially those who speak to their interest in a greener economy and community. Further media comes from this and brings in more people who want to help create positive change.

A worker from the slaughterhouse or the farm might come forward to someone involved in the campaign, as has happened before, to share their experiences there. Unions and people passionate about mental health and human injustices related to it put together a paper with both anecdotal evidence from the worker, and detailed, more widespread studies, which show how harmful working in a slaughtering system is for the mental health of people who, naturally, do not want to commit violent acts. Amongst their community, they create infographics and spread information, which leads a whole new group of people to take part in the campaign. Some of the people from this community decide to offer free counseling support to those who have worked at the factory farm and slaughterhouse. Meanwhile, others create a program to assist those people who no longer want to work within this unjust system: legal support, retraining, communal support.

Some people notice that the supermarket brands tied to this factory farm are creating advertisements that are misleading, presenting a fantasy version of the shortened lives of these chickens, one totally different than the reality exposed by the whistleblowers. A video comparing the two is made, and some people share it and contact advertising and consumer authorities about the falsehoods being presented through marketing. The pressure causes the advertisement to be removed from circulation. People interested in cooking offer plant-filled recipes to those newly shocked by how the chickens they were buying came to them. There's a list online where all the campaign content is centralized, so everyone knows how they can help. Some of these recently shocked people decide to join in.

Perhaps during the campaign, so that some of the central victims can be spared while efforts continue, some chickens are rescued from the factory farm or off the back of trucks about to enter the slaughterhouse. These chickens are free to live peacefully at a secure, private sanctuary. Their stories, and joyful images of their freedom, propel people to continue advocating and working for them and those who are not yet free.

This may sound far-fetched, but this is mass mobilization, and many hands make for light work. With so many injustices involved in the factory-farming and slaughtering of animals, people with different interests and passions can come together as part of a largely horizontally organized effort to create broad and positive change. This sort of communal, dedicated effort could see the pillars propping up this factory farm topple. And as this sort of campaign is repeated, the industry itself might well shrink, leaving room for something better. Something built for and not at the expense of our fellow animals, us people, and the planet.

The need for numbers in the rally for social justice is well documented, as is the need for non-violent, direct action. In-depth research spanning hundreds of campaigns over the last century has shown that when a small minority, 3.5 percent of a population, engages in sustained, non-violent protest, that population "has never failed to bring about change."[12]

> In 1986, millions of Filipinos took to the streets of Manila in peaceful protest and prayer in the People Power movement. The Marcos regime folded on the fourth day. In 2003, the people of Georgia ousted Eduard Shevardnadze through the bloodless Rose Revolution, in which protestors stormed the parliament building holding the flowers in their hands. While in 2019, the presidents of Sudan and Algeria both announced they would step aside after decades in office, thanks to peaceful campaigns of resistance.[13]

Today, the founders of the Extinction Rebellion movement have quoted this exact research as a significant inspiration to their efforts.[14] A similar Animal Rebellion group now also exists and advocates for a just, sustainable, plant-based food system, and supports the wider environmental advocacy of the previously mentioned group.

If we are ever going to dismantle such a vast system of injustice, it's going to take a sustained effort from a large number of people. When a large number of people are involved too, the going is a lot easier for the individual, who can fall back on others when they need a break, as we all do. This system, which is rooted in the slaughter of animals, is intertwined with so many other forms of oppression and, frankly, if we don't ally ourselves with those invested in these interconnected issues, none of us have the numbers to make the kind of widespread change we yearn for. Imagine if even a small portion of people involved and particularly invested in different social justice issues came together to tear down a common barrier to justice. We would be unstoppable.

It will not be easy, as there will continue to be immense pressure back on us, but it is all possible.

Chapter 8

Metaphorical Fences to Be Broken

What we need to address if we're ever going to achieve a world where we and our fellow animals are seen as individuals deserving of safety, not numbers in a production line.

Changing How Animals Are Seen by the Law

As whistle blowers make their way through barbed-wire fences, too there are many metaphorical fences we must break through. In a deeply political world, reforming and writing legislation is key. The protections animals have, in farms, and in fact in most instances, are pretty useless. In the case of farmed animals, most of the time, they're barely worth the paper they're written on. The root of why this is, is because animals are things. Not in reality, but in law.

Legal personhood creates the only entities who are recognized by law as the subjects of rights and duties. It is this personhood that gives us privileges and protections that legally cannot be eschewed. Actions of others may of course violate our rights (often at a systemic level and without justice), but such acts are still illegal.[1] Contrarily, in the case of animals, the legal system does not and cannot possibly see them, let alone truly protect them. They are things, they are human property. A piglet liberated from a factory farm is considered stolen property, just as a phone is stolen. If someone took "my" dog, it would be considered "pet theft," not "abduction."

When someone is a "thing," they are owned, and the only laws that protect these "things" are those that call upon the owner to properly provide their duty of care. This is where animal welfare laws come in, but it is also where they fail. These laws are flimsy, and with lobbying, they can be changed at the whim of "thing" owners like farming groups, because these protections are not inherent to the individual animal. It is how whaling bans are put in place and lifted again, how wild species are protected from slaughter and consumption, until they aren't anymore.

The Nonhuman Rights Project (NhRP) works to change the status of animals from "things" to "persons." This way, their protection and safety should be inherent, unable to be swayed by any "owner." In 2013, the director of the project, Steve Wise, started with what should be the most "conservative" or "safe" animal to attempt to give legal personhood to—a chimpanzee called Tommy. Tommy and his species share 98 percent of our DNA, are cognitively complex, emotional, culturally rich, and developed beings. Importantly, they are also not of huge economic interest like a pig is.[2]

Tommy was locked in a cage in New York, and he had a history of exploitation in the television industry. Wise found him completely isolated, watching a nature documentary on the small television in his mostly empty, mesh crate. Recalling a similar legal strategy used to free an enslaved person named James Somersat in 1772, Wise and his team asked the courts to issue a writ of habeas corpus for Tommy. Habeas corpus, meaning "you shall have the body," demands a person who is restrained of their liberty be sent to court so they may perhaps be freed. This 1772 case was the first to offer an enslaved Black man freedom in this legal manner, because at the time, legal personhood did not extend to such people.[3]

While these rights to liberty (in theory) are now extended to all human persons, the same is not true for all animals. And so not to Tommy, either. But here is where it gets interesting. "Natural persons," or humans (the animal homosapien), are not the only "people." "Legal" or "juridical" persons are not humans—large corporations are afforded legal personhood all the time. Interestingly, in New Zealand in 2017 a river was extended legal personhood.[4] Thanks to the diligent work of Indigenous Maori people, the river, which is a part of spiritual and physical entity Te Awa Tupua, is seen by government law as they have seen it all along: As a living being deserving of protection. This means that this river is safe from pollution, degradation, and other human activity to the river's detriment. So, non-humans, whether they be businesses or rivers, can be legal persons, but animals are not afforded this safety.

Why is personhood considered synonymous with humanity? What is it to be a "person," a "natural person?" It is not to have a certain level of intelligence, because as Sunaura Taylor's *Beasts of Burden* reminded us, not all persons share the same levels of intelligence or the same capacity to operate within society as we generally consider "normal." It is not to work, it is not to speak a complex and audible language, it is not to read, wear pants, write, or do any other thing many human persons can do, but that many other human persons are not able to. Is to be a person instead to have autonomy, to have wishes, to have preferences, to act on them, to react, to feel, to think? To enjoy the world surrounding or to be fearful of it, to cower, to consider, to be gleeful, to be guilty? Non-human animals experience the world through their own autonomous thought and action, they view it through the lens of their own emotional and thoughtful internal worlds, just as we do.

Despite all of the personality possessed by our fellow animals, a large part of why judges and law officials rejected the notion that a chimp could be a "person" was because other animals cannot uphold the same duties and social responsibilities of a natural person. For example, to vote, or to be held accountable for their actions in law. Of course, many natural humans do not need to fulfil these responsibilities to be considered persons. Think of infants or some people with mental disabilities. Infants can't be sued in court, but they have rights. Further, these persons have guardians appointed to them, who have a responsibility to care for them, but who are not their "owners" because they are not things.[5]

While other animals may not vote, they often already are held accountable for their actions in law. Take, for example, the shooting of Harambe in Cincinnati Zoo, following his attack of a child who ended up in Harambe's enclosure where he was held captive. Perfectly legal and totally unjust, the person who killed Harambe was not legally persecuted and didn't even need to make claims about protecting the child to avoid such. Harambe was the zoo's "thing" to deal with as they saw fit—owned by the zoo, imprisoned by the zoo, killed by the zoo.[6] Harambe was "held accountable" for his actions, for having somewhat offensively engaged with the child who had been allowed to invade the small space Harambe was offered in this world. For frightening the people who had paid to come gawk at him. The child is fine now, Harambe is dead—the only potential legal consequences of all of this may have been for the child's parents to sue the zoo on their child's behalf.

Nonhuman Rights Project has not yet been able to win any non-human animal their legal personhood, with many courts refusing even to take up the issue. Tommy to this day is not free. However, his case has forced an uncomfortable question to be discussed more broadly. One judge, Eugene M. Fahey, issued an opinion in which he stated that the refusal of courts to take up the issue "amounts to a refusal to confront a manifest injustice. . . . To treat a chimpanzee as if he or she had no right to liberty protected by *habeas corpus* is to regard the chimpanzee as entirely lacking independent worth, as a mere resource for human use, a thing the value of which consists exclusively in its usefulness to others. . . . The issue whether a nonhuman animal has a fundamental right to liberty protected by the writ of *habeas corpus* is profound and far-reaching. It speaks to our relationship with all the life around us. Ultimately, we will not be able to ignore it. While it may be arguable that a chimpanzee is not a 'person,' there is no doubt that it is not merely a thing."[7]

This idea of "independent worth" is one that, particularly under a ferociously capitalistic system, is largely ignored. Even as human persons, our worth is often dictated more by our usefulness, our labor and consumption, than by anything inherent within us—something I and many combat, often struggling with feelings of unworthiness when not producing or achieving something. But it is far more deeply rooted in our view of non-human animals and of the wider natural world, too. Do we see rocky mountain outcrops and admire them, or imagine the resources within them we can exploit, mine, sell? Do we see the soft feathers of a goose, their tender breast, and see a sensitive, gentle creature, or a filling for our pillows, flesh to dine on? If a paper book could play music, I'd queue Pocahontas' "Colors of the Wind" right now.

If we come back again to legal personhood specifically, rather than a broader but important consideration of independent worth, we can see that legal personhood is so controversial because it prioritizes life over profit, in a global system that does not.

If Tommy the chimpanzee had been afforded legal personhood, he would have been freed from his cage and sent to South Florida, where a sanctuary for rescued chimps offers those like him protection, freedom to roam, play, socialize. Other chimps who have lived there include those who survived being shot into space by NASA, or who had been subjected to years of agonizing testing and experimentation. The sanctuary guards over these animals. In Argentina, a chimp named Cecilia was successfully granted recognition as a non-human legal person with "inherent rights." She was freed from her zoo confines and taken to a vast, wild sanctuary.[8]

If, in what would be considered an even wider stretch, the same legal personhood were extended to pigs. They would no longer legally be confined to factory farms, mutilated, and slaughtered. If it were extended to turkeys, they would no longer be legally artificially inseminated. Fish would have rights prohibiting hooks to be forced painfully through their cheeks as they're ripped from their watery home to be waved around like a prize and photographed, held up, and dying for photos used on dating apps. In fact, nothing about what's done to animals that you've read in this book would be legal anymore. All that violence, gone in one blow.

It is a true and worthy question: "Where would it end?" when considering legal personhood being given to non-human animals or non-humans generally. If a river is extended legal personhood, what about all the natural environment surrounding it? What will we be able to do with that land? Who is guardian? What does it mean for us? But we need to have a level of rationality about this. In an imperfect world, all we can ever do for anyone is avoid harm as far as is practically possible, working to extend what is practical every day. It's absurd to pull such legal arguments to extremes and fear a tomorrow where stepping on an ant sends you to prison. It would be equally absurd to pretend not to see the difference between such an impossible to live with law, and the protection and liberation of individuals who, despite their sentience, are rendered production units in an enterprise that makes money from their bodies, whether as meat, skins, pets, test subjects, or forced workers.

If we can begin to look at legal personhood not as "how close is this animal to being human" but instead as "what do human animals have that makes us worthy of freedom and safety, and who else do we share these qualities with," the world will certainly change. And it should, seeing that the shared quality is one we are aware of: sentience. This change will not be overnight; it won't even be fast—one chimpanzee receiving legal non-human personhood has not freed all other chimpanzees—but it's a beginning, and it will be important to creating a legal system that sees all those who suffer in our society. By the numbers, those suffering and dying under land-based animal agriculture every day are the same as the lower estimate of all those who have died in human war conflict—ever. Over 194 million land-dwelling individuals.[9] That's certainly a large number of someones to begin thinking about more seriously in law.

Changing How Money Is Used to Oppress Animals

Law and politics, the system in which we live, makes it so that if you have money you have power. Animal enterprises have a lot of money at their disposal to ensure that their "products" are seen as healthy, sustainable, and ethical. It's difficult for a predominantly grassroots movement to compete with advertising budgets like that of, for example, the many multibillion-dollar brands owned by JBS Foods, the single largest animal-processing (slaughtering) company in the world. The enterprise supplies flesh-based products to 190 countries. It preaches about their "always do the right thing" philosophy, their commitment to sustainability, social responsibility, and animal health and safety, which are "top priorities" for them.[10] JBS has an annual revenue of about $50 billion USD,[11] and every week JBS USA alone slaughters 200,000 cattle, 500,000 pigs, 45,000,000 chickens, and 80,000 calves, sheep, and goats.[12] They have continually been found guilty of and involved in almost monthly scandals, including bribing authorities to falsify expiration dates on meat sold globally, illegal deforestation on stolen Amazonian land, supplying meat and skins from farms where modern-day human slavery practices occur, beating and hot-face branding cattle, and failing to meet even meager animal "welfare" legal recommendations.[13] Despite all of this, JBS-owned companies that sell flesh in stores advertise themselves as a good choice for caring consumers, with JBS and brands owned by it referring to "animal welfare" and "humane" treatment.

The power of advertising is immense, and it is frightening when it is not based in any kind of truth. Many would be surprised to know, for example, that the USDA has stated the words "healthy" and "nutritious" can't be used in advertisements that the American Egg Board creates, because of the level of saturated fat and cholesterol content in them.[14] Instead, they can use legally undefined words like "nutrient-dense," and create TV advertisements where children do extraordinary things, saying "if you want to be incredible," people should "eat incredible."[15] The underlying message being that if you eat eggs, you could increase your brain and motor functioning just like this "incredible person" has.

Money is spent by the animal-industrial complex to purposefully confuse people's perceptions of realities they've been informed of by peak health bodies. Despite beef's being labeled as a Group 2A carcinogen by the World Health Organization and recognized as not only causing cancer, but also being linked to heart disease, diabetes, and premature death by *Harvard Health*, Meat and Livestock Australia advertises a different story.[16] One of their campaigns, in their words, targets "time-poor families who value nutrition highly." Particularly, it targeted and measured the change in behaviors of "mothers limiting red meat consumption due to health concerns"—something that they saw reduced by 20 percent after their purposefully misleading advertising campaign was complete.[17]

Perhaps most of all, though, money is spent convincing people something kind happens in a slaughter-based fashion or food supply chain. A 2020 Lilydale brand "free-range chicken" advertisement is the perfect example of this. It showed a farmer listening to chickens through a baby monitor, sitting outside with a handful of chickens who enjoyed roaming rolling hills, sitting on hay bales, being covered from rain by the doting, umbrella-holding farmer. The music sings, "thank you for being a friend." The strapline is heard: "dedication you can taste," and the ad closes with the farmer cutting up a carrot, a lit oven on in the background.[18]

There's a lot to unpack here, even beyond that the advertiser was unwilling to show their roast carcass "product," knowing it would confront people who just looked at happy chickens. The ad also portrays free-range farming fictionally. Other than the obvious lack of umbrella-holding, Lilydale, following national certification requirements, only provides free-range access to birds once they're fully feathered, at about 21 days old.[19] According to an email I received from Lilydale, these birds, who live longer than most, are killed when at least 33 days old. At night, when the chickens are indoors, they're required to receive only one square metre of space "per 28kg of live birds" (almost 62lbs of birds in less than 11 square feet). When chickens are slaughtered, they're only a few, if not a couple of kilos light (say 6lbs).[20] Try to picture what 28kg or 62lbs worth of small birds standing on top of each other in one square meter, or about 11 square feet, actually looks like. Opposing what the ad portrays, for the majority of Lilydale-owned chickens' lives, they are not free-range, they're crammed on top of each other, and then about two weeks after they've been outside for the first time, they're dead.

What's far more troubling than any of this, though, is that I pay for the research behind these carefully planned-out advertisements—in fact, we all do. Also, despite spending a significant amount of my time working to inform the public about the cruel realities of the wool industry, for example, and the more ethical and sustainable alternatives to it, I help pay for the marketing and development of the wool industry.

In Australia, alongside the government funding of marketing campaigns worth hundreds of thousands of dollars to "counter animal activists" messages',[21] animal industries are subsidized. These industries pay a levy to the government on their goods—the slaughtered animal carcasses, milk, wool, or hair they produce. This levy is then returned to these industries to be spent on research, development, and marketing. What's interesting is animal industries then also receive dollar-for-dollar government-matched funding on this levy, up until a certain threshold.[22] For example, Meat and Livestock Australia was given about $80 million from the Australian government—from tax-payer money—just for research and development. The peak bodies for each animal "product," like pork and wool, receive the same kind of matched funding.[23] In this way, animal liberation is political; my everyday life may not be funding the slaughter of animals, factory farming of pigs, separation of calves and cows, tail docking of sheep, or brutal shipment of live animals to other countries for slaughter, but my tax payments do.[24]

Industries responsible for horrific violence against animals, serious health risks for consumers, unethical treatment of workers, and environmental destruction should not receive government funding. And yet this is a global problem.

In the United States, legislation protects the owners of enormous factory farms from the impact of supply and demand. Essentially, while more people are "voting with their dollar," buying more ethical and sustainable alternatives to animal skins, flesh, milk, and eggs, our votes aren't counting. The system is rigged. For decades, animal production systems have been protected in that if their revenue drops, the government will simply cash them out through "revenue guarantee" programs.[25] These protections especially help the enormous factory farms and feedlots of America, which confine billions of individuals. In 2013, farms with more than one million dollars in sales received 35 percent of government support, despite making up only 4 percent of total farms. Sustainable plant-based farmers are given near nothing in comparison. Until this legislative protection is removed, nothing can truly change in agriculture in the United States.[26]

While enormous operations continue to make and be given money to raise animals for slaughter, small, American family farms, as mentioned earlier, are increasingly owned by these large conglomerates (some 90 percent of poultry farmers). As a result, together these smaller farms are hundreds of billions of dollars in debt, despite the revenue from the sale of chicken flesh increasing. This is because these massive companies own the animals on smaller farms, pay the farmers what they want for them, and control how the animals are treated and confined.[27]

The existing Farm Bill that ensured this monetary support was only strengthened by President Donald Trump, who in 2018 signed into law an $867 billion farm bill, while simultaneously making it more difficult for people to get food stamps. Trump continued to give more money to farmers later, including a $23.5 billion addition within the wider American $2 trillion coronavirus stimulus package. This was despite COVID-19's not having closed farms as it had other industries, and despite meat, poultry, and egg sales, surging due to panic buying so intense it caused shortages. This isn't to say that money and support of any kind of farming is not necessary, but when lobbying moves that money and support to large corporations and unsustainable, unjust industries, something is wrong.[28]

How is this all possible? Farmers are a very small percentage of the human population, with farming protection directly benefiting less than 2 percent of the overall US population of humans. While we all benefit from agriculture, the types that are most funded do not benefit our planetary or personal health.[29] Farmer interest, and even more so, the interest of those parent companies, who essentially own smaller farms, seem to come before safety and justice for animals, the livelihoods of people trapped running these factory farms, the wellbeing of those surrounding them, and our environment.[30] A kind of "development paradox" exists where, despite a decline in the overall economic importance of agriculture, animal agricultural systems stand apart in the protectionism surrounding them. This is despite a general increase in free-trade policies in the United States and Europe that see supply and demand dictate which industries thrive or shrink. There is importance to some agricultural protectionism, as we all need to eat; however, it lends itself to manipulation by big food corporations that attempt to dictate what we eat despite the negative consequences.[31]

Much of the immense funding of farmers came as a direct result of intense lobbying efforts by major corporate farming groups, like Perdue chicken; the Perdue family has personally hoarded a net worth of around $3.2 billion.[32] This bloating wealth continues thanks to widened loopholes in the Farm Bill, which allowed relatives of mega-factory-farm owners, who had never even stepped foot inside the crowded sheds, to receive tax payer–funded subsidies.[33] The reason for the absurd amount of financial support is clear. Lobbying works. So, let's talk more about it.

Congressional members who sit on committees and draw up drafts of bills related to agriculture are heavily influenced by rural farming constituencies whom they want votes from. They're also massively swayed by industry lobbying groups, which they are tied to and supported by. These groups, which represent those producers receiving disproportionate subsidies, reward the legislative efforts of members of Congress supporting their will. They offer generous and much-needed campaign contributions.[34] Essentially, the animal–industrial complex pays to ensure they get financial support, and farming voters walk if they don't get it. Even if that funding is killing the land and heating the planet, harming animals and our health. This is important because rural America, where most farmers live, has more electoral power.[35] Essentially, where these people live means their votes are counted as more than they really are. It's the reason Donald Trump won the 2016 US election over Hillary Clinton despite having received fewer individual votes—he won the rural farmer votes. If that seems confusing and wildly unequal, that's because it is.

Corporate lobbying that influences politics exists everywhere, though to varying degrees and through different avenues. It exists in Australia.[36] It exists across Europe, where nearly one-fifth of all agricultural subsidies go to animal industries, despite far more vegetable, fruit, seed, and cereal crops being produced.[37] It exists in Canada, where only 11 percent of all agricultural subsidies go to plant-based farming and production, while a whopping 72 percent goes solely to the dairy industry and the other 17 percent goes to the remaining animal slaughtering systems. The subsidy breakdown in Canada is, while absurd, unsurprising when you know that the most active lobbying group in Canada is the Dairy Farmers Consortium. This lobby group even out-ranks the Mining Association of Canada, the Canadian Association of Petroleum Producers, and other Big Oil groups.[38] If this sort of political power, driven by financial power, is not disrupted and redistributed in a way that is more equitable and focused on the wellbeing of us all, little will significantly change.

Changing How Words Can Be Used to Hide Animal Violence

People care about animals. Whether or not we always align this sense of care with our actions is another story. This is a story that's easier to understand when we remember the myths we are fed, largely, through the labels and marketing that we wrap parts of dead animals in. In fact, studies have shown that in Australia, 95 percent of people are concerned with the wellbeing of farmed animals. There "is a gap between societal expectations and the regulatory reality," "animals are seen as sentient beings that have capabilities, rights, and freedoms," and "the majority of the public is concerned about how farm[ed] animals are treated." After activists release footage of violence in animal agriculture, "the public is most concerned about practices that are depicted graphically in the media"—because these are often the only practices the public knows about or understands beyond the sterile and deceptive language used by animal industries to describe such practices. Because of this, "the public's distrust of the industry and government, and the perceived lack of transparency are driving outrage."[39] Similarly, research shows that "American consumers are overwhelmingly concerned" about the wellbeing of farmed animals, and that "consumers are confused by what food labels mean when it comes to the treatment of animals raised for food."[40] This confusion is due to the massive "ethics-washing" of products based in violence and destruction.

Every day, we are absorbing buzzwords and terms animal enterprises use to convince us we're not acting out of alignment with our care for animals. We see terms like "hormone free," "sow stall–free," "cage-free," "humane," "high–welfare," "natural," and "free-range" spouted by animal industries spending hundreds of millions on advertisements. But these terms mean very little to animals themselves. Across Europe, for example, there is no harmonized system of animal welfare standards for labeling.[41]

Words like "humane" generally have no legal definition that demands any kind of consistency between farms, despite the majority of consumers thinking otherwise.[42] In the book *Grilled* by Mercy For Animals president Leah Garcés, a certification later banned in 2006 is referred to: the "Animal Care Certified" label created by United Egg Producers. This "codified the norm" of factory farming, where hens were offered less than an A4 sheet of paper worth of space—unable to stretch their wings. However, until Compassion Over Killing's tireless effort banned the certification, the care label convinced people that something better or more caring was happening.[43]

Only in 2016 was a legal definition for "free-range" relating to eggs introduced in Australia, where one bird is allowed one square meter of space each, and outdoor access is "meaningful and regular"—though these words aren't defined further, so are up to the discretion of farmers.[44] In regard to chickens raised for meat, the RSPCA states that "even free range chickens spend most of their time indoors," and yet a large amount of their own marketing images and images from their accredited and other free-range farms show pictures of broiler chickens outside in the grass, because that's what sells chicken flesh best.[45]

The RSPCA itself is an important example of how deceptive accreditations can be. So many people across nations see the RSPCA logo and feel comforted that the animals they are eating were well cared for. Many people don't realize that the RSPCA receives royalties from the farms and abattoirs they accredit every time they sell approved animal flesh or eggs.[46] Perhaps this is why their supposedly "humane" standards of farming and slaughtering are so far from what people picture in their minds. When pigs being burnt alive from the inside with CO_2 gas were first recorded, the RSPCA removed their accreditation of the associated slaughterhouse.[47] At least, it seemed so publicly when the facility removed the certification label from their website, despite gassing being one of two approved stunning methods in RSPCA standards.[48] A few years later, while still not promoting their accreditation, a parliamentary submission by the slaughterhouse showed that they were still approved by the RSPCA and still are today.[49] The RSPCA hid their accreditation not for the wellbeing of the pigs but for their reputation.

The RSPCA not only receives royalties from brutal gas and blunt-force trauma killing, but on farming practices that are far from public expectation.[50] RSPCA certification allows factory farms to pack 17 broiler chickens into one square meter, for example.[51] Hens in RSPCA-approved egg farms are allowed to have the tip of their beak seared off with heat without pain relief, despite their own acknowledgement of the acute and chronic pain this often causes.[52] Birds have a similar proportion of opioid receptors to humans, which indicates the way we process pain in the brain to be similar. I cannot fathom the pain of part of my lip being cut off.[53]

Similarly, "ethical" butchers make no mention of legally painful and bloody castration, tail docking, or dehorning. Instead, they babble on about how the meat they sell is "ethically raised" and "sustainable"—without any legal definitions for these terms, and without any data supporting the sustainability claim. Terms like "local" are often used as though they're synonymous with "ethical," the underlying argument being that if a sheep has a captive bolt shot into her brain just a few hours down the road, it's somehow acceptable.

This is where we really get to the crux of the issue. Not only are these terms incredibly misleading, selling us lies through totally misrepresentative images and "cruelty-free" claims that mean near to nothing, they're forgetting something critical: All these animals are killed. One wool sweater brand gives "sheep adoptees" (buyers of sweaters) regular updates about their "happy sheep" and how well they're doing. They even let buyers name them.[54] I asked the brand what they told their adoptees when they slaughtered the sheep, to which I did not hear back. When buyers have asked if the photos they share of named sheep are indeed "their" sheep and not any random sheep, there's no answer. I did a bit of digging and some of "their" sheep images have existed far longer on other wool websites, used as stock images.[55]

The respected "Responsible Wool Standard" and "Responsible Down Standard" certifications are equally discounting of the whole slaughter thing, with both unbothered by it despite maintaining standards that are supposed to protect animals. The down standard, for example, primarily means that the ducks and geese aren't live-plucked, but are instead ripped from life and then plucked.[56]

We are misled to believe this is the way things have to be, that there isn't a sound, compassionate alternative. The reality is that there is an alternative, a path forward, but instead we're deceived. We are also distracted, told to focus on trivial issues, like what should be legally referred to as a "sausage." Animal enterprises and even some government parties across Europe, the United States, and Australia are working to put in place bans on words like "hamburger," "milk," and "leather" from being used for products made without animals, like vegan burgers, oat milk, and bio-based and other materials replicating leather.[57] These industries claim consumers are "confused" by these terms, despite there being a lack of any evidence to prove this.[58]

While these industries push fear mongering of public deception by oat milk and veggie burgers, they mislead the public themselves. Advertisements for animal materials like fur, which claimed to be eco-friendly and natural, have even been banned by advertising and consumer authorities, labeled misleading.[59] The fur industry was appalled by this decision, despite their own funded studies showing even synthetic faux fur to have a lower climate impact, and that very little animal fur significantly biodegrades—as little as 6.6 percent.[60] This is due to the heavy use of toxic chemicals including formaldehyde and chromium in the processing of both fur and skins.[61] Did you know "new leather smell" is the smell of those carcinogenic chemicals?

Far tighter legislation around labeling is required to combat these weaponized and false campaigns. And if enacting more strict labeling laws means vegan products also can't be called "milk," "leather," or otherwise, so be it. While no one has questioned the existence of coconut milk for its long existence in Thai cuisine, sure, let's say we really will start saying "soy, oat, and coconut drink" not "milk." Let's just call vegan leathers what they are—polyurethane synthetic material, polyurethane and apple powder blend material, pineapple leaf fibers coated in bio-resin, wholly plant-based material. Let that be done, so long as the "real" leather industry gets real, too, and brands label their expensive handbags as made of chemically tanned calf skin.

Words have always been manipulated to better their markets, to alter the presentation of things that don't sound particularly appealing, or to create new categories of products. Language has always and will continue to evolve. As it does, we need to collectively understand what it means. If vegan "butter" has to become "spread," a legally undefined claim of "humane" surely should not be slapped onto plastic packaged carcasses. We cannot let the meaning of important words, such as those about benevolence and compassion, exist only as marketing tactics for cruel industries.

Changing Public Perceptions of Animal Advocacy

Because of the misleading and sometimes outright fraudulent labels on products made from animals and their exploitation, our perception of these products is skewed. But animal enterprises have worked, paid, lobbied, and strategized to ensure anti-speciesist activists are perceived in a very specific and false light, too.

Among the storm of terroristic labels, proposed and passed ag-gag laws, and farmers presented as endangered by those who care for animals, are the stories of people damaged by these things. Of course, the ultimate damage is done to our fellow animals, who are continually unheard and avoided in discussions of their lives and deaths, but the human impacts are worth understanding, too.

In late 2019, an activist named Mia went to a rabbit factory farm in Spain and rescued 16 rabbits from their confinement and eventual slaughter. The rescue didn't go to plan, and she and her fellow animal advocates were found by the owner of the farm, who Mia said "was extremely aggressive, strangling activists." The police were called to the scene, and Mia and her friends agreed to leave peacefully with some rescued rabbits. Peacefully until, down the motorway from the country farm, the farm owner and likely neighboring farmers had chased after them, pursuing them in cars and eventually shooting at Mia and her few friends. Mia recounts her experience:

> We tried to lose them down a side road but they were on our tails. They blocked us into a dead end and surrounded the car with five other farmers' cars. They were banging on the windows, shouting and threatening us. We called the police who arrived after an hour. They diffused the situation and escorted us to a "safe place." We asked them to escort us home but they refused and said we would be okay. They let us go and ten minutes later back on the motorway one of their cars pulled up alongside us and shot at us. The window exploded in my face and there was a lot of blood from all the glass.[62]

The video of Mia speaking with a panicked, shaky voice, with shattered glass in her lap and her face as blood drips down her cheek and colors her fingers, went viral. On a mainstream national news show in Australia, a female journalist, after watching the footage and stating that Mia claimed the farmers "beat, chased and eventually shot at her," simply said: "Good. Sorry, but good. It was going to come to this." The panel goes on to discuss trespass, the risk of a farmer's livelihood, the fact that she "stole from their business," and how that was not okay. A man mocks her, pretending to cry, acting as a burglar who stole a DVD player from a home, upset to be beaten up and shot at, comparing the situations. "What else do they expect? This should be a lesson to those other militant vegans who like to wear masks and storm properties in the dead of the night." The live audience cheered as the panel smiled gleefully.[63] When I first watched this, and every time I have since, I have been mortified. The demonization of people who do not accept commercialized brutality, and so who break unjust laws to protect those brutalized, has led to this. All the lobbying, all the labels and advertisements pushed by animal enterprises to call us terrorists and militants, had got us here. To a woman in journalism, who had been known as a feminist, standing in support of gun violence against a woman who had saved 16 lives, followed police instruction, and left the farmer's property.

Violence against women is rife, and activists are not immune. I know women who have been sexually assaulted by farmers. I also know queer activists who have had slurs and graphic descriptions of violence slung at them by farmers. I also know Cara. She is caring, has rescued and rehabilitated countless animals and provided them sanctuary, and works in disability care for humans, too. When Cara's activism led her into the public eye, she was doxed. Cara's image, home address, and number plate were posted into a private men's Facebook group with over fifty thousand members with images captioned "first to rape the bitch wins." One message called her a "walking, talking corpse . . . trust me when I say your life isn't safe." People followed her in her car, constantly drove past her home, threatened to kill the animals in her care, threatened to rape her, kill her, do unmentionable things to her.[64]

While we must understand that many farmers and slaughtermen work out of necessity and are good people numbed into doing terrible things in a speciesist, carnistic world, serious issues of patriarchy and gender-based violence still exist in this industry. Often more so because of the normalized violence they participate in every day. If it weren't for the myth of "violent militant vegans" being pushed by the industry and endorsed by the government, perhaps our mainstream media would be showing the horrific violence that occurs in these factory farms. Perhaps they would be outraged by the violence against activist women. Instead, they are mocking women who are subject to extreme threat and attack when they try to free animals from their suffering. Imagine if these women had been freeing kittens from factory farms and slaughterhouses; speciesism and a pushed public perception of farming has truly changed how we see animals, activism, and those who partake.

Not only is public perception of anti-speciesist activists altered by the efforts of the enterprise, but so too the perception of the wider vegan community. The perception of the wider vegan community is also caused by patriarchy and racism. "They want to take your hamburgers" was proclaimed to a conservative audience by former White House aide Sebastian Gorka, referring to the Green New Deal. When opposing Kamala Harris' announcement that she would change American dietary guidelines to have a reduced amount of red meat for environmental and health reasons, Mike Pence said that he's "got some red meat" for her, to his audience of Farmers and Ranchers for Trump.[65]

The majority of vegans are women. As a result, terms synonymous with femininity (because that's so bad) and weakness like "soy boy" have gained popularity in alt-right spheres that see masculinity as tied by necessity to domination, to the right to cause animal suffering, to slaughter and hunt. Advertisements with quotes like "100 percent manly man, 100 percent pure beef" only exacerbate this ridiculous rhetoric that food, or compassion, ought be gendered.[66] Veganism is also seen as a "white thing," ignoring the reality that Black Americans are statistically more likely to be vegan than any other American ethnic groups, and that the roots of veganism are largely in India, or that many Indigenous groups have eaten predominantly plant-based diets throughout history and had a relationship with animals far less manipulative than colonial white people (who, you'll remember, created factory farming).[67] Veganism is not a "white thing," and its being presented that way is the fault of our community for not amplifying the many strong voices of color in our movement. Many of these voices existed long before veganism became common amongst white people.

This lack of accurate representation is not only inequitable, affording white vegans more success in business, more space in academic circles, more positions of power, but also harmful to our cause. When entire communities of people do not feel welcome or comfortable in a movement meant to be about justice and liberation, something is wrong. We will never be an effective movement for animal liberation if we are not supporting other liberation movements and welcoming all those who would like to be involved, creating spaces where they feel safe, seen, and heard. Different people offer different perspectives and understandings of the complexities of the world. Of how we can navigate them and assist those around us while working in alignment with the vegan, liberationist lenses we hold to our core. If we make our community more inclusive, we inevitably will change what mainstream veganism looks like, for the better.

Chapter 9

The Movement in the Mainstream

As more "extreme" animal liberation activists have worked for the cause, veganism has moved from the fringes and into the mainstream. There are both positive and negative implications to this, and navigating a growing movement can be complex.

Plant-Based and Vegan Labels

It is so important that we look at and present mainstream veganism as diversely as it truly is, for the sake of human social justice, and so that a wider range of people can identify with veganism and all it has to offer the world. If a more diverse group of individuals can see that there are vegan people like them, creating their cultural food, thriving on plant foods and giving back to their communities, a more diverse group of individuals will be likely to consider how they too can act upon their environmentalist, humanitarian, and anti-speciesist tendencies. Everyone has anti-speciesist tendencies to some degree; most of us do not believe that dogs or kittens should be killed, that instead, they deserve their right to freedom and to life regardless of their lack of human-ness. We may not realize that these animals are killed in puppy and kitten mills, behind greyhound racing tracks, or in medical testing. However, we feel on a more intuitive level that a human should not have the right to take away the life of one of these animals.

Veganism and plant-based eating have become more mainstream than ever before. There are new vegan products on supermarket shelves every week, billboards for the newest vegan ice cream, advertisements that feature comical vegan characters, brands that sell animal products branching out, catering to an audience of people wanting to eat less or no meat at all. This is encouraging, as even forgoing animal flesh every Monday has positive environmental outcomes.[1] Too, when supply and demand is not skewed, every barcode we scan is a digital vote that stems up to food producers. In this case, when producing vegan foods becomes more profitable on a large enough scale, fewer animals may be bred for slaughter. It's exciting too, in that as more affordable and widely available vegan foods come into the market, this generally healthier, certainly more sustainable and ethical way of eating becomes more accessible to a wider range of people, including those who are poorer or are time-poor. This isn't to say these foods are totally cruelty-free or sustainable, but they are certainly far better.

However, there is a deep missed opportunity in plant-based eating's having gone mainstream rather than anti-speciesism itself. We have centered a way of living that is more aligned with anti-speciesism and collective liberation, rather than the social justice movement itself. Veganism is an important, and ultimately critical form of allyship toward our fellow animals and our shared planet. It is a tool for dismantling it and an act of solidarity. But it is not the sole solution to this oppression. When a tool, but not the system of oppression it works to combat, is understood, it is more challenging to create a just transition to something better. We cannot effectively focus on a solution without an understanding of the problems it helps to solve.

As feminists we don't call ourselves equal-payers, or consenters. We don't centralize our movement around a particular word describing any one act, principle, or way of treating women, which should inevitably run off of holding feminist values. Paying women equally to men for the same job, ensuring the bodily autonomy of women, and making enthusiastic, informed consent the standard should inevitably come from a world in which sexism is dismantled. Similarly, while it may be a long while off (as are the "end goals" of most social justice movements), veganism is one affirming action of a community dismantling speciesism. But why should anyone be interested in veganism if they don't understand how animals are harmed, why it matters, or what speciesism is? Why should I be interested in feminism unless I understand how women are harmed because of their gender? Or that women are deserving of all the rights and safeties men have, *because* they are not lesser, and *because* I understand sexism's warping of the inherent worth of beings? Without this first level of understanding, everything after it stands seemingly feeble and irrelevant.

By centralizing one solution to one major result of speciesism, we have missed opportunities to address other impacts of this form of oppression. Diet is, of course, critical to these discussions, considering the billions of land and trillions of sea animals who are killed for consumption every year. Diet is also critical in other roads to justice when we consider the rights and treatment of farmers, climate justice, and our community health and wellbeing. However, diet is not the sole answer to speciesist problems. If we all ate vegan food, we may still kill animals for clothing and testing purposes. If not that, then for entertainment through cruel companion animal breeding systems, animal racing and betting, zoos, and aquariums. We might still consider "nuisance" animals worth killing, like the native Australian kangaroo who nibbles our crops, or allow duck shooting for the purpose of human "recreation." The food we eat is simply a symptom, not the root of speciesism. So, a vegan diet is not a silver bullet with which to kill oppressive ideology with.

When we promote a vegan diet without taking the time to raise awareness of speciesism itself, inevitably some symptoms of this oppressive system continue. It's why when I first started eating a vegan diet, I didn't think it was an issue to continue wearing someone's skin as shoes (that is, until the Elira incident). It's why I didn't see what was wrong with buying a life, like buying a puppy (because I didn't see what was wrong with that power imbalance, of "owning" and buying someone, let alone know the realities of puppy-farming). It's why people buy vegan leather handbags and wear them to the horse races in a silk dress, or get the vegan burger, their animal-tested lipstick smudging off as they eat it.

In fact, "vegan" products are becoming blurred themselves. Some beauty products are labeled vegan because they are free of animal derivatives, but they're tested on animals. Of course, it's positive that there aren't crushed bugs, animal fats, or wool grease in these products, but animal cruelty still exists in the making of them, in testing labs and the cages inside of them. This is an important example of the need to dismantle speciesism more broadly and not consider a wider range of "vegan products" alone as a sign that animals are close to their freedom. Ultimately, while dollar votes can be powerful, we are not going to buy our way to liberation, ever. Animal products are products of oppression, but not the source.

Anti-speciesism is a social justice movement, and veganism is one of the most effective ways we can reduce our compliance with an oppressive system. Reparations for Black and Indigenous people are one powerful way we can combat the effects of racism. Ensuring that consent and bodily autonomy is taught or that survivors of sexual violence receive justice are powerful ways to instill feminist values into society. However, none of these things are solutions. If we are not willing to consider what oppression is at its root, what it means for us and those here with us, we'll never see a more truly just world.

"Personal Choice" and Mainstream Social Justice

When we forget to position personal veganism as a part of a wider societal move beyond oppression, other unintended consequences rear their heads. "Go vegan!" calls for personal vegan transformations, isolated from calls for a societal shift in recognition of animal rights, can feel like a deeply personal critique. And with this comes change-halting defensiveness.

Animals are most widely killed for food and clothing. Food is deeply personal, as is clothing. There can be significant cultural meaning in both, ways to connect with others and express oneself. When veganism is presented in the mainstream as the core message of the animal liberation movement, many people feel like their "freedoms" are being taken away. Requests to change the way someone lives, when speciesism as a form of oppression is unclear to someone (in a deeply speciesist, carnist world), can feel insensitive, a sign of personal or cultural disrespect. Whether or not this is the intention of the request, these feelings brought about are barriers to progress for animal protection and freedom.

If discussion of animal liberation were as widespread as discussion of veganism, plant-based food, and fashion, we'd see this social justice movement build and develop faster. It's unsurprising, though, that products brought about by the movement are the focus in a world driven by unfettered and glorified consumption.

Let's imagine that mainstream discussions about animals moved farther from animal-free products and closer to animal freedom. Perhaps the removal of freedoms animal experience might be better understood, not only in the freedoms that are lost for animals who spend their lives in cages, who are subjected to painful procedures, who are eventually killed, but freedoms on a more fundamental level. The right for an animal to be really seen, by law and by people. The freedom to live as an individual, for their own enjoyment, in their own right, rather than as a commodity or tool for the benefit of others.

Perhaps, then, calls to live a vegan lifestyle and to avoid products that directly harm animals, denying them their freedoms and lives, may be considered less like a critique, and more like a solution to a problem. A problem that people would want to solve, considering that we, on the whole, feel a real affinity to our fellow animals and can't bear to see them suffer. Perhaps more people would take individual action for those animals outside of the food system, too.

An interesting thought on personal choice and freedom comes from Ha-Joon Chang, who wrote *23 Things They Don't Tell You About Capitalism*. "Free market" capitalism is defined as an economic system in which prices are determined by unrestricted competition between privately owned businesses. When explaining the myth of the "free market," Chang explains the many policies and laws that mean it is not totally "free," but which mostly no one has a problem with. Child labor used to be seen as against the principles of a free market, for example. None of us consider the abolishment of legal child labor (though it persists today) across many nations to be a denial of our freedom to do what we want. Instead, we see it as an important step to ensuring the freedoms of children, as the right thing to do. So, Chang argues that what we see as "free" is always subjective and politically driven. We are not annoyed and we do not feel unfree because we aren't allowed to hurt or demand work from children, because we don't believe it right to do so. This comes from our (still incomplete) understanding of children as autonomous, sentient beings who deserve their innocence, to play, to be free. They may not have the same levels of rationality or intelligence as us, but we do not see this as making them lesser, at least not to the extent we do other animals.[2]

Perhaps if our understanding of animals were addressed, before our consumption of animals, what we consider a removal of our freedom would change, too. For a little while I felt I missed eating animals and wished I could wear those gorgeous leather boots. Now, the idea is entirely unappealing, because I see flesh and skin. I see animals as individuals and not products. Veganism is not a restrictive lifestyle; it is a set of choices based upon an understanding of autonomy and anti-speciesism, as well as environmentalism, and a sense of justice for all the marginalized people harmed in animal production industries. It is a continued act driven by ethics, the same way some actions are compatible with anti-racism and others are at total odds with it.

This reframing of what we are free to do, and what we want to do, is important in so many aspects of life. There are very few exclusively personal choices because none of us exist as islands. We are deeply social beings, and everything we do has an implication for the planet and those we share it with. The more that root issues of oppression are centered in mainstream discussion, rather than symptoms, the sooner these symptoms will lessen. If we encouraged discussion about feminism and racism to be as broad and all-encompassing as the root oppressive ideology they branch from, we wouldn't just have more than T-shirts with "woke" slogans on them. We would demand an end to fast fashion systems where T-shirts are made from unsustainably sourced cotton farmed by exploited people of color, and sewn by exploited, underpaid, predominantly brown women. We wouldn't understand these oppressions only through manifestations of them, but in the ways they are tied up ideologically.

Social justice movements today are flawed when they are limited by the idea that oppression exists in a vacuum. Animals are far from the realm of concern amongst many people working for other forms of liberation, with their rights not considered a true part of total social justice. Many people interested in social justice become genuinely angry at the suggestion that our fellow animals and their rights be included in this collaborative movement for a more just world. This idea stems from speciesism and a belief that other animals and their oppression are less important than that of humans, who need to be dealt with first. Or further, that by working to liberate other animals, we are ignoring the liberation of humans. But we cannot be for liberation sometimes; a true fight for liberation cannot exist in isolation. This works both ways, for human and "beyond human" advocates alike. It would be far more effective to identify what oppression is and dismantle it when we see it, whether it manifests in the treatment of Black, Indigenous, queer and trans people, women, disabled people, or other animal people, beyond the human.

A lack of collectivism in our idea of liberation stops us from seeing that our choices are not personal. Most of the greatest things about living on this planet come from our connections—with other animals within and beyond our species, and with the planet. If mainstream social justice worked through a more collective, collaborative framework, people interested in social justice issues like women's and animal rights would inevitably become better anti-racist allies, they would become better LGBTQI+ allies. It is not logical to consider only one form of oppression as a concern, because there are not multiple forms of oppression, only different symptoms damaging different individuals.

This collective approach would see more people passionate about social justice becoming vegan, as mainstream advocacy wishes for, but, more important, becoming anti-speciesist. Our consumptive habits would be considered in a larger sense, and systemic cruelty would be avoided and dismantled in a far broader way. Some people would continue specializing in the efforts to work with specific oppressed groups, others allying with them, and others at least not contributing harm to them. Our movements and communities would look both similar and utterly different. They'd be greater, they'd be more effective.

Palatable Activism

While anti-speciesism is on the fringe, far from our communal circle of concern and compassion, the kinds of activism that can penetrate societal carnism and speciesism work for different kinds of people. The degree to which a person understands their fellow animals as individuals will change what impacts them, what drives them to transform. Footage of animals being mistreated or slaughtered may be unpleasant, but not change much for someone who does not believe animals to be wholly sentient, or who believes they are lesser, and so we have a right to violently dominate them regardless. When people don't understand, they don't connect. My misunderstanding of fish was, again, why I continued to eat them but not land-dwelling animals for a year. It's why most of us don't wear fur but wear leather most days, despite both being someone's skin.

The root of anti-speciesism is recognition of animals as individuals who deserve personal agency. Who have a right to act autonomously and live freely, rather than for our decided uses under exploitative dominion. These are rights we all have, whether they are denied or accepted. It's easier to accept this when we see individuals, not monolithic groups.

I see the individuality in the people around me most, not when I see them suffer, but when I see the glimmer in their eye as they speak with passion. When I hear their laugh, see them spending their time how they love to most. This is perhaps a shortcoming of awareness-raising that rests exclusively on exposing suffering without showing how life could be or what joy looks like. This was an idea that I mulled on after reading Roxane Gay, Black feminist writer, review the critically acclaimed film *12 Years a Slave*. She spoke to her exhaustion in seeing almost all film representations of Black people being of them suffering. Roxane wrote on her wish to see films where characters live out the full Black experience, the life of a unique individual. Only seeing someone in their suffering is not seeing them as complex beings with thoughts, feelings, wants, and pleasures.[3] Solely through depictions of suffering, we do not see someone who deserves freedom from suffering, who understands they are suffering and who would choose joy, every time.

For similar reasons, one form of advocacy, perhaps often overlooked as activism at all, is the sharing of happy videos. Videos that are effective in deconstructing the base layers of speciesism that homogenize whole species and deny individuality, deny personhood. *The Dodo* is a great example of this. The Dodo is a platform that shares sweet videos of wild and domesticated animals overcoming adversity, fostering relationships, finding freedom, being supported and helped by humans, expressing joy, enjoying connection, and play. Videos of fish interacting, seeking companionship and play from each other and divers, made me consider them in a way I never had before. Videos and stories of abused pitbulls made me realize that a bred-for-fighting breed of dog, which I had been taught was vicious and mean, was not. Pitbulls can be gentle and are often wonderful with human children, especially when an individual dog is removed from the environment that encouraged and demanded aggression from them, and that fostered fear.

Seeing animals outside of the mold they are forced into is powerful. This more palatable sort of content that encourages kindness toward animals also supports the effectiveness of other types of advocacy. If we have only ever considered chickens as thoughtless animals, undercover footage of them being gassed to death in egg production systems won't be upsetting. If we think that fish don't have the capacity to feel pain, let alone joy or excitement, watching them asphyxiate, seeing their strained breathing, their writhing in a hopeless attempt to be safe, will feel unimportant.

The Dodo once shared the story of Monstro, a ten-year-old fish. His carer Lacey saw him looking "so sad," black in color, sitting at the bottom of a store tank. With dedicated care and attention, Monstro, who was lethargic and covered in lesions on his stomach from sitting on the tank gravel all day, totally changed. After a week, he began eating. He became encouraged to move and exercise. Over time, his coloring totally changed, and he became golden orange and red. Monstro transformed from a "lifeless, dull, sickly" fish to one his doting carer described as "a beautiful, sunny fish" who is "active and happy." He has companion fish he loves to engage with, even sharing life with a partner fish he spends most of his time with.[4]

Monstro's story has been watched at least 3.5 million times, undoubtedly by many people who eat other fish with all the same capacities for thought and feeling as Monstro. Commenters fawn over Monstro, with people remarking: "I never realized fish had emotions like this," "who knew that fish could be depressed and recover! I'm in tears," "I didn't think I'd cry over a fish," and "now I do not want to eat fish." On days I feel really dreadful about the world, I like reading comments on *The Dodo*.[5]

These feel-good forms of activism for animals, which solidify the individuality of all those who deserve respect and love, are often tied to whistleblowing and other "extreme" forms of activism. Here's what I mean. Before footage from the late 1990s was released from Huntingdon Life Sciences, showing beagles being used for animal testing, no one knew what this really looked like. This made claims that tests were humane easy to make. The undercover investigator who worked there for ten weeks, documenting everything, allowed the world to see these dogs caged in cells painted in their blood, tubes forced down their throats as they struggled and yelped, cut open and bleeding out into sinks. This brave activism has allowed for campaigning to be evidence-backed. It meant campaigns on behalf of beagles exploited for medical testing gained wider support.[6]

Kevin Kjonaas was one of the activists jailed for organizing the Stop Huntingdon Animal Cruelty campaign. Today, Kjonaas works for the Beagle Freedom Project. The president of this organization is Shannon Keith, who created the documentary *Behind the Mask* about the ALF, and who was Kjonaas' defense attorney in his trial. This organization helps rehome beagles and animals who have suffered in testing facilities, so they are at least not killed after all they've survived. In numerous American states they have successfully passed their signature Beagle Freedom Law, or Right to Release, mandating the adoption of dogs and cats from facilities. This law, which is proposed federally too, means that research facilities are obliged to find homes for animals that previously were killed, because it was decidedly more convenient. These laws mandate the release of test subject animals to rescues who find loving homes for them. All around the world, Beagle Freedom initiatives now rehome animals and work to have similar legislation passed.[7] The success of these campaigns is in part due to our human love of happy stories. Kjonaas has been on national news, speaking about legislation with his cheery beagle companion sitting on his lap.[8] Footage of rescued beagles feeling grass under their feet and sunshine on their backs for the first time in their lives has gone viral, lapped up by a world of dog lovers who, until the SHAC campaign, had no idea what happened to beagles in labs.

The topic of dogs is one that reminds us that speciesism exists not only in the dichotomy between those who are human and those who are not, but within and between other species groups, too. Activism that focuses on freeing dogs is palatable to a mainstream audience who loves dogs. In contrast, activism focusing on chickens is more difficult to resonate with people because we are all fed the carnistic myths that we need to eat chickens, that it is normal and natural, and that chickens don't really "matter" the way dogs do, anyway. Yet, dogs are still considered sub-human, and advocating for them can also help people see through speciesist dogma. Many of the activists who have dedicated most of their waking hours to helping free animals from farms and slaughterhouses first considered animal rights because of campaigns about puppy farms or convenience killing in the greyhound racing industry. Once one animal is placed in our minds as deserving total freedom, it's far easier to realize the same is true for everyone else.

Looking at the dichotomy between humans and other animals, activism that "feeds two birds with one scone" is far more inviting to a community of people who may not connect exclusively to animals beyond our own kind yet. When a more foreign concept like animal rights is presented alone, it can be unpalatable and ignored by wider communities. By addressing multiple symptoms of oppression at once, or specifically, say, by addressing the leather industry in a more collective way, more people are likely to support the cause. A campaign that encourages people to wear "next-gen," animal-free leather because cows are slaughtered is probably going to be less effective than one that depicts the leather industry's woes in its entirety. Sharing that wider story, that cows are objectified, mutilated, and killed, and that too, farm, slaughterhouse, and tannery workers suffer mental ill health, forced labor, and disease in environmentally destructive supply chains polluting our communities, gives many reasons for many people to get behind the cause. While this is more complicated, the world is complicated.[9] It's a mess, so it's not surprising that there are multiple symptoms of oppression behind one product like leather.

Widening our circle of compassion can seem exhausting. But in a lot of ways, change-making could be simplified if the mainstream notion of social justice was one of collective liberation, and if our activism was born from that.[10] Social transformation could come more naturally if we could come together and understand a common root cause behind what at first seem to be isolated incidences of oppression-fueled anguish. We see that each form of activism is striking at a different root of one invasive, thorny, and poisonous plant. This sort of goal requires activism not only in the forms we see on these pages and in the streets, but also in the forms in our heads. It all starts with deconstructing the myths we've taken in over time, about who deserves freedom: from violence, to live, to feel joy.

Animal Sanctuaries

Many of the heart-warming stories that make for palatable ways of introducing anti-speciesist discussions to social justice come from animal sanctuaries. With approximately 200 million land-dwelling, farmed animals being slaughtered every day, providing sanctuary and refuge to some thousands of animals may feel like a tiny drop of goodness in endless amounts of blood.[11] But it's everything to those whose blood is saved from spilling.

Some animals who live at sanctuaries have been rescued from farms and slaughterhouses uncovered as part of investigations. There is something very powerful about comparing footage of the horrors an animal has been spared from that others unfortunately could not have been, with the lives those rescued are now free to live. Seeing the bliss of one animal who is safe makes the reality of what happens to all those like her so much more potent.

Some animals living in sanctuaries have been surrendered by farmers, who, like most of us, do feel some care for other animals, but who have been conditioned to see animals as products and means to ends. In the Australian meat and wool industry, every winter lambing season some farmers call rescue groups and ask if they can take in lambs who are weak and dying. Similarly, in the dairy industry, sometimes people beginning work on a farm discover what happens to all the male newborns and try to find homes to spare some of them. Some years a handful, or maybe 50 newborns, may find homes, but that same farm may kill hundreds more like them. There simply will never be enough homes for this method to counteract all the violence of the industry, but it can be a powerful way for people within the industry to consider the lives of animals differently. I once had a farmer tell me that he never knew people could care for or think of animals the way I did, and that it made him think. As farm transition projects expand, engagement between animal advocates and farmers plant seeds for another way forward.

The end of animal slaughter and consumption, and the end of speciesism, isn't coming any day soon. There is a long road ahead before such a substantial societal shift arrives. In the meantime, animals lose their lives every day, and any animal who can be spared that unfair fate deserves just that. By sharing the stories of those rescued, individual liberated animals become advocates for all those left behind.

Animals and their stories are powerful. Edgar's Mission is an Australian farmed-animal sanctuary, named after the first pig who founder Pam Ahern cared for. There, mother cow Clarabelle and son Valentine live freely together, their story shared globally. When Clarabelle was surrendered to the sanctuary, rather than sent to an abattoir as most "spent" dairy cows are, Pam knew she was pregnant. It's not uncommon for pregnant cows to be slaughtered. Clarabelle had gone through the dairy cycle of forced impregnation through artificial insemination, birth, and separation of her newborn many times. One day, it was clear to Pam and those working at Edgar's that Clarabelle had given birth, but they couldn't see her calf anywhere. They watched her from a distance and learned that every few hours Clarabelle would go to a hidden spot—behind a tree in high grasses and offer her calf milk. Then, she would move her calf to a new hidden spot. Clarabelle would then go back to the rest of the herd, glancing back every so often at the spot where her baby was hidden. A few days–old calf was finally spotted in the forested area of the sanctuary.[12]

Clarabelle was fearful of letting humans get too close to her calf because she remembered what had happened to every other much-loved baby she'd birthed. Dr. Temple Grandin, renowned animal behaviurist, wrote that once a fear-based memory is formed in the mind of an animal like a cow, she cannot be free from it. As with humans, fearful memories are formed in the amygdala, making them strong, vivid. Such a reality and such a story has connected with many empathetic people, and in particular mothers who think of the love of their children.[13]

Billboards with the precious face of a still fuzzy piglet that read "call me Penelope Sue, not dinner," have been erected around Australia by Edgar's Mission, particularly at Christmas time.[14] A message of kindness and of the individuality of animals has spread widely with this sort of inviting activism. Similarly, the United States' Barn Sanctuary has allowed the stories, struggles, and triumphs of rescued animals to be felt and celebrated by people globally through their television series. The Discovery Channel's *Animal Planet* shows are watched internationally. *Wildlife* documentaries, "deadliest catch" shows promoting recreational hunting, and veterinary shows are watched by enormous audiences. Among this channel's shows is *Saved by the Barn.* The series follows the hard work of carers at Barn Sanctuary, like founder Dan McKernan, to rehabilitate injured and ill farmed animals. As people cheer on recoveries and feel sorrow for the terrible situations these animals have come from, a profound shift in their perception of farmed animals can occur.

When we connect with individual animals at any of these sanctuaries, or in the care of rescuers, we are reminded that as precious as they are, they are not special. They are just more fortunate. I think, for example, of Anwell. A newborn male goat saved from the dairy industry, he did not survive more than two nights. He'd been surrendered from a farm we were told would otherwise drown him and all the other newborns. Until he and the other kids were collected by carers, they had been left in a shed—no milk, no warmth, no comfort. They all had a form of gastro that, in fragile newborns, can be deadly. They had seemed alright at first, and I'd softened at the warmth of their bodies resting together, their wiggling tails, their zestful bounding and little sniffs and kisses of their nose against mine. When Anwell crashed quickly, it was scary. The inside of his mouth was cold, his body almost completely limp. He cried out sometimes, but other than those quiet and strangled, devastating sounds, he already appeared dead.

I whispered to him, telling him it would be okay. I knew it probably wasn't true. I asked him to stay. I knew it was probably too much to ask for. Most of the goats we had been caring for hadn't been named yet, but I decided to name Anwell sooner because I didn't want him to die without a name. "Anwell" means "beloved," and though he was, he was no more capable of love, joy, or fear than any other goat. He was not blessed with any more personality, capacity for feeling, or thought than any of the other animals killed in each passing moment, by our hands.

The goats who survived with the high level of care they received from vets and other carers are advocates for themselves, for Anwell, and for all those animals who die without names, without love.

The stories that make our hearts sore render the fortunate ones more special. The fortunate stories make the sore ones ache harder. Animals who live freely are the best advocates for all those like them, and they are a gentle entry into the much-needed deconstruction of speciesism in a society yet to mourn the killings and deaths of so many precious individuals.

Part Three

Moving Forward

While we can and must talk about social justice, the freedoms and rights of us all, none of this will matter on a dead planet, or a planet we cannot survive on any longer.

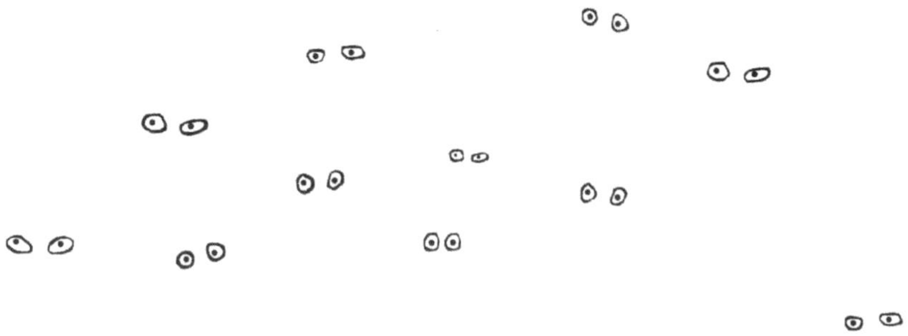

Chapter 10

The Time Is Now

There is no more time for philosophical chewing of the cud around the liberation of all beings. There aren't decades ahead for debate. This all matters now, is happening now, on a planet pained by our treatment of those we share it with. Our utter dislocation from the planet we belong to and destroy has, on average, led our singular species to cause a 60 percent decline in the size of living animal populations since the 1970s.[1] Our insistent perversion with invading healthy biomes and the wildlife within it means that I write this while locked away under COVID-19, stage four "state of disaster" conditions, able to leave home once a day for a limited time, wearing a mask and staying away from everyone around me. This is the second state of disaster my home of Australia has seen this year, the 2019–2020 bushfires being the first. More than 12,600,000 hectares of native land were swallowed in flames and burnt, and even far-away cities choked in the toxic smoke. Three billion animals were killed and misplaced.[2]

Over 30 years ago we were first warned of global warming, and today, we're seeing the effects: bushfires, bleached coral reefs, melting ice caps, heating oceans, prolonged droughts, floods, and monsoons.[3] It's scary to become used to the erraticism of today's climate—hailing one day and reaching previously unseen hot temperatures the next. What is merely unnerving for me, though, is life threatening to so many.

The humans who have contributed the least to the dysfunctional, disjointed system causing it are those who will experience the most devastating effects of the climate crisis. They are the Indigenous people of the world, who have a relationship with the land they belong to, which is far more symbiotic than the white, colonial, pillaging mindset could ever feel without serious deconstruction. White history for so long has been about taking from Indigenous human and non-human animals and land. We need to learn what environmental harmony could look like. Aboriginal man Tom Dyrsta said, "We cultivated our land, but in a way different from the white man. We endeavoured to live with the land; they seemed to live off it. I was taught to preserve, never to destroy."[4]

There is no more important time than now, for us to consider our relationship with all those around us, those that we "other." Sometimes in the silence, I remember the grumbling groans from animals in darkened factory-farm cages, stalls, and slaughterhouse holding pens they stand weary in. The cries of animals we drew out from their wild homes only ten thousand years ago, so we may hold dominion over them, hanging the balance of their lives in our every move, meal, and manufacturing. They are the largest group of beings on the planet and are being killed at a rate like never before.[5] These animals live in our created terror, and so do we to a differing degree. Our harming them also harms free-living animals and ourselves, within an unsustainable, collapsing system, which we were wrong to think would do anyone good.

Global Warming and the Climate Crisis

As per the Paris Agreement, if we don't stay below an increase of 1.5 degrees Celsius, the domino effect that will play out on our planet will be frightening beyond belief.[6] To prevent this, we need to remove greenhouse gases from our atmosphere, and we need to dramatically reduce our future emissions. This will require both short- and long-term solutions, particularly as different gases stay in our atmosphere for different lengths of time. Methane, for example, is enormously more potent than carbon in the short-term, warming our atmosphere for about 12 years, whereas carbon does for 100, if not many years longer.

In 2006, the Food and Agricultural Organization of the United Nations released a report called *Livestock's Long Shadow*.[7] For what was really the first time, the impact of animal agriculture on climate was addressed. Unfortunately, a comparison between animal agricultural and fuel emissions from global transport within the report has since been slightly misquoted for years. This slip-up has allowed for industry-paid scientists to discredit the whole report.

The error made a direct comparison of both sectors in their entirety—for example including the emissions involved in the mining of materials for vehicles. This not quite right regurgitation of information has made the comparison seem illegitimate. The real, data-backed comparison the United Nations made, is as follows: The greenhouse gas emissions, that relate to the animal agricultural sector are more significant than the emissions that come from all transport fuel exhaust.[8] Think of every car in peak hour traffic, every ship, every truck, every plane in the sky burning fossil fuels as they go. This is a hugely significant and confronting statistic, one accepted broadly by rational scientists, including those writing IPCC reports calling for a plant-based shift.[9]

Beef is talked about a lot in relation to greenhouse gases, but people easily forget these same animals are being exploited for dairy and skinned for leather. And, it's not only cattle we need to consider when acting for the planet. All animal agricultural products contribute disproportionately more to the climate crisis than plant-based foods and materials do.[10]

If we do focus on cows, we see that eating even the most "sustainably" raised animals, rather than protein from peas, results in 36 times more greenhouse gas emissions.[11] Similarly, one pair of shoes made from cow skin leather, rather than the most common synthetic leather, polyurethane, results in about seven times the emissions. Synthetics aren't our solution, but it's telling that a fossil fuel product's climate impact is dwarfed by one from Big Ag.[12]

In part, these steep emissions are due to enteric fermentation—essentially the passing of gas by ruminant animals like sheep, alpacas, goats, and cattle. Enteric fermentation is of particular concern in relation to methane. Because of methane's fairly short life in the atmosphere, if we stopped breeding these animals for the purpose of their slaughter, within 10–20 years we could see enormous change in the greenhouse gas emissions in our atmosphere.

However, it's too late for just a reduction, or even an end to greenhouse gas emissions to save us. We need to sequester the emissions that are already floating about our atmosphere, and for that, we need to address longer-lasting gases, like carbon. And for *that*, agricultural land needs to be reassessed. If we compare cow flesh and peas again, six times more land is required for the same amount of protein to be produced.[13] This is an issue because whether we work technologically, saving more emissions from being released through conversion to solar or wind energy, or if we work naturally, using trees to suck carbon from the atmosphere, we need land for this. Instead, right now, more land is being cleared for agriculture than for anything else. This is particularly frightening when we consider that even if dramatic emission reductions were seen across other sectors like transport and energy, the impact of consuming animal-based products alone, continued as projected, would mean global temperatures would more than likely rise beyond two degrees Celsius.[14] This would take us to an environmental tipping point that would likely cause irreversible destruction.[15]

Destruction of Land

Trees turn carbon into oxygen, they themselves being over one-third carbon. Older trees "communicate" with a network of those around them. With the help of fungi, trees exchange and share the nutrients they are more able to receive—as they are larger and more able to access light to photosynthesize with. Trees offer nutrients to the soil around them, they offer refuge and food to animals, they offer us all our lives.

Yet, in 2019 we lost a soccer field of untouched, pristine forest every six seconds. The majority—one-third—of this loss was in Brazil, largely in the Amazon rainforest, the lungs of the Earth.[16]

The farming of cattle for beef and leather is responsible for 80 percent of the Amazon's deforestation.[17] The other major driver of this deforestation is soy production, of which 80 percent goes toward animal feed for factory farms, including fish farms.[18] Brazil is the world's most significant "beef" exporter, and third most significant bovine skin exporter. Still, people claim soymilk is the cause of our problems.[19]

The destruction of land for the sake of our desire to eat animal rather than plant foods is not unique to Brazil. Animal grazing and monoculture crops grown for animal feed—largely going to pigs and chickens—is a widespread leading cause of destruction. In Australia, 54 percent of land use is for animal grazing alone.[20] Meanwhile, 63 percent of European arable land is used for animal agriculture.[21] A staggering 85 percent of the United Kingdom's agricultural land is down to animals.[22]

And 41 percent of US land in the contiguous states relates to animal agriculture.[23]

In fact, half of all habitable land—so forget glaciers and barren land—is used for agriculture, and of this land, 77 percent is used for grazing animals for slaughter, factory farms, and crops grown to feed these animals.[24]

The problem is that animal-based foods offer only 18 percent of the world's calories and 37 percent of total protein.[25] This is a phenomenally inefficient system that causes immense releases of carbon locked away in forests, biodiversity destruction, species endangerment, and soil erosion.

With a transition away from animal-based agriculture and consumption, global farmland could be reduced by 75 percent and we could still feed the world.[26] What we could do instead with this land, what we could finally give back to nature and so to ourselves and everyone else here, is genuinely mind-blowing. Imagine if this much land could be rewilded, full of trees, native plants, fungi, amphibians, insects, mammals, reptiles. They would breathe new life into this planet if we let them.

It's about not only how much land is used, but also the level of impact on that land. Degradation has ruined land "productivity"—a variable representing land cover through vegetation density and vigor—on over 23 percent of the global land surface.[27] When we cover such a significant portion of the Earth with animals like cattle, goats, and sheep who have hooves, we cause the erosion of what fertile soil is here to create and support life. There is a pervasive and grave misconception that rolling green hills and fields full of sheep are natural and ecologically beneficial. This argument is based on the fact that cropland visibly looks less natural, even though if we only cultivated plant foods and materials, as we know, there would be more land available for genuinely natural landscapes. I say "genuinely," because, indeed, green pastures are not natural. These landscapes are in a state of arrested development when both the purposeful addition of nitrogen and ruminant animals who are farmed en masse destroy and halt the potential growth of the diverse range of plant, insect, and wild animal life needed for a thriving ecosystem.

Take, for example, the diverse and important grasslands of Patagonia or Mongolia. In the first half of the twentieth century, Patagonia, Argentina, was second only to Australia in wool production. Today, Mongolia is the second largest producer of cashmere. The sharp hooves and the teeth of these herbivores have demolished both areas to the point of widespread desertification and degradation.[28] Mongolia has not halted its production of cashmere despite warnings, caught up in rising global demand for cheap cashmere, harming local economies, goats, and grasslands alike. Goat herders state that they are saddened to "watch their grasslands disappear," but with the demand for the material supporting them, feel they have little option. Conversely, Patagonia Park "destocked" the land, removing all sheep and farmed animals. Since then, project biologists have said they are "impressed with the speed at which these grasslands have regained their vitality" as those working to restore Patagonia Park "watch the land heal and transform at an astounding rate."[29]

Destruction of Ocean

Our land massacre spills into our waters, fresh and salty. Eutrophication, when a body of water becomes overly enriched with minerals and nutrients, results in excessive algae growth and, in turn, oxygen depletion. Nitrogen and phosphorus cause eutrophication and are found in great levels in animal agriculture, largely due to the fecal waste from the animals we raise to kill.[30] Fish factory farms and the waste released from them similarly harm the natural oceanic environments around them.[31] Eutrophication kills fish en masse, both in fresh waterways running off of farms and in the oceans they lead to, where ocean acidification occurs and "dead zones" are created.[32] Marine life cannot be sustained in these areas.

The awful treatment of fish in factory-farm sea cages poses a threat to wild fish populations, too. The forced, tight enclosure of fish means that disease and infestations spread quickly. Amoebic gill disease, for example, is a parasitic disease that is considered one of the most detrimental to farmed fish worldwide.[33] The parasite deteriorates their gills, making it difficult for the fish to breathe, and leads to heart collapse and death when left untreated. Sea lice also commonly infect farmed fish populations, infesting fish who are literally eaten alive by parasites. Their skin hangs off of them, and the red raw flesh under their scales becomes exposed as their bodies are riddled with lesions.[34]

Not only is this horrific for the affected farmed individuals, but also is awful for wild populations of fish who contract the parasites.[35] Fish regularly escape from sea cages, with these "trickle losses" and larger escapee events resulting in parasites, being free to run rampant.[36] Even without these escapes, if a wild salmon just swims by one of these sea cages, they can contract sea lice. There are grave implications to this. Scottish wild salmon populations are at their lowest levels, despite no commercial fishing of the species occurring in the United Kingdom, due to both environmental and parasitic influence.[37] In Canada, some studied regions saw 95 percent of wild juvenile salmon populations killed by lice infestation.[38] Such industrial destruction led Argentinian legislators to unanimously pass a world-first salmon farming ban in 2021.[39]

"Property in our societies has more value than life. Property is sacred, life is expendable."[40] Captain Paul Watson of Sea Shepherd's words reverberate loudly through the ruinous reality of our relations with those living under water. Dedicating his life to the animals of the sea, in *Watson* he explains how endangered bluefin tuna continue to be captured and slaughtered, because the fewer of them there are, the more expensive they become. Southern bluefin tuna are critically endangered, but industries raking them out of the ocean are unconcerned, because they have a plan.[41] Mitsubishi, which deals with nearly half of all bluefin tuna imports, is freezing warehouses full of the enormous fish at -60°C (at which point cellular degradation is practically paused). The purpose? An independent fisheries consultant believes it's to watch the species go extinct, then sit on a pile of gold.[42] For those interested only in money and profit, it's a brilliant idea; a threatened bluefin tuna carcass sold for three million USD in 2019. Extinction has never been so profitable, apparently.[43]

And it's not only tuna who are disappearing. Every day, a similar number of fish are caught and killed as there are people living across China, Nigeria, the United States, and Europe—nearly 2.7 billion (at time of writing). Of large fish species, 90 percent are gone, with more facing extinction almost entirely because of human action.[44] Too, 90 percent of sea areas where fish live and are ripped from are now drained of these individuals or are exploited to the point that the fish, to differing degrees, struggle to recover.[45] They are unable to mate and breed as quickly while their populations are slaughtered. It is unthinkable how many sea animals are killed every day, with enormous purse seine nets up to 2,000 meters long and 200 meters deep (~6,561ft x 656ft), as well as hundreds or thousands of sharp hooks strung along lines that extend across tens if not one hundred kilometers of sea.[46] Imagine every single stressed fish or other incidentally caught shark or dolphin, their arduous struggling and writhing to be free. Imagine every single slow, painful death as they're hauled out of their home and unable to breathe.

The deaths of these individuals could lead to the death of us all, to the death of our shared planet. About 70 percent of "Earth" is covered by ocean—perhaps a poor planetary name.[47] If we did have a future of fishless or practically fishless oceans—which is predicted as possible—the entire ocean ecosystem could fall apart.[48] If we made fish extinct, species that rely on their existence for food, like some whales and sharks, as well as dolphins, seals, and penguins, would die out, too. Without all these species creating the symbiosis that is nature, algae, kelp, plankton, krill, and worms would all seriously struggle, too. The ocean, due to its phytoplankton, produces up to 80 percent of our oxygen, which is the reason this planet is habitable for anyone on land. Without these smallest of species, we are nothing.[49]

The Sixth Mass Extinction

Today we are in the "Anthropocene," the period during which human activity has been the dominant influence on climate and the environment. Our treatment of the animals we breed, cage, slaughter, rip from oceans, and shoot in grasslands, and of the land we effectively slaughter for these purposes too, plays a significant role, as we've seen.

Within this period, we are seeing the sixth mass extinction our planet has faced. A mass extinction period is when more than 75 percent of the species on the planet become extinct. I spoke to Chris Darwin, conservationist and descendant of Charles Darwin, about it after having visited his home in the Australian Blue Mountains. There, we worked with a small team on a campaign exposing false species conservation claims in the native crocodile-killing industry.[50]

"This extinction period has been caused by one species, which has never happened before. One species, homo sapiens, having named themselves 'wise man,' has taken over the productive capacity of the planet and has channelled it away from the other species, effectively. That is quite extraordinary. In the process of doing that, homo sapiens are causing the extinction or rarity of all of their closest cousins. They all are in steep decline and have a threatened status on their names." Think of the orangutan, whom we are slowly making homeless and lifeless through deforestation.

This is the sixth mass extinction period. There have been five others, the most well-known being at the end of the Cretaceous era, when all the dinosaurs died out. The one at the end of the Permian era was even worse . . . it was almost a close call with the total extinction of the species on the planet.

Why does it matter? We live on a small, moist lump of rocks, spinning in the desert of space, and the only reason why it is liveable on this lump of rock is because of the services the other species on this planet give on a daily basis—an hourly basis, per-second basis . . . Most things of value on this planet are produced by the other animals. As you destroy them, the ecosystem services, the life support system of the planet, starts to deteriorate.

From the fossil records we see it took the planet up to 10 million years to start to recover [from past mass extinction periods]. These are not small events. Of all the signs that humans have been living on this planet, if we do complete this mass extinction event, it will be the most permanent impact of our existence.

That we built cars, landed on the moon, created the internet, or built skyscrapers won't matter, only that we wiped out well over half of all animal life on Earth.

Extinction rates are up to one thousand times higher because humans are in the picture.[51] We credit ourselves as highly intelligent, but we simply have not learned how to live in symbiosis with the rest of the planet and its earthlings.

In the last 40 years, we have already lost so many creatures. The Pinta Giant Tortoise, the Mexican Dace ray-finned fish, the Christmas Island Pipistrelle bat, the Splendid Poison Frog, the Saudi gazelle, and the Kauaʻi ʻōʻō honeyeater bird, and a Great Barrier Reef island–residing rodent named Bramble Cay melomys are just a few.[52] We cannot allow our actions to kill off more.

The United Nations has identified agriculture as one of the global primary causes of biodiversity destruction. This destruction is led by inefficient agricultural land use, eaten up by the rearing of animals.[53]

Our Dysfunctional Relationship Harming Ourselves

We threaten our own species with our callousness, too. As the Earth continues to warm, as salty waters rise, fresh waters dry up, rain falls less, and natural disasters become the norm, we will see climate refugees needing to seek asylum all over the world. People indigenous to the Pacific Islands, for example, are threatened by the extreme risk that some of their island home countries may in the next 10 to 15 years become "submerged under water," according to the United Nations.[54]

Far more catastrophic bushfire-condition days and more frequent, hotter heat waves in Australia mean the new normal may not be bushfires like those we saw in 2019 and early 2020, but ones far worse.[55] The 2019 Tropical Cyclone Idai struck the southeast coast of Mozambique and led 1.85 million people to need assistance, with 146,000 people internally displaced.[56] The World Bank estimates that, without intervention, across Latin America, sub-Saharan Africa, and Southeast Asia, 143 million climate refugees will be forced to leave everything behind for safety by 2050.[57] These are distressing realities, especially when considering those who will seek refuge internationally, as our "global community" is often not communal at all, denying people their human right to seek asylum.

Another significant reason people may need to seek asylum is due to resource scarcity, leading us back to the inefficient and disastrous animal agricultural system.[58] Only 55 percent of food crops directly nourish people, with the rest going to animal feed (36 percent) and bio-fuel (9 percent). When we use 100 calories of grain to feed animals, (we'll soon slaughter grown-on land that could instead cultivate a whole range of crops for human consumption) we get only 12 calories back from chicken carcasses, 10 calories back from pig carcasses, and 3 calories back from cattle carcasses.[59] The 9 billion human mouths we must feed by 2050 would be more secure if more of the food we grew actually fed us.[60] Otherwise, we perpetuate a system of great food waste in a world where, globally, 820 million people do not have enough to eat.[61] Western, heavily animal-based diets are sustaining those more fortunate while leaving others around the world hungry when they do not need to be. The Romantic Era's "strict vegetarian" activists against classism were right.

Heavily animal-based diets are sustaining some bodies, but only through an extremely short-sighted lens. COVID-19 has already raised alarms about the dangers of zoonotic diseases, pathogens that have jumped from non-human to human animals. Since it spread across the world, many more zoonotic disease outbreaks have sprung up. At the time of writing, two Australian egg farms have tested positive for avian influenza, with one shed of 21,750 birds all testing positive.[62] They were slaughtered, as were the nearly 39,000 chickens in a San Luis farm who also were determined to carry a strain of highly pathogenic avian influenza.[63] A new swine flu with reported "pandemic potential" has already infected 10 percent of industry workers, and "as many as 4.4 percent of the general population" also appears to have been exposed.[64] In Denmark alone, 17 million mink on fur farms were killed because they tested positive for COVID-19.[65] Experts have given warning that the global trade of exotic animal skins, built on both farmed and wild captured reptile exploitation, can contribute to the spread of diseases in humans.[66] If we continue to meddle with nature by trapping animals in factory farms, by hunting and butchering them, more of these diseases are going to hurt us, too.[67]

If we look deeper at factory farms and the human health risks they pose, we also have to talk about antibiotic resistance. Bacteria are rapidly dividing and mutating all the time, and so they are constantly adapting to their environment. This means that infectious bacteria can rapidly become resistant to the antibiotics we fend them off with. The World Health Organization recognizes this as one of the biggest threats to global health today.[68] Why? Because it can affect anyone, of any age and ethnicity, and can cause things that we now consider trivial to become death sentences. In a post-antibiotic era, we will go back to how things used to be; an infected cut or minor injury could kill you, dental and surgical procedures could be life threatening. Today, some STIs and infections like tuberculosis and pneumonia are becoming harder to treat with decreasingly effective antibiotics.

The more we use antibiotics, the more in danger we are of bacteria's becoming resistant to them. We animals don't become resistant to antibiotics, the actual pathogens do. This all relates to factory farming because 73 percent of antibiotics used globally are linked to animal agriculture.[69] Farmed animals fed these medicines are generally not sick but are given our most important medically invented gift for the sake of prevention.[70] For the sake of profit, it's easier to forgo individual care and address a large group of animals, who are at risk of infection from living in overcrowded, grimy squaller, for the short period of time they are allowed to live.

These antibiotics, which are medically important to humans, are also sometimes prescribed simply to increase growth rates. This causes animals to become fatter faster, so more money can be made from shorter lives before sooner slaughter dates.[71] With such heavy use of antibiotics, bacteria resistant to them are on the rise, and resistance seen in farmed animals has tripled since 2000.[72] These disease-causing, antibiotic-resistant bacteria can be transmitted to humans not only through direct contact, but also through eating these animals.[73]

The first man to receive antibiotics accidentally scratched his face with a rose thorn as he walked into his garden. Before he was given the penicillin, his entire face had swollen, his eye had been removed, he had abscesses that needed draining, and his remaining eye had to be pricked to relieve swelling pain. Within days of receiving antibiotics, he began to recover. He unfortunately died when there was not enough of the drug yet to help him through to full recovery. We don't want to be in that world again.[74]

And just to continue on this very merry route, even if none of the above will hurt us in our lifetimes, eating animal foods is hurting us, today. But actually, we can make it merry, so let's look on the bright side. The impact of choosing not to eat animals and what comes from them is outstandingly significant to our overall health. Dr. Mehr Gupta explains, with the support of numerous peer-reviewed studies, that plant-based diets reduce the risk of developing cardiovascular disease, diabetes, cancer, and chronic kidney disease. In some specific metabolic diseases it can even be an effective treatment option.[75] While a plant-based diet is certainly not a cure-all and everyone is different, these are incredibly significant findings, especially considering that some of these diseases are top killers of people all around the world.[76]

Hurting our fellow animals is also hurting us, in countless, devastating ways.

Chapter 11

Systemic Change

Change can't only come from individuals, but from us as a collective. We need systemic solutions that help create a more just, sustainable world for all of us animals.

A System for Us All

We all deserve to live within a harmonious societal system. One that, rather than destroying the natural environment we love, depend on, and are a part of, protects and even contributes to it. One that, rather than jeopardizing our mental and physical health, nurtures it. One that, rather than seeing the lives of any individuals as expendable, for the sake of production and profit, produces only that which is in our best interests, necessary for a good life. Simply, we all deserve to live in a system that values life.

This is not the system we live in. This is not what we get from stripping the Earth back to barren land where forest once stood, humbly tall and seeping with life, where now, animals selectively bred for commodification graze non-native grass covering degraded soil until their not-far-off slaughter date. This is not what we get from a system where industry is ultimately uninterested in individuals: those they profit from, those laboring under them, those dying under them. This is not what we get from a system where consumption is central, and this consumption sees the concaving of our planet around us, the killing off of our compassion and connection to life.

We've seen the way our planet is struggling with the impact of a system built on dead animals, exploited beings on an exploited planet. If we continue as we have, we will see not only the worsening of this environmental collapse, but also the societal and economic collapse that shall follow. Some decades ago, the Club of Rome think tank commissioned an MIT systems professor and his team to produce computer modeling based on environmental data to see what our future might look like. This work developed the studies of "population, agricultural production, non-renewable resource depletion, industrial output and pollution" and how they impact us all. The first of 45 study reports, the Club of Rome's 1970s publication *The Limits to Growth* was written by these researchers and shared a non-technical explanation of their findings as well as a message that remains vitally important in our perpetually growing economy today: "The global system of nature in which we all live—probably cannot support present rates of economic and population growth much beyond the year 2100, if that long, even with advanced technology."[1]

The research team's data and modeling showed that the way we see growth is deeply problematic, because it is rooted in the constant extraction of natural "resources" from a planet with only so much to offer. At the time of release, the report and book were criticized as "doomsday fantasy," the idea of a finite planet that we accept today, mocked. These early findings have been supported by far more recent research by other scientists, including those which specifically sought to discover if the original data was indeed valid and on track with a more modern reality.[2]

Beyond the frightening and accurate foreshadowing, *Limits to Growth* came with hope, too: We can create a society in which we can live indefinitely on Earth if we impose limits on ourselves and our production of material goods to achieve a state of global equilibrium."[3] We could thrive if we stopped equating progress with growth. The real growth of our economy, our system, and our society is not in the infinite supersizing of the goods and services a country produces annually (gross domestic product, or GDP) nor the subsequent destruction of our finite planet which follows. Genuine societal growth is in our ability to learn and progress toward putting the lives of each individual and the environment we are a part of first, valuing the quality of these lives rather than the quantity of things we own and dominate.

This is what we need. A system that sees the independent worth of individuals and the Earth, first. All animals have independent worth. A chicken does not exist to be eaten as a cutlet, a koala does not exist to be "awwed" at until we destroy their homes and lives for cattle farming,[4] cattle do not exist to be laced up as shoes, a human does not exist merely to labor in the production of stuff we don't need. Stuff made from animals, plants, and minerals we consider only to be resources, not individuals or delicate parts of a phenomenal ecosystem of life. There's nothing wrong with admiring and caring about things; about art, beauty, and what we can make. But no thing is so beautiful that it should be worth more than life itself.

It can be hard to picture what this different sort of system might look like, and it can also be hard to realize how far removed we have become from nature, how much of it we have decimated. Dr. Helen Harwatt, a Food and Climate Policy Fellow at Harvard Law, told me that she thought the reason for our unknowingness of the extent of our destruction of the natural environment is due to "shifting baselines" we experience between generations. "Our parents and our grandparents will probably remember different insects and animals compared to what we remember, or they might remember more of an abundance of them compared to what we see now. But we have grown up in a much more barren and depleted ecosystem, so it's seen as normal."

Our current, exponential growth form of capitalism demands our economy must grow forever and constantly. Nothing in the natural world grows forever, but many economists for a long time have decided that, essentially, how much stuff and money we make should. More economists today are arguing that this pursuit of growth is not only insensible, but also "quite dangerous," among them Peter Victor, an economist and environmental scientist. Dangerous, when GDP growth is favored over things that would benefit us all, like work to cut greenhouse gas emissions, which would help save the planet as we know it, but also would reduce GDP by trillions of dollars. GDP is privileged too, over the development of good social housing and systems that ensure everyone has their basic needs met, and met with respect.[5]

This endless pursuit of growth is also dangerous because as collective liberationist activist and educator Iye Bako further notes, this intense and rapidly growing form of capitalism is monstrous in that it relies on the exploitation and dehumanization of others. Largely brown workers, for example, like some people in India or Bangladesh, are underpaid and poorly treated in systems that produce our mobile phones, accessories, and many of our clothes. This sort of treatment of white Americans, Australians, or Brits would never be tolerated. But, this aggressive form of capitalism relies on a racism rooted in dehumanization, which means these people are seen as "less valuable, as commodities, used as a resource to produce more commodities."

This often-unconscious labeling of others as "sub-human" allows us to render these "others" as "animals" whom we deem acceptably objectified and exploited. This pipeline thinking from "non-human" to "non-being" is clear in the labeling of animals with numbers, not names, within systems commodifying them. Mostly hidden from our sight, and intentionally so, when I spoke to Iye she said that this meant "we don't have social relationships with these animals, we've lost our connection to the Earth and all of nature's creatures because through capitalism, we see ourselves as separate from our ecosystem. Land, labor, and individual beings are seen as resources, not as individual entities or a part of nature. Because everything is separated off, we don't have the ability to comprehensively understand that there are other beings here who have lives that they want to live." So, despite many animal species, and even trees, facilitating the redistribution of food and water, playing integral parts in the maintenance of life, we do not value them. Instead, a small percentage of humans hoard wealth they will never be able to spend within many lifetimes, built on the backs of these exploited individuals and their environment.

Economists suggesting a move away from GDP-centric thinking and toward the prioritization of policies that pursue the safety and wellbeing of all we coexist with, are important, but such ideas are not actually new or revolutionary. Indigenous people lived and thrived without GDP and with a far more balanced relationship to nature for thousands of years. What's more, modern GDP itself only came into existence in response to the Great Depression, which ended in the 1930s, in an effort to improve accountability around what was really happening in an economy.

While GDP may help us understand and applaud how much stuff we're making, it helps us with little else. Measuring a country's GDP is not measuring the wellbeing of those living in that country—the creator of the system himself noting this as the case.[6] There are many different systems, like the doughnut economic systems that prioritize social equality, environmental protection, and regeneration, being taken more seriously now, instead.[7] Too, other metrics for success are being considered, with New Zealand's former prime minister Jacinda Arden adopting the Happiness Index, announcing national budget changes that focus on improving the lives of New Zealanders.[8] This progressive policy, which explicitly places wellbeing as an objective before economic growth, also isn't actually new. The Kingdom of Bhutan began using this Index in 2008, measuring psychological health, living standards, community vitality, and environmental and cultural resilience. This index is then used to inform government policy. There are many systems that would better suit us all on this planet, both ancient, newly formed, and fusions of both, which do not accept environmental or living harm and unhappiness for the sake of a growing economy.

Some animals are considered keystone species in their particular ecosystem because they are so irreplaceable that without them, everything would fall apart. Some sharks, predatory birds, beavers, and even starfish hold this role. However, humans are considered hyper keystone species, due to our treatment of animals as resources, which so quickly devastates keystone species and everyone else who relies on them.[9] As humans, we "unite the entire world in a chain of falling dominoes" if we're not careful.[10] We are just a small part, though currently a disproportionately impactful part, of a far wider, wonderful, and complex ecosystem we will likely never fully understand. Our greatest growth will be in finding symbiosis within this ecosystem again, while continuing to live and create culture, art, food, clothing, and joy. Without that symbiosis, we live at the expense of the life of everything and everyone outside of our singular species. And we can't live that way for much longer. A symbiotic society would be a successful society.

Politicians, People, Fighting for Change

Every day, politicians sit, debate, and pass policies that impact all of us. Short of a French-style revolution, for us to ever see a society that does not systemically other, undermine, and undervalue living beings and our planet, our deeply political world needs politicians to pass policies effecting this change. It's important for us to feel connected to politics and policy change, and not as though they are something far away and untouchable to the majority. Politicians aren't as far away from us as we think. They are individual people, representatives we can speak to and share concerns with. We pay them, they work for us, they must eventually listen when a large number of people rise and speak up. Though, of course, that's all easier said than done. When no change comes exclusively from the top down, the best politicians are involved and supportive of grassroots movements.

Leaders and politicians who seek genuine social and environmental justice, while doing deeply important work, often have closed our fellow animals off from their circle of concern and compassion, missing opportunities for policies that may deliver us a more truly and collectively liberated world. Fortunately, around the world there are more politicians and political parties that have sprung up from dedicated communities, which seek to include our fellow animals in discussions of justice.

In 2006, the Dutch Party for the Animals (Partij Voor De Dieren) was elected to 2 of 150 parliamentary seats. In 2017, the party won 5 seats, and today has 92 elected representatives across different levels of parliament, from European, to national, regional, and local levels. This was the first party that successfully sought to invite discussions of animal oppressions and the oppressions that intertwine with them, into the political sphere. The party gives priority to sustainability and compassion over short-term economic gain, standing for environmental policy that considers clean, renewable energy, greenhouse gas emission reduction, and the need for a transition to an environmentally and more ethically just, healthy, plant-based agricultural food system.[11]

Underlining that all violence and crises concerning climate, food, economy, biodiversity, and animal wellbeing are connected, the party started the Animal Politics Foundation. Sharing knowledge and support with other political parties that also seek justice that extends to our fellow animals, such parties now exist globally—in Canada, Finland, Sweden, Greece, Portugal, Brazil, Switzerland, and Denmark, to name a few.[12]

In Australia, the Animal Justice Party has three members of parliament (MPs) at the time of writing, with others in local council positions, too. The party's unity principles address animal, civil, LGBTQI+, disability, refugee and worker's rights, as well as environmental and economic justice. The first woman elected into parliament within the party, Emma Hurst, quickly banned the sale of fur in the city of Sydney. She has advocated within parliamentary inquiries for the end of animal use in entertainment, of painful animal mutilations on farms, and for legislative reform around domestic violence impacting both human and other animal victims. Threats and actual violence against companion animals are extremely common in domestic violence situations.[13]

Meanwhile, the first Victorian MP, Andy Meddick, has voted to protect important natural ecosystems, banned recreational wombat hunting in the state, voted in favor of workplace manslaughter laws, and supported workers' unions, passing workplace manslaughter laws to protect people.[14] He has sat on the inquiry board looking at the impact of animal activism on agriculture, which ultimately saw many draconian ag-gag laws defeated in Victoria. He has sat on a parliament health board and promoted plant-based diets. He has passed Birth Certificate Reform, changing and affirming the lives of trans people like his children, and secured reform protecting both native and those animals too often killed for convenience in shelters and pounds.[15]

While some animal advocates have misguidedly critiqued the party for advocating for marginalized humans and not focusing solely on our fellow animals, a party that truly stands for animal justice works for the collective liberation of us all, unbound by species. Our separation of ourselves from our animality has stopped the wider social justice movement from seeking to free everyone, regardless of their species, and has perpetuated the degrading of some humans to "sub-human," then treated accordingly. As a party predominately focused on those beyond humans, which is needed in a parliament predominately avoidant or opposed to making animal abuse illegal, also protecting people and planet is not a disservice to other animals. It is the solidarity required for collective liberation.

Even outside of animal-specific parties, more leaders are helping to create a world where we are all free, regardless of our identity. Dr. Mehreen Faruqi is a federal senator for the Greens Party in Australia, which focuses on environmental issues and social justice, which environmental justice cannot exist without. A migrant from Pakistan, a feminist, a member of the vegan society, and an environmental and civil engineer, Dr. Faruqi became the first Muslim woman to sit in Australian parliament and to become a senator. She campaigns and works to see Australia create effective, safe, and comfortable social housing and fairer rental rights, stating that "housing is a human right."[16] She operates an "anti-racism in Australia" strategy alongside the Victorian state's first Aboriginal senator, Lidia Thorpe, working to tackle anti-immigrant racism. Working without a species-based barrier to justice, Dr. Faruqi is also a spokesperson on animal welfare—with less liberationist policy work than the Animal Justice Party and its members—and other issues, calling for an end to greyhound racing, animal testing, live export, and culling of native wildlife populations that have been devastated by bushfires.[17]

The United Kingdom's Animal Welfare Party looks far beyond welfare to liberation. They work to see subsidies redirected away from factory-farming and the slaughter of animals, to a transition toward plant-based, sustainable agriculture. Their policies work to phase out animal experimentation through binding targets for reduction and funding, and with support for alternatives that are effective, safe, and free from animal cruelty.[18]

In the United States, Cory Booker is the first African American senator from New Jersey and is also vegan, focusing significant efforts on cruel factory farming of animals, and on the environmental injustice caused by it; injustices that he calls further "assault on Black bodies." As part of his wider effort to create a socially and environmentally just America, the senator speaks consistently about the detrimental health impact on communities of color living around factory farms and their pollution. "The determining factor of whether you live around toxicity . . . is the color of your skin." Impaired drinking water, antibiotic resistance, and air pollution are just some of the issues these communities deal with. Cory also addresses safety concerns for meatpacking workers who are largely people of color too, and on the driving out of small farmers by multinational corporations that often pollute without consequence.[19]

Most significant to his work in this area is the senator's 2019 bill and coalition alongside Elizabeth Warren and independent farmers, which seeks to pass the Farm System Reform Act.[20] Reintroduced in 2023 alongside Representative Ro Khanna, this bill would phase out the largest existing factory farms and ban the building of new factory farms, as well as expansions on existing operations. It would impose "liabilities and costs of pollution, accidents and disasters on the agricultural conglomerate that control[s] the market rather than on the independent farmers who contract with them." Perhaps most significantly, it would create a $100 billion fund to support debt relief and assist factory-farmers in transitioning into other forms of agriculture—such as plant-based agriculture. This sort of legislation, if passed, would be life changing and even saving for countless animals, communities of color, and the environment. A reduction of mega-factory-farms would ultimately mean a reduction in cheap "meat" products and so the number of individuals killed for them. It would mean real progress toward a healthier, more just food system.[21]

The once president of the Brooklyn borough and now mayor of New York, Eric Adams, was the first Black person to hold his former position, and the second for his current role. With a large Black and brown population in the borough in particular, this kind of reflective leadership, which stands for the protection of a marginalized, oppressed, yet innovative, resilient, and vibrant community, is critical. Eric once followed a common, "junky" American diet and had type-two diabetes with vision loss and nerve damage in his hands and feet. He had high blood pressure and cholesterol, and an ulcer. Within three weeks of eating a wholefood, plant-based diet, his vision came back, and within three months, his body became healthy again; his diabetes went into remission, his ulcer and nerve damage disappeared, and his blood and cholesterol levels returned to a healthy state.

Today, while a number of his positions and actions have not aligned with collective liberation, the mayor says that "you can't abuse living beings and expect for it not to abuse you in the process," as we "come from the same core" so must "determine how we are going to take care of ourselves and our mothers" and also "of mother earth." Wanting to show his community that they could be more in control of their health and not need a lifetime of medicine in many cases, Eric has set himself a mission to foster a more mentally and physically healthy community. Black communities in America experience significant disparities in chronic conditions, access to mental and physical health care, and preventative screenings. Eric has stood up against a lack of government action and worked to set up initiatives regarding extremely high suicide rates among Black youth. He has, despite the requests for retraction by the North American Meat Institute, set up Meatless Mondays at New York City public schools and successfully seen the Department of Education effectively ban carcinogenic processed meats from being served in these schools.[22]

What's more, as part of New York's Green New Deal, which tackles the city's climate footprint, Eric led the "green action" against processed meat and beef, with not only schools, but also hospitals, prisons, and municipal offices confirmed to reduce their beef purchases by 50 percent. He has also worked with forty doctors of color to promote the health benefits of wholefood plant-based diets, especially as people of color were dying at higher rates from COVID-19 due to pre-existing conditions. Hoping it will extend across further hospitals, Eric has set up a pilot lifestyle medicine clinic in the oldest hospital in America, Bellevue. This clinic, with the help of doctors, nurses, dieticians, and coaches, will work with patients to educate and change their eating patterns, helping communities prevent and even reverse diet-related health issues.[23]

The work of these politicians is powerful and critical, and, importantly, it is only possible because of the grassroots movements supporting their work and making their position of power reality through election. The political drive for animal justice and the good that offshoots from that is speeding up, with many more laws passed around the world to protect our fellow animals, all of these beginning from grassroots movements.

Positive Law Change

Grassroots activism—and the political campaigning for the rights of animals that comes from it—has already led to some significant changes for the lives and protections of our fellow animals. Every time a law changes for these individuals, even when in the scheme of total liberation it may seem like a small step, something powerful has happened. Not so long ago even the idea of "animal welfare" was mocked by the majority, so even the most basic welfare laws that have passed for animals beg the question of what else is possible as we continue to demand justice for our other animal kin.

A pivotal example of work bridging grassroots activity and political campaigning for animals is the Oscar's Law campaign, which seeks to end puppy farming in Australia.[24] The campaign is led by founder Debra Tranter, and at the time of writing, President Georgie Purcell, who was also the chief of staff for Andy Meddick MP. Today, Georgie is an MP herself, working for our fellow animals, us humans, and our planet. This move only highlights the power of grassroots campaigners working in the political field.

Currently, it is impossible to practically ban the factory farming of puppies while dog breeding exists, as there are no legal definitions as to what a puppy factory farm really is. Instead, they need to be regulated out of existence, limiting the number of dogs who can be exploited under one operation, and made financially impractical for such operations to exist. Thanks to the campaign, this goal has already been achieved in the state of Victoria, saving thousands of dogs from lives of misery.

At the time of the change, the previous Liberal (conservative) government had made it legal to use blunt-force trauma to kill runt puppies on farms, as well as to deny soft bedding to breeding dogs who could instead be offered a wooden plank to sleep on. While opposing the Liberals in the election, the Labour Party (which is more politically liberal) made an election commitment, and once in power they passed legislation that saw these laws reversed, the codes of practice for dog breeding changed, and puppy-farming effectively banned through regulation.

This substantial legal feat may well also occur in other Australian states where the issue is still being challenged. Georgie says this is the result of a chain of tactics: whistleblower exposés followed by the creation of media moments around them, garnering of public support, and exerting political pressure. The Victorian campaign ran an exposé of the conditions inside puppy farms supplying pet shops in the state. This led to protests at pet shops linked to these exposed farms, which often in turn led to shopping centers canceling store leases in fear of reputational damage. The campaign ultimately worked to break the puppy farm supply chain, as Victoria has now banned the sale of puppies and kittens in store entirely.

Another important tactic deployed is the juxtaposition of heart-warming stories of puppy-farm survivors, living their newly happy and safe lives, with upsetting documentation from the kinds of puppy farms they were saved from. One of the most chilling examples of such a confronting story focused on Strawberry, the less than one-year-old mother boxer dog who, in a New South Wales puppy farm, was left to slowly die in 2020. Some of Strawberry's unborn puppies were found rotting inside her, while surviving pups were sold in stores in Western Australia. Concerned citizens held a vigil for Strawberry on Western Australia's parliament steps, bringing their beloved companion dogs, flowers, candles, and placards. The government was lobbied to make a change on her behalf, and for all those like her. At the end of 2021, landmark "Stop Puppy Farming" legislation passed in Western Australia.[25]

The ban on foie gras sales in New York City is another triumph of grassroot activism. This feat came largely due to the work to organize a movement of individuals, activists, and whistleblowers, by Voters for Animal Rights. When the news of the ban's success broke, *The New York Times* wrote, "One chef's reaction: What's next? No more veal?."[26] Similarly, when mandatory pain relief was first discussed in parliament in Victoria, Australia, the chairman of the New South Wales Farmers Wool Committee stated, "The concern is, where will this demand for pain relief stop?"[27] This is an extraordinary statement, one that shows the industry's greatest fears to be a demand that they reduce the pain they inflict on animals. The fear for animal exploiting industries each time a law is passed, even one based in "welfare" and not true liberation, is that this law is one step toward just that.

The laws that are passed today to protect animals are around those forms of exploitation and cruelty that are considered not only abhorrent, but unjustified. An indictment of vanity, the animal protection laws most widely adopted are those banning testing of cosmetics on rabbits and rats, as well as other rodents. Cosmetics testing on animals is now banned in 42 countries and counting around the world.[28] While many of these laws, like those in Australia, aren't as exhaustive as they should be, allowing for cosmetics ingredients that are also used in other industries (like the therapeutic, household cleaning, agricultural, or food industries) to still be tested on animals, and for the importation of animal-tested cosmetics, they are meaningful.[29]

These cosmetics testing laws mean that we have, on an enormous scale, recognized that external, personal beauty is not more important than the wellbeing of other individuals. With increased education, advocacy, and awareness, perhaps this sentiment may be extended to mean that not only should cosmetics not be tested on animals, but that they should not contain ingredients from exploited or slaughtered animals, either. While a wide range of animal-free cosmetics exists, guanine is found in sparkly eyeshadow, highlighter is often made from fish scales, crushed bugs are in red lipsticks, snail mucin is in face creams, hair and skin care products are often made with animal fats, and lanolin used in lipsticks, balms and other cosmetics comes from the wool and meat industry, killing sheep.

Perhaps most interesting though, are laws passed in a growing number of places, including Australia's capital territory (though not the whole country), the European Union, New Zealand, and Quebec, recognizing animal sentience; the ability of animals to, on a psychological and physical level, feel both pain and pleasure.[30] These laws are of particular importance because they serve as ammunition against violent but standard practices in industries built on exploitation; if we know the animals on factory farms and fishing boats both suffer and rejoice, how can we justify causing the former?

Some of these laws, like the capital territory's, also recognize the "intrinsic value" of our fellow animals: "animals have intrinsic value and deserve to be treated with compassion and have a quality of life that reflects their intrinsic value."[31] How does this kind of legal act sit comfortably next to commercial kangaroo shooting, cosmetics filled with animal fats, or the existence of operating slaughterhouses?

German law, as another example, sees other animals as "fellow creatures," and says that no harm should be done unto an animal "without good reason." Following this, German law now forbids catch-and-release fishing. Switzerland, which has an animal welfare act that protects the dignity of non-human beings, has even made the keeping of single parakeets, guinea pigs, and other social creatures illegal, to protect them from loneliness. Yet, in both of these countries the flesh of other social creatures is reduced to a simple snack, eaten each and every day and seen as normal—as it is in every country.[32]

The hypocrisy of these laws may be maddening, but it is a tool for more radical progress, too. After all, what is the "good reason" for causing harm to animals when we do not need to? It is easy for us to define cosmetics testing, foie gras eating, or fur wearing as an unnecessary cruelty. These are for the sake of vanity, they are mere luxuries. There are good alternatives. While it's less widely accepted, is all of our commercialized animal killing not vain and needless crime, particularly as there are alternatives? When we have the choice to do something better, how could there ever be a "good reason" for commodifying, confining, and slaughtering our fellow animals? Is our best reason simply convenience?

In 1986 a global moratorium on commercial whaling was imposed in response to devastated whale populations and global outrage toward the violence these mighty cetaceans were victim to.[33] This worldwide commitment could give us hope for the possibility of similar global species protections. It won't be any day soon, but, as Helen Harwatt suggested, perhaps there may be a global animal treaty someday. Perhaps before then, more species will slowly be added to the list of those who are, by global law, protected from killing for the sake of commercial gain.

Supported Agricultural Transition

One of the most powerful steps our governments could make toward a fairer world for animals—whether human or beyond us—and for our planet would be to financially support the transition to a just agricultural system. This would be a system that is plant-based, rather than built upon the commodification and slaughter of those we live on Earth with, and would focus far more on the regeneration of the planet than on what can be taken from it. Of course, we need agriculture, but we take far more from the land than we give back, and, on a finite planet, this model is doomed.

Regenerative plant agriculture values the environment and recognizes that a healthy ecosystem allows us to have long-term food security, climate security, and a stable planet to live with. It is farming in a more balanced, give and take agri-environmental system, rather than one that pushes the absolute boundaries of what the planet can offer. This is farming that's future-proofed for coming generations. This sort of agricultural system also really loves dirt. It works to rebuild soil health and protect precious topsoil and the living organisms within it. We need healthy soil for fertile land that can grow a biodiverse range of plants, some we can eat, and some that are home to a wide range of wildlife species. It is important that this new, regenerative agricultural system be not only environmentally just, but also just in a broader sense. The needless slaughter of billions of animals is not sustainable nor innovative in any way, and if we're reinventing agriculture to be more just and sustainable, maintaining the status quo of commodified animal killing just doesn't seem in the spirit of things. This new agricultural system should value life; not only of the Earth, but of all its creatures.

Regenerative practices are already being implemented in some plant-based agriculture. Rotational and diverse cropping benefits soil bacteria and reduces disease threats. Cover plants between nut and fruit trees protect soil from erosion. Farmers foster an ecosystem where bugs naturally keep each other in balance, in turn reducing and removing chemical pesticides. Green (plant) "manure" and compost fertilizes plants.

Some regenerative agricultural practices are also being used by some people rearing animals, but with the claim that farmed animals are essential to this sort of system. This is not accurate. The widely applauded rotational grazing of farmed animals has been found in an analysis from Oxford and Cambridge, across over three hundred sources, not to cause a meaningful net reduction in greenhouse gas emissions as has been claimed.[34] Peer-reviewed assessment of some of the most famous studies and proponents of using animals as a "climate solution" while we eat and wear them has found misinformation and suspect, biased funding sources. Farmers who are reducing the number of animals they raise and kill for the sake of soil, land degradation, and desertification prevention are reducing their environmental harm. However, the best thing that could be done with this land for the sake of biodiversity and carbon sequestration is for it to be transitioned toward plant growing, or rewilded.

The use of land for inefficient animal agriculture incurs a "carbon opportunity cost" of sorts, with a study published in *Nature Sustainability* showing that if by 2050 we have transitioned to an entirely plant-based agricultural system, we would see the long-term, secure, and sustained storage of greenhouse gases equivalent to 99–163 percent of our carbon emission budget of 1.5 degrees Celsius. This budget is the total amount of carbon emissions we have left before it's all out of our hands. This, combined with the also necessary clean energy revolution, would be utterly future-changing.[35]

Because wildly more efficient plant-based agriculture delivers far more calories with far less land than animal agriculture, in this new, plant-based agricultural system, much of the land animals have been living on and degrading could be given back to nature, supporting biodiversity: up to 3 billion hectares.[36]

Animal life is necessary for a thriving ecosystem, but these need to be wild, free-living animals, not those born unnaturally to be killed. While many farmers may need to farm less in a more efficient system, this doesn't have to mean job loss, but instead, job transformation. Some farmers would simply transition their focus to cropping. But, just as many farmers raise animals for slaughter and also grow crops, cropping could exist alongside carbon sequestration and land restoration efforts on current grazing land.

Opportunity for a just transition is important for farming people, too, as running farms that are often in debt and heading toward an environmental breaking point is detrimental to many farmers' mental health. In Australia, research has found that farmers are more likely to have suicidal ideation or complete suicide.[37] Too, depression surrounding economic security fears and the struggle that comes with watching environmental degradation has been shared by animal farmers.[38] So many farmers feel a deep connection with the land they farm on and distress at watching it decline. Being paid to care for the land, planting native flora, assisting in carbon sequestration and the regeneration of totally wild natural systems, could be a wonderful and achievable reality, particularly when supported by eco-tourism.

The funds for this future already exist. All of the public funds governments spend subsidizing animal agriculture could be put toward this transition.[39] While the United Nations states that 90 percent of farm subsidies fund "harmful" operations, and every fifth subsidy dollar funds the meat industry, these funds could be used far better, for everybody. Politicians representing constituents involved in animal farming may feel a need to push for these subsidies to stay in place, with a sense of duty to protect these people. However, this is short-sighted and offers only a false sense of security when solid, long-term solutions are required to combat environmental problems that, if not addressed, will be catastrophic.[40] The Agriculture Fairness Alliance, in the context of their at-risk farmer legislation, which supports transition away from dysfunctional animal agriculture, said it best: "Farmers need a hand up, not a handout."[41]

Additional government funding for carbon farming, and even animal- and Earth-friendly wildlife and ecotourism, could come from other avenues, too. Now, value is placed on what can be extracted from the Earth—trees too often being seen as holding more value when they're cut down than when they're standing old and tall, creating oxygen, cleaning our environment, and creating homes for wildlife. If we put greater value on the natural environment and its health, and in turn, all of our health, we could see dramatic changes. A carbon tax has been introduced in some parts of the world to recognize the environmental impact carbon release has and to hinder massive emissions.[42] In a similar spirit, carbon sequestering efforts by carbon farmers could be supported by governments around the world, even directly from these taxes where they exist or from current agricultural subsidies.[43]

While a just transition is no doubt a huge cost, when considering the current financial cost of animal agriculture, we should include the additional economic burden forced upon sick people and our health-care system, due to known health risks associated with animal-based foods like flesh and milk. A study from Oxford University found that, if by 2050 we really all had switched to a plant-based diet, literally eating the fruits (and vegetables, fungi, grains, nuts, and pulses) of our new agricultural system, we could enjoy a cumulative 129 million years of life saved. The costs of illness avoided by this change in diet could result in economic benefits of, at the very least, one trillion US dollars globally, every year.[44] These funds could be redistributed to ensure food, climate, and social security for everyone.

Regenerative, plant-based agriculture that allows for rewilding is a more natural solution to a human-made problem, and is one supported by some of the best available scientific analysis.[45] With more rewilded land comes an opportunity for Indigenous land sovereignty, giving back to people who have seen the introduction of grazing animals destroy their native land. In so-called Australia, for example, Aboriginal people have a wealth of knowledge surrounding land care management. With the use of controlled burns to prevent devastating bushfires, these people have increased the fertility of land and grown food native to it, benefitting rather than harming it. When colonizers came with sheep to exploit for wool and meat, native yam pastures and grasslands soon disappeared.[46] Too often Indigenous people are simplified and homogenized, made out as only "hunter gatherers" to make them appear less "evolved" or innovative than white people. In reality, some different Aboriginal communities across the country could be considered some of the first bakers, who, relative to their climate, grew different types of wild rice, fruits, and vegetables, sometimes also building dams to source water for crops.[47] A plant-based food system should be one informed by Indigenous techniques about what edible vegetation grows best within an ecosystem.

An agricultural revolution is happening now. Plant-based, regenerative farmers, including the dedicated and compassionate Jay and Katja Wilde from the earlier mentioned film, *73 Cows*, now speak and are involved with scientists' calls for European agricultural policy change, which could support this much needed shift.[48] It is inevitable that these grassroots agricultural movements continue to grow and thrive, but in order for the global environmental revolution to flourish, we need it to be accessible to all farmers and communities, and animal agriculture must not be funded any longer. Support for this transformative system must come.

Chapter 12

Innovative, Organizational, and Grassroots Change

Propelling systemic change, and sprouting larger organizations committed to a more just world, is the grassroots movement at the forefront of ethical evolution. Here we look at the work coming from both these grassroots collectives and those individuals who have built innovative businesses and organizations that help propel a world without exploitation forward.

Abolition and Working with Those Considered "the Opposition"

The grassroots of the animal and total liberation movement often form and shoot out from soil in the places we least expect it. Vivisectionists, slaughterhouse workers, and farmers continue to be integral players in the success of dismantling speciesism and replacing it with something better, as they look for something better for themselves, too. It's not so surprising that those most intimately aware of the violence perpetrated within these industries, who have suffered through mental anguish because of them, should often become powerful voices for change.

Again, we must see ourselves as a collective. All of us who are oppressed, whether due to our species, class, race, sex, or something else, we are the same and deserve the same. When we consider our most vital needs, when everything else is stripped back, our considerable similarities far outweigh our considerable differences. Just the same as humans and our fellow animals are similar in the ways that matter most, animal advocates, farmers, vivisectionists, and slaughterhouse workers all want the right to act freely, with autonomy, and in safety. In working for other animals to have these rights too, it is in our collective best interest to remember that oppression is a structure that cannot be selectively dismantled. Harming other animals harms people, and demonizing people who harm animals within a system harming them too is not a radical liberatory act.

While someone working in a slaughterhouse may seem at odds with work to dismantle oppressive systems, they are no more unaligned from animal or total liberation than someone who consumes the bodies that come from their work. By demonizing those closest to the greatest symptoms of speciesism, we forget that we helped build the wider system, and that we will all benefit from its undoing. The greatest difference between slaughterhouse workers and "us" is not how complicit we are in this system. It is in the close proximity to violence a person working along the animal slaughter supply chain is, and how the mental anguish from this can make them a victim of this industry too. A survivor, a potential storyteller.

There is complexity to advocating for illegal trespass to record what goes on in farms and slaughterhouses while also holding space for the people who work in these places. However, transparency and the justice that trickles off of it are ultimately positive for us all, even if it comes with levels of discomfort in getting there—as it always will. Violence is not something any of us benefit from. One of the most powerful stories I've read in opposition to industrialized animal slaughter, from a human perspective, came from an anonymous slaughterman. Shared via *BBC News*, the "confessions of a slaughterhouse worker" spoke of the commonness of prospective workers fainting as they walked through their potential new workplace. Of visibly upset men cracking hardened exteriors at the sight of calves they had just killed, of depression and suicidal ideation, of numbing and coping mechanisms, of a sobbing co-worker, of another who took his life, no longer able to stand it.[1] The pain of slaughterhouse workers and the immense suffering and robbery of life faced by animals do not cancel each other out; they complicate things. One thing is simple and certain though: everyone deserves far better.

There is a power in willingness to work together. Movements working together, like animal rights groups and union groups aiming to slow down production lines in slaughterhouses, are creating win–win situations. Mercy For Animals President Leah Garcés (running an organization founded by Milo Runkle, who was previously on track to be a fifth-generation farmer)[2] stated to me that the cost of animal consumption is externalized by an industry that "relies on treating workers and animals as expendable." Garcés said this just after telling me about an Oxfam report that saw poultry slaughterhouse workers wearing diapers after being denied toilet breaks.[3] If just some of these costs were internalized, if slaughtering lines were slowed down to reduce injury and workers were paid a living wage and provided health care, fewer animals would be able to be killed as quickly. Flesh would cost more, fewer animals would be killed.

Working alongside people with experience in this industry is not weakening an anti-speciesist position; it is extending our circle of compassion—something we ask other social justice advocates to do for our fellow animals. It is also effective. In her book *Grilled: Turning Adversaries into Allies*, Leah shares her experience working with people in the chicken slaughtering industry. Having worked for nearly two decades to bring an end to chicken factory farming and chicken slaughter all together, when Leah found herself in the living room of Craig Watts, a chicken factory farmer, all she wanted was to get footage from inside his farm.[4]

Craig had got in contact with her and was willing to show the inside of his Perdue chicken-supplying farm to the world, something that had not happened in a decade. Uninterested in him personally, Leah says that when they planned to meet, she was looking for a fight and not a solution, and certainly not a friend. Upon speaking with Craig, Leah "felt ashamed." Ashamed that she had never considered why someone would make the choice to become a factory farmer: to keep the land their family had handed them, to keep food on the table for their family. She had never realized that it may not be a purposefully cruel or cold choice, or that it could be a "choice" people like Craig felt trapped in by debt and circumstance. Craig and many farmers Leah has met since have been "disgusted by their choice of work, the way the chickens get sick, the way they get diseases." Many of these farmers said that they would never eat chicken, and that "if America knew" how chickens were treated, "they wouldn't either." She claimed, "I realized they hated the industry as much as I did."

When I spoke with Leah, she talked about assuming positive intent in people, and the unavoidable discomfort and need for humility in her work. While it can be difficult to feel empathy for someone who partakes in the slaughter of another being, empathy and the extension of compassion never made a situation worse. Often, too, in Leah's experience, this empathy-extension widens the range of people opposed to factory farming whom she could work with, who want to do good. She said that "there's other bricks to pull out from this factory-farming wall than cages and crates," now understanding that for many farmers, if they had another choice, they'd simply do something else.

By working with Craig and seeing him not as her adversary, but her ally, even her friend, they achieved more than she ever had before for chickens. The footage from Craig's farm broke international news, which led to Craig's being involved in a historic whistleblowing case, blowing the lid off the utterly false "humanely raised" claims Perdue had been spewing over television commercials for so long. The exact adverts that had started it all when they made Craig feel ill, knowing it was a total lie. One he had to bust open.[5]

Having formed a strong mutual respect with Craig by advocating not only for the animals in his sheds, but for him and other farmers who hate being trapped in an industry exploiting them and the chickens they hate to raise for slaughter, Leah began the Transfarmation Project. As part of this project, Craig's broiler chicken sheds are being turned into the perfect space to grow mushrooms for people to eat, with other farmers in the program also moving away from animal slaughtering supply chains, towards fungi and hemp. This story of alliance is one critical for all animal advocates to consider. When we deny others the same right to develop or change that we have, we miss opportunities.

Everyone needs to be a part of the solution, and no one deserves to be left behind; it's this same principle that sees miners being involved in climate activism and work to move to renewable energy. When we come to someone ready to fight, not to find resolution, we will never see that solution, or this kinder world, begin to bloom—like the fungi in Craig's ex-broiler sheds now will.

Grassroots, Innovation, and Growth

Another important and often forgotten part of grassroots activism is innovation. Innovation, the creation of a new way of doing or making something, is powerful because it offers positive, tangible solutions to coincide with advocacy work, which raises awareness of the problems inherent to current ways of doing and making.

Innovation exists on small and large scales, with both having profound impacts. Innovation offers new possibilities in the way we live, and it can look like a lot of things. It could be an accessible vegan food business providing a more nourishing option to a local community. It can be a small start-up with a big idea that's sure to grow, like non-animal growth serum–derived cell-based meat that's more affordable and accessible than slaughter-based flesh.[6] It can be the development of more sustainable and just bio-materials replicating feather down, wool, and fur. These kinds of solutions help build a future where we, our fellow animals, and the planet are eschewed for profit's sake.

Say we called for the end of wool, exposed the cruelty behind it for sheep, as well as slaughterhouses, and shearing workers. Say we demanded the end of native habitat theft and demolition for the industry, impacting Indigenous human and animal communities. Little would be able to change if there wasn't a better way being offered up, too.

Similarly, we need to face up to the reality that not everyone cares about animal liberation, Earth, or collective liberation. While I sway between idealism and pragmatism, the empathetic and ever pragmatic Sebastiano Cossia Castiglioni, who has helped numerous ethical, vegan start-ups grow to compete with and cut back the profit margins of slaughter-based foods, thinks about the numbers. He told me that "it is important to acknowledge that, even though we do it strategically, not because we think it's morally right, a fundamental part of winning the battle for the animals is to make alternatives widely available and desirable." If alternatives to cruel and destructive products are more "appealing, efficient, functional, inexpensive, delicious, and available worldwide," their existence, together with the use of all other strategies we've looked at here, will save many more animals than if we rely only on ethics and empathy. Basically, while market disruption may not be the thing he's most passionate about, it's what he thinks will win. Regardless of the reason for a reduction of animal consumption, a huge reduction will mirror a huge reduction in animal suffering. On the path to liberation, disruption and reduction of suffering is desperately needed, so long as we don't lose sight of where we are going, and why.

There are lots of people who work for animals with these ideas in mind. Tying together innovation and allyship with humans stuck in speciesist industries is Miyoko Schinner. Now in her early sixties, in the 1980s Miyoko was vegetarian for the sake of animals, but then learned about veganism, as she (as is common across Asian communities) had stomach pains, which she realized were associated with her dairy consumption. In conjunction with learning more about the cruelty inherent to dairy, the health benefits of a completely vegan diet led her to make the switch.[7]

Miyoko loved and loves cheese. Full of ideas and a desire to share an ethical, enriching way of living with the world, Miyoko opened a small restaurant where she began to create vegan cheeses. She also wrote a book called *Artisan Vegan Cheese*, which she hoped would help others enjoy the same foods she was, without the cruelty or stomach pains she had felt. Today, Miyoko sells her vegan cheeses far and wide, with both artisanal and more affordable ranges, to anyone looking to make a more ethical, sustainable, or healthy choice when they eat.[8]

What's most interesting and innovative about Miyoko, though, is her combining purpose-led business with activism and charity. Today, Miyoko's Creamery supports Miyoko's rescued farmed animal sanctuary, Rancho Compasión: the peaceful, visual embodiment of a more just world she strives for, surrounded by animal slaughtering farms. The sanctuary runs tours and allows liberated animals to advocate for themselves when people connect with them as individuals rather than as commodities.[9]

Miyoko also works with people who rear animals. Some people in businesses built on animals fear for their future livelihood as they watch the rise of vegan food and fashion alongside the continued struggle of their own industry, sometimes only able to continue due to government support. "We want to help bring farmers along with the change we think is necessary to tackle climate change and reduce the environmental footprint of farming." Today, Miyoko is offering financial support to dairy farmers who are willing to convert to growing potatoes and legumes, which are used in the making of some of her cheeses.[10]

The people who work in industries that exploit our fellow animals are often the ones least spellbound by the myths we are fed about how natural and normal animal "products" are, or of how ethical and sustainable they are. When Carmen Hijosa, who grew up in the traditional Spanish countryside of Asturias, moved overseas to begin a career, she worked cleaning and baby-sitting while she studied. Her studies ultimately led her to build a brand creating "luxury" animal skin bags. Later, she became a consultant for the World Bank, helping make "better" leather export products for countries including Colombia and the Philippines.[11]

In her work in this position, she saw things that "completely changed" her way of thinking about the products she was using, and that made her realize that making animal-derived products wasn't helping anyone. Instead, seeing people working in the leather supply chain, she realized that "leather making is one of the worst ecological and social disasters of all." The billions of animals killed in these supply chains, and the devastating chemical use and pollution that see tannery workers in countries like Bangladesh have a life expectancy of less than fifty years, convinced Carmen. But what impacted her most was connecting with other mothers like herself. With her own young child at home, speaking to Colombian women in the leather industry she learned that they, and other women in other countries she met, had to leave their children with their grandparents farther out into the countryside. They weren't paid enough to care for them in their own homes, near their work. The fact that these mothers saw their children perhaps once a month impacted Carmen deeply.[12]

This led Carmen to work with local weavers, crafters, researchers, scientists, and farmers to create a better way, which she hoped would bring "people, ecology, and economy together." This was how Piñatex, a leather alternative material made mostly from pineapple leaves, was made. The leaves of pineapple plants, not of the fruit themselves, are normally discarded, but with the creation of this material, they are sold, providing an additional income stream to farming communities. The leaf fibres are meshed together and coated in a plant-crop-based bio-resin, making for a partially biodegradable material with a far reduced environmental and social impact than cow-skin leather, created without funding animal slaughter. Carmen's material now replaces these skins in shoes and bags all over the world, while she continues to share her message of social justice and our responsibility to those we share the Earth with. She also advocates for lessened consumption more broadly, asking not only what shoes ought to be made of, but if we really need another pair at all.[13]

A third example of innovation borne from necessity was thought up by then twenty-two-year-old Francesca Chaney. Francesca, a young Black woman, "saw a need in her community for affordable vegan food and got to work." Francesca is based in Bushwick, Brooklyn, where the poverty rate is higher than those citywide, and where a large Black community lives. She found that she didn't have many healthy options, which she wanted to fuel herself with as she studied at school and worked three jobs. From making herself fresh juices, to selling them at festivals and through her cousin's apothecary, Francesca worked toward her vegan restaurant, Sol Sips. Sol Sips provides hearty, nourishing food to Francesca's community, at accessible prices, and every Saturday food can be bought on a sliding scale where people pay as they can, reflecting their economic privilege. Francesca also works with other community members passionate about health and wellness, offering free cooking classes as well as a number of free meals given to those suffering during times of crisis, including the COVID-19 pandemic.[14]

Innovation that makes wellness and ethics accessible is fundamental to the growth of a movement working toward a just world for all. We need solutions. We can campaign, we can fight for the removal of unjust laws and funds into unethical industries, but if there isn't an alternative, if we can't offer a solution, we will get stuck. Innovation at its best recognizes that community care is at the real root of any movement. All three of these women, Miyoko, Carmen, and Francesca, have provided an ethical alternative, and a way to make life better for the individuals they connect with, be it through literal lives saved, healthy food, economic security, or the peace that comes from these. None of us can pour from empty cups, and this is why justice for people, our fellow animals, and the planet must be seen as one.

Community Care Is Radical Activism

Going back, deep down to the very grassroots of activism, there is the radical, non-violent kind of activism tjat has already been covered; pressure campaigning, literal animal liberation from factory farms, and the like. However, what is radical is not just that which involves painting banners or wearing balaclavas. In a world severely lacking kindness and generosity, and in which these limitations come at the detriment of people's ability to act on their anti-speciesist tendencies, community care is radical activism for all animals.

Veganism, being one of the most substantial lifestyle changes one makes to align with anti-speciesism, is more complicated for some people than others. Some, or many people make excuses that are more about their unwillingness to be vegan than anything else. (Read, previous me, saying that I couldn't be vegan or do more for animals because of an intolerance that made it more difficult, but which had nothing to do with my buying lots of pairs of leather shoes just because I liked them). Some people, though, genuinely struggle to live vegan or to eat a plant-based diet for a multitude of reasons and lacking of privileges. People who feel aligned with anti-speciesism may still not be able to eat or consume in accordance with these values all the time, because of poverty, a lack of awareness or access, disability, or another issue. Some people might just be desperately trying to keep afloat themselves.

Yelling at struggling people isn't activism, or if you want to call it so, it's at least ineffective activism. What's far more effective, helping both us and our fellow animals, is listening to struggles people want to share, listening to animal advocates from different communities, and working to foster positive changes that might remove barriers to veganism. We are a diverse movement full of people aware of both roadblocks and solutions that can help spread veganism and help all animal communities, our own included. This knowledge is important, as it bolsters our theoretical understanding of these issues, which makes our movement more caring, considerate, and inviting. It also guides our tangible actions to increase accessibility to total liberation.

Issues of accessibility overwhelmingly impact already marginalized communities, like communities of color. Black communities in low-income areas as well as people living in rural areas have less access to supermarkets full of fresh, healthy foods, so are more likely to live in what is called a food desert, a form of environmental racism in many instances.[15] Food security is out of reach for many Aboriginal and Torres Strait Islander peoples in so-called Australia, too.[16] Often, as the film *They're Trying To Kill Us* discusses, this is by design, a covert and systemic form of racism that further perpetuates a kind of segregation, worsening the opportunities for these people to build themselves up the way white people are given the resources to.[17]

The Food Empowerment Project (FEP), created by lauren Ornelas, is a vegan group that seeks to create a more just and sustainable world through food. A part of their wider range of work is in conducting focus groups in low-income Black and brown communities. This information is passed on to public officials to encourage policy change and informs other grassroots efforts to improve access to just, healthy food. FEP also shares resources on eating justly on a budget and how to grow food.[18] Urban gardening as a form of resistance against oppression and to combat food injustice is powerful, taking place across Black communities.[19] These efforts, and those offering free nutritional and cooking courses for marginalized people, like the Woke Foods Co-Op, are worthy parts of the liberation puzzle.[20]

Around the world care-based activism is growing. There are shelters for people experiencing homelessness, people who are hungry, or who are at risk all across many countries, and there are local groups that offer to regularly supply and cook food in them. When this food is nourishing, sustainable, and free from violence against animals, food justice takes place in two forms. This kind of intersecting activism is already happening and is a perfect example of the grassroots activism that serves a wide group of individuals.

Our understanding of the othering of our fellow animals, which places them as undeserving of consideration, can inform our understanding of how this same disenfranchisement affects humans, and vice versa. Dangerous dehumanization built on animality's being deemed "less than" is the root of a whole host of oppression. Bringing together humans and our fellow animals being abused and mistreated can be mutually healing and transformative.

Renowned journalist, vegan, and former attorney Glenn Greenwald, together with his husband, David Miranda, a Rio de Janeiro council member, are building the Abrigo Hope shelter. The shelter is a temporary home to animals while they find adoptive families, and they are taken care of by humans who are also homeless, providing them with decent, stable work and the security that comes with it. With human homelessness and abandoned animals both being serious problems in Brazil, the shelter will offer support to two groups that are regularly othered and ignored. Glenn referred to his conversations with people experiencing homelessness, sharing that the isolation, invisibility, and dehumanization of living on the street was what they found most painful. Many of these people came to care for abandoned dogs, sharing food and company with them on the street. Working with this existing connection between humans and our fellow animals, Greenwald hopes that the shelter model will lead as an example of how we can address multiple forms of injustice together.[21]

When we care for others, we are activists, whether the label resonates or not. We are creating a world that is kinder and more just than that which we have today. Animals exploited and killed for human greed deserve to be front and center in their own movement, as every group surviving oppression does. But, when we see movements for the liberation of different communities come together, something profound happens. As Aph Ko says, many of us suffer under a "common source of oppression,"[22] deemed sub-human, so our liberation must be common, grappled toward, together.

Creating a Unified Liberation Movement

With the knowledge of a common source of oppression, largely thanks to the work of Black femme thinkers and writers, comes an obligation to dismantle not simply a specific expression of oppression, but the whole ideology itself. While people work and focus their energy and expertise on ripping down specific bricks from a wall of harm, there is still only one, monstrous wall. It is for this reason that there cannot truly be such a thing as "single issue activism" if it is to be effective activism. This isn't to say focusing on specific bricks is bad, as it would be impossible to ask any one person or group to tear down all the bricks, all at once, themselves. But, if we are so focused on our individual bricks that we don't take a step back and see the rest of the wall, and the rest of the individuals around us trying to rip it down, we will be missing vital opportunities to do better. lauren Ornelas once said that "to think a world without exploitation of non-human animals can exist where racism, sexism, ableism, and LGBTQ+ discrimination still exists is ignoring the root of why animals are exploited," and the same can be said for a belief that any one form of discrimination could vanish while the others remain intact.[23] What continues to pervade us as we deconstruct these forms of oppression is the perception of "disability" and following lack of "humanity" sitting behind it all. Our concern with humanizing ourselves in order to be liberated from oppression "leads at once to the recognition of dehumanization,"[24] which would not be a tool of oppression if we were comfortable in our animality. We can never be comfortable in this while we continue to justify violence based upon a species-based label.

Our understanding of human as a political identity that means fitting into certain boxes continues to alienate and discriminate against those who don't fit into them. Whether it be people of color, women, queer or trans people, disabled people, or non-human people—those we simply refer to as animals—this identity of "human" is one that was developed with the intention of elevating white men above those supposedly below them. Those below them are "reduced" to animals, monkeys, bitches, birds, and monsters. If I am a "bitch," I'm considered belligerent, aggressive, dominant, controlling, and, more literally, a female dog. If a man is considered a "bitch," or a "little bitch," he is weak, submissive, pathetic, and, ultimately, feminine.[25] Even our most supposedly beloved animals are the namesake of those we aim to belittle, because they still are "sub-human," as we hope to subtly deem women, or any other human we refer to as animal.

While an understanding of the interwoven nature of oppression is vital to seeing the downfall of it, we need to go further, still. We need to ensure that our movements, for the protection and liberation of animals; Black, Indigenous, and humans of color; women; and so on are not at any level replicating or enforcing the oppression of some group. When we fight to be free and liberated, we must not be fighting to prove our "humanity," because this means fighting for our right to be oppressor ourselves. We are not being "generous" to Black people, feminine people, or other animal people in offering them rights, because we are not "offering" them anything at all. If we were offering them something, we would be maintaining our status of unequal power, which allows us to take away this "generosity" at any time. We must not be self-righteous or stand above others but rather recognize in ourselves not just our privileges, but also our capacity to be oppressors. As is noted in the *Pedagogy of the Oppressed:*

> Discovering [oneself] to be an oppressor may cause considerable anguish, but it does not necessarily lead to solidarity with the oppressed. Rationalizing [our] guilt through [patronisingly "supportive"] treatment of the oppressed, all the while holding them fast in a position of dependence, will not do. Solidarity requires that one enter into the situation of those with whom one is solidary; it is a radical posture. . . . True solidarity with the oppressed means fighting at their side to transform the objective reality which has made them these "beings for another."[26]

This kind of true solidarity cannot exist from way up high, but rather from recognizing the agency oppressed beings themselves have. Even our fellow animals, named constantly as "voiceless," shriek terror in slaughterhouses and become agents of their own liberation, as we see in the many stories of cattle and pigs, for example, who escape abattoirs and run through town and forest to their freedom.[27] Christopher Sebastian suggests that "we should be inclusive to the point of centering disadvantaged voices and allowing them to be the architects of liberation. That would be the most transformative thing we could do." Problems constructed by one oppressive hand cannot be solved alone by the same.

If we are to see true liberation, then, we certainly cannot accept the oppression of some in the efforts to free others. It is just as counter-revolutionary to promote animal-tested, animal-body-filled lipstick in the name of women's mental health, as it is to sell girl power T-shirts made by impoverished brown women. It is deconstructive of actual Earth liberation to raise funds for wild animals harmed by bushfires with the barbecued bodies of other animals. This kind of collective liberation movement is more complicated, and it is "not a gift, not a self-achievement, but a mutual process."[28] It is something that cannot be reached if not in its totality.

If we saw our movements, our causes, our fights, our passion, and our burdens as united rather than adversarial, we could transform everything. If we did not see ourselves as all so utterly separated, if we stopped acting as if there weren't enough liberation to go around, if we saw ourselves all as simply animals, we would hold the weight of this much needed change together. The wall would come tumbling down.

Epilogue

Individual Change, A Call to Arms

Ultimately, everything is personal. Whether or not we see a future where we are all collectively free is up to us.

At the beginning of this book, I said that you may feel uncomfortable, but that by the end you would feel better, more hopeful. I hope you do. Perhaps there is a sense of connection with those around you. I am hopeful that the privilege we have as humans is clear, as clear as the obligation that comes with that privilege, to do our individual part to deconstruct the hierarchy we all fall under, which looks farthest down upon our fellow animals.

Aurora Levins Morales wrote that "solidarity is not a matter of altruism. Solidarity comes from the inability to tolerate the affront to our own integrity of passive or active collaboration in the oppression of others, and from the deep recognition that, like it or not, our liberation is bound up with that of every other being on the planet."[1]

Carol Adams wrote that "dominance functions best in a culture of disconnections and fragmentations,"[2] and this culture can be resolved through simply living relationally.

We must recognize, understand, and interrogate not only our privileges and our ability to oppress, but also our ability to connect. To bring together. Simply holding space for each other, allowing each other to just exist, to just be, is both basic decency and somehow today revolutionary. It is through giving up the exclusivity of freedoms and rights that we have enjoyed and taken for granted, that we have denied others, that we can build this just world we all ache for.

It is a more peaceful existence, even when it involves great resistance and great struggle, to unpick the tapestry of injustice that has been cloaked over us and those around us. Neutrality in the face of injustice is not enough,[3] and to interfere with it is to live in accordance with the goodness that rests warm inside us all.

The next page of this book is blank. It is space for you. It is to write what you will do next. Everyone has a place in a revolution, one that will create an ecosystem of equilibrium.

Recommended Reading and Watching

Reading

Adams, Carol J. *The Sexual Politics of Meat: A Feminist-Vegetarian Critical Theory*. New York: Bloomsbury Academic, 2015. First published in 1990 by Continuum International Publishing Group.

Braitman, Laurel. *Animal Madness: How Anxious Dogs, Compulsive Parrots, and Elephants in Recovery Help Us Understand Ourselves*. New York: Simon & Schuster, 2014.

Chang, Ha-Joon. *23 Things They Don't Tell You About Capitalism*. New York: Bloomsbury Press, 2010.

Foer, Jonathan Safran. *Eating Animals*. New York: Little, Brown and Company, 2010.

Freire, Paulo. *Pedagogy of the Oppressed*. Translated by Myra Bergman Ramos. New York: Bloomsbury Academic, 2018. First published in English in 1968 by Herder and Herder.

Garcés, Leah. *Grilled: Turning Adversaries into Allies*. London: Bloomsbury Sigma, 2019.

Harper, A. Breeze. "Connections: Speciesism, Racism, and Whiteness as the Norm." In *Sister Species: Women, Animals and Social Justice*, edited by Lisa A. Kemmerer, 72–78. Chicago: University of Illinois Press, 2011.

———, ed. *Sistah Vegan: Black Women Speak on Food, Identity, Health, and Society*. New York: Lantern Publishing & Media, 2020.

———. "Vegans of Color, Racialized Embodiment, and Problematics of the 'Exotics.'" In *Cultivating Food Justice: Race, Class, and Sustainability*, edited by Alison Hope Alkon and Julian Agyeman, 221–238. Cambridge: The MIT Press, 2011.

Harari, Yuval Noah. *Sapiens: A Brief History of Humankind*. Oxford: Signal Books, 2014.

Hardy, Rich. *Not as Nature Intended: An Undercover Journey into the Secret World of Animal Exploitation*. Unbound Digital, 2020.

Hurst, Ren. *Riding on the Power of Others: A Horsewoman's Path to Unconditional Love*. Danvers, MA: Vegan Publishers, 2015.

Joy, Melanie. *Beyond Beliefs: A Guide to Improving Relationships and Communication for Vegans, Vegetarians, and Meat Eaters*. New York: Lantern Publishing & Media, 2018.

———. *Powerarchy: Understanding the Psychology of Oppression for Social Transformation.* Oakland, CA: Berret-Koehler Publishers, 2019.

———. *Why We Love Dogs, Eat Pigs, and Wear Cows: An Introduction to Carnism.* Newburyport, MA: Red Wheel, 2010.

Katcher, Joshua. *Fashion Animals.* Boston: Vegan Publishers, 2019.

Ko, Aph, and Syl Ko. *Aphro-Ism: Essays on Pop Culture, Feminism, and Black Veganism from Two Sisters.* New York: Lantern Publishing & Media, 2020.

McArthur, Jo-Anne, and Keith Wilson, ed. *Hidden: Animals in the Anthropocene.* New York: Lantern Publishing & Media, 2020.

Nocella II, Anthony J., and Michael A. Slusher, eds. *Terrorists or Freedom Fighters?: Reflections on the Liberation of Animals.* New York: Lantern Publishing & Media, 2004.

Pachirat, Timothy. *Every Twelve Seconds: Industrialized Slaughter and the Politics of Sight.* New Haven: Yale University Press, 2011.

Pascoe, Bruce. *Dark Emu: Aboriginal Australia and the Birth of Agriculture.* London: Scribe Publications, 2014.

Patterson, Charles. *Eternal Treblinka: Our Treatment of Animals and the Holocaust.* New York: Lantern Publishing & Media, 2002.

Potter, Will. *Green Is the New Red: An Insider's Account of a Social Movement Under Siege.* San Francisco: City Lights Books, 2011.

Regan, Tom. *The Case for Animal Rights.* Berkeley: University of California Press, 2004.

Sebastian, Christopher. *Christopher Sebastian.* Blog, accessed September 29, 2023. https://www.christophersebastian.info/blog-1.

Simon, David Robinson. *Meatonomics: How the Rigged Economics of Meat and Dairy Make You Consume Too Much—And How to Eat Better, Live Longer, and Spend Smarter.* San Francisco: Conari Press, 2013.

Singer, Peter. *Animal Liberation: The Definitive Classic of the Animal Movement.* New York: HarperCollins, 2009.

Slusher, Michael A. *They All Had Eyes: Confessions of a Vivisectionist.* Danvers, MA: Vegan Publishers, 2016.

Spiegel, Marjorie. *The Dreaded Comparison: Human and Animal Slavery.* London: Mirror Books, 1997.

Taylor, Sunaura. *Beasts of Burden: Animal and Disability Liberation.* New York: The New Press, 2016.

Zaraska, Mart. *Meathooked: The History and Science of Our 2.5-Million-Year Obsession with Meat.* New York: Basic Books, 2016.

Watching

Argo, Allison, dir. *The Last Pig.* ArgoFilms, 2020. First released in 2017. https://vimeo.com/ondemand/thelastpigmovie.

Cappelli, Rebecca, dir. *Slay.* Let Us Be Heroes, 2022. https://www.waterbear.com/watch/feature/62fe1af430a9286bbf6a380d.

Chilcott, Lesley, dir. *Watson.* Giant Pictures, 2019.

Cowperthwaite, Gabriela, dir. *Black Fish.* Magnolia Pictures, 2013.

Delforce, Chris, dir. *Dominion.* Farm Transparency Project, 2018. https://dominionmovement.com/watch.

Ed, Earthling, dir. *Land of Hope and Glory*. Earthling Ed, 2017. https://www.landofhopeandglory.org/.

Hakansson, Emma, dir. *Willow & Claude.* Collective Fashion Justice, 2022. https://www.willowandclaude.com/watch

Hennelly, Denis Henry, and Casey Suchan, dir. *The Animal People.* Finngate Pictures, 2019.

Lockwood, Alex, dir. *73 Cows.* Lockwood Film, 2018. https://lockwoodfilm.com/73-cows.

Lockwood, Alex, dir. *Test Subjects*. Lockwood Film, 2019. https://testsubjectsfilm.com/.

Monson, Shaun, dir. *Earthlings.* 10th Anniversary Edition. Nation Earth, 2015. First released in 2005. https://www.nationearth.com/.

Notes

Introduction

1. Food and Agriculture Organization of the United Nations. "FAOSTAT." Accessed September 29, 2023. http://www.fao.org/faostat/en/#home.
2. Humane Society International. "The Fur Trade." Accessed September 29, 2023. https://www.hsi.org/news-media/fur-trade/.
3. Mood, Alison. "Worse Things Happen at Sea: The Welfare of Wild-Caught Fish." Fishcount.org.uk, 2010. http://www.fishcount.org.uk/published/standard/fishcountfullrptSR.pdf.
4. Sweetlove, Lee. "Number of Species on Earth Tagged at 8.7 Million." *Nature*, August 23, 2011. https://doi.org/10.1038/news.2011.498; Ritchie, Hannah. "Humans Make up Just 0.01% of Earth's Life—What's the Rest?" Our World in Data, April 24, 2019. https://ourworldindata.org/life-on-earth.

Chapter 1: This Is What We Know About Animals and How We Justify Their Use

1. Low, Philip. "The Cambridge Declaration on Consciousness." The University of Cambridge, July 7, 2012. http://fcmconference.org/img/CambridgeDeclarationOnConsciousness.pdf.
2. Warren, Jeff. "Why Whales Are People Too." *Reader's Digest Canada*, updated June 14, 2016. https://www.readersdigest.ca/culture/why-whales-are-people-too/; "Declaration of Rights for Cetaceans: Whales and Dolphins." *Journal of International Wildlife Law & Policy* 14, no. 1 (March 14, 2011): 75. https://doi.org/10.1080/13880292.2011.557946.
3. Marino, Lori, and Christina M. Colvin. "Thinking Pigs: A Comparative Review of Cognition, Emotion, and Personality in *Sus Domesticus*." *International Journal of Comparative Psychology* 28 (2015): 1–23. https://doi.org/10.46867/ijcp.2015.28.00.04; Bekoff, Marc. "Are Pigs as Smart as Dogs and Does It Really Matter?" *Psychology Today*, July 29, 2013. https://www.psychologytoday.com/au/blog/animal-emotions/201307/are-pigs-smart-dogs-and-does-it-really-matter.
4. Singer, Peter. *Practical Ethics*. Cambridge: Cambridge University Press, 2011.
5. Brown, Culum. "Fish Intelligence, Sentience and Ethics." *Animal Cognition* 18, no. 1 (2015): 1–17. https://doi.org/10.1007/s10071-014-0761-0.
6. Marshall, Michael. "Timeline: The Evolution of Life." *NewScientist*, updated April 27, 2023. https://www.newscientist.com/article/dn17453-timeline-the-evolution-of-life/.
7. Jane Goodall Institute UK. "Chimp Facts." Accessed September 29, 2023. https://www.janegoodall.org.uk/chimpanzees/chimpanzee-central/15-chimpanzees/chimpanzee-central/21-chimp-facts.
8. Slusher, Michael. *They All Had Eyes: Confessions of a Vivisectionist*. Danvers, MA: Vegan Publishers, 2016.

9. Joy Melanie. *Why We Love Dogs, Eat Pigs, and Wear Cows: An Introduction to Carnism.* Newburyport, MA: Red Wheel, 2011.
10. Graça, João, Maria Manuela Calheiros, and Abílio Oliveira. "Moral Disengagement in Harmful but Cherished Food Practices? An Exploration into the Case of Meat." *Journal of Agricultural and Environmental Ethics* 27 (2014): 749–765. https://doi.org/10.1007/s10806-014-9488-9.
11. Hartman, Steve. "Cattle Rancher's Wife Goes Vegan: 'Every Marriage Has Its Issues.'" *CBS News*, March 4, 2016. https://www.cbsnews.com/news/cattle-ranchers-vegan-wife-turns-ranch-into-animal-sanctuary/.
12. Streeter, Sara. "Children Love Animals. Let's Keep It That Way." Faunalytics, December 6, 2022. https://faunalytics.org/children-love-animals-lets-keep-it-that-way/.
13. USDA National Agricultural Library. "Humane Methods of Slaughter Act." Accessed September 29, 2023. https://www.nal.usda.gov/awic/humane-methods-slaughter-act.
14. RSPCA. "What Does the Term Humane Killing or Humane Slaughter Mean?" Accessed Spetember 29, 2023. https://kb.rspca.org.au/knowledge-base/what-does-the-term-humane-killing-or-humane-slaughter-mean/.
15. *BBC News*. "Femicide: Women Are Most Likely to Be Killed by Their Partner or Ex." February 20, 2020. https://www.bbc.com/news/newsbeat-51572665.
16. Sherman, Brian, Ondine Sherman, and Katrina Sharman. "From Paddocks to Prisons: Pigs in New South Wales, Australia Current Practices, Future Directions." Voiceless, December 2005. https://voiceless.org.au/wp-content/uploads/2011/09/Voiceless_Report_From_Paddocks_To_Prisons_Dec_05.pdf; Parker, Christine, Rachel Carey, and Gyorgy Scrinis. "High Welfare Labelling for Pig Meat." The University of Melbourne, 2018. https://rest.neptune-prod.its.unimelb.edu.au/server/api/core/bitstreams/9e10abd2-565c-5cbc-83cb-851eb8fc275a/content; Voiceless. "Broiler Chickens." Updated September 2018. https://voiceless.org.au/hot-topics/broiler-chickens/#footnote17_ciom0y0.
17. Anthis, Jacy Reese. "US Factory Farming Estimates." Sentience Institute, updated April 11, 2019. https://www.sentienceinstitute.org/us-factory-farming-estimates.
18. Compassion in World Farming. "New Interactive Map Exposes UK Factory Farming Hotspots." July 17, 2017. https://www.ciwf.org.uk/media/7431377/new-interactive-map-exposes-uk-factory-farming-hotspots.pdf.
19. Argo, Allison, director. *The Last Pig.* ArgoFilms, 2021. https://www.thelastpig.com/; Comis, Bob. "Happy Pigs Make Happy Meat?" *HuffPost*, updated December 6, 2017. https://www.huffpost.com/entry/happy-pigs-make-happy-mea_b_4790902.

Chapter 2: This Is What We Do to Animals

1. Food and Agriculture Organization of the United Nations. "FAOSTAT." Accessed September 29, 2023. http://www.fao.org/faostat/en/#home.

2. ASPCA. "A Growing Problem: Selective Breeding in the Chicken Industry: The Case for Slower Growth." 2015. https://www.aspca.org/sites/default/files/chix_white_paper_nov2015_lores.pdf.
3. Ibid; PoultryHub Australia. "Meat Chicken (Broiler) Industry." Accessed September 29, 2023. https://www.poultryhub.org/production/meat-chicken-broiler-industry.
4. ASPCA. "A Growing Problem: Selective Breeding in the Chicken Industry: The Case for Slower Growth." 2015. https://www.aspca.org/sites/default/files/chix_white_paper_nov2015_lores.pdf.
5. Gura, Susanne. "Livestock Genetics Companies." League for Pastoral Peoples and Endogenous Livestock Development, 2007. http://www.pastoralpeoples.org/wp-content/uploads/2020/01/livestock_genetics_en.pdf.
6. RSPCA. "How Are Meat Chickens Farmed in Australia?" Updated November 24, 2020. https://kb.rspca.org.au/knowledge-base/how-are-meat-chickens-farmed-in-australia/; Julian, RJ. "Rapid Growth Problems: Ascites and Skeletal Deformities in Broilers." *Poultry Science* 77, no. 12 (1998): 1773–80. https://doi.org/10.1093/ps/77.12.1773; Knowles, Toby G., Steve C. Krestin, Susan M. Haslam, et al. "Leg Disorders in Broiler Chickens: Prevalence, Risk Factors and Prevention." *PLoS One* 3, no. 2 (2008): e1545. https://doi.org/10.1371/journal.pone.0001545; RSPCA. "Meat Chickens." Accessed September 29, 2023. https://www.rspca.org.au/take-action/meat-chickens.
7. Farm Health Online. "Sudden Death Syndrome: Commonly Associated with Broiler Systems." Accessed September 29, 2023. https://www.farmhealthonline.com/disease-management/poultry-diseases/sudden-death-syndrome/; Dinev, Ivan. "Diseases of Poultry." The Poultry Site, accessed September 29, 2023. https://www.thepoultrysite.com/publications/diseases-of-poultry/238/pulmonary-hypertension-ascitis-syndrome-in-broiler-chickens.
8. RSPCA. "How Are Meat Chickens Farmed in Australia?" Updated November 24, 2020. https://kb.rspca.org.au/knowledge-base/how-are-meat-chickens-farmed-in-australia/; RSPCA Australia. "RSPCA Approved Farming Scheme Standard: Meat Chickens." August 2020. https://rspcaapproved.org.au/wp-content/uploads/2022/03/2020_08_MEATCHICKENS_Standard_v1.1.pdf; PoultryHub Australia. "Alternative Poultry Production Systems." Accessed September 29, 2023. https://www.poultryhub.org/production/alternative-poultry-production-systems.
9. RSPCA. "How Are Meat Chickens Farmed in Australia?" Updated November 24, 2020. https://kb.rspca.org.au/knowledge-base/how-are-meat-chickens-farmed-in-australia/; Delforce, Chris, director. *Dominion.* Farm Transparency Project, 2018. https://www.dominionmovement.com/.
10. Animal Liberation. "Goat Truth." Accessed September 29, 2023. https://www.alv.org.au/goat-truth/.
11. Katcher, Joshua. *Fashion Animals.* Danvers, MA: Vegan Publishers, 2018.
12. Ibid.

13. Pickett, Heather, and Stephen Harris. "The Case Against Fur Factory Farming." Respect for Animals, 2015. https://www.furfreealliance.com/wp-content/uploads/2015/11/Case-against-fur-farming.pdf; The Associated Press. "N.Y. Bans Anal Electrocution of Animals for Fur." *NBC News*, April 30, 2008. https://www.nbcnews.com/id/wbna24389992#.X4Ubci1L1bV.
14. Pickett, Heather, and Stephen Harris. "The Case Against Fur Factory Farming." Respect for Animals, 2015. https://www.furfreealliance.com/wp-content/uploads/2015/11/Case-against-fur-farming.pdf; Collective Fashion Justice. "Issues in the Fur Supply Chain." Accessed September 29, 2023. https://www.collectivefashionjustice.org/fur; Dalton, Jane. "Caged Animals Resort to Cannibalism on 'High Welfare' Fur Farms Linked to Britain's Most Upmarket Brands and Sellers." *The Independent*, November 23, 2018. https://www.independent.co.uk/news/uk/home-news/fur-farms-animal-welfare-cruelty-cannibalism-mink-foxes-coat-jacket-a8647616.html.
15. Hakansson, Emma, Carly Halliday, Danielle May, et al. "Under Their Skin: Leather's Impact on Animals." Collective Fashion Justice, February 2023. https://static1.squarespace.com/static/5f5f02dd9b510014eef4fc4f/t/63fe6c7a4305dc76ee40a43c/1677618365889/Leather%27s+impact+on+animals+report.pdf.
16. Ibid; RSPCA Australia. "RSPCA Approved Farming Scheme Information Notes: Dairy Calves." January 2021. https://rspcaapproved.org.au/wp-content/uploads/2022/03/2021-01_DAIRYCALVES_InformationNotes.pdf; Commtrade International. "Torello Trade Final." YouTube video, 2:50, February 8, 2019. https://www.youtube.com/watch?v=6ppejDI7rGc.
17. Hakansson, Emma, Carly Halliday, Danielle May, et al. "Under Their Skin: Leather's Impact on Animals." Collective Fashion Justice, February 2023. https://static1.squarespace.com/static/5f5f02dd9b510014eef4fc4f/t/63fe6c7a4305dc76ee40a43c/1677618365889/Leather%27s+impact+on+animals+report.pdf.
18. Feldstein, Stephanie, Emma Hakansson, Joshua Katcher, et al. "Shear Destruction: Wool, Fashion and the Biodiversity Crisis." Center for Biological Diversity, Collective Fashion Justice, 2023. https://static1.squarespace.com/static/5f5f02dd9b510014eef4fc4f/t/6496bcd0963cea10ced9ba24/1687600350969/Shear+Destruction+wool+report+2023.pdf.
19. Ibid; ACIL Tasman. "The Value of Live Sheep Exports from Western Australia." RSPCA Australia, March 2009. https://www.rspca.org.au/sites/default/files/website/Campaigns/Live-export/Live-exports-vs-the-meat-trade/ACIL%20Tasman%202009%20-%20The%20value%20of%20live%20sheep%20exports%20from%20Western%20Australia.pdf; Hunt, Karen. "Demand for Animal Leather Dives as Consumers Flock to Synthetic Clothes and Shoes." *ABC News*, July 25, 2019. https://www.abc.net.au/news/rural/2019-07-26/animal-skin-prices-plummet/11347588.
20. ACIL Tasman. "The Value of Live Sheep Exports from Western Australia." RSPCA Australia, March 2009. https://www.rspca.org.au/sites/default/files/website/Campaigns/Live-export/Live-exports-vs-the-meat-trade/ACIL%20Tasman%202009%20-%20The%20value%20of%20live%20sheep%20exports%20from%20Western%20Australia.pdf.

21. Clark C. Survival of the Fittest. [Internet]. Sydney: ABC, 2012 [cited via Animal Liberation Victoria and Web Archive 2020]. Available from: https://web.archive.org/web/20170321074341/http://www.abc.net.au/landline/content/2012/s3581122.htm; Grant, Rose. "Lamb Deaths Emerging as a Welfare Issue." *ABC News*, updated August 10, 2012. https://www.abc.net.au/news/rural/2012-08-10/lamb-deaths-emerging-as-a-welfare-issue/6114940; Animal Health Australia. "Australian Animal Welfare Standards and Guidelines for Sheep." January 2016. https://www.integritysystems.com.au/globalassets/isc/pdf-files/sheep-standards-and-guidelines-for-endorsed-jan-2016-061017.pdf; Sheep Standards and Guidelines Writing Group. "Sheep Standards and Guidelines: Tail Docking." January 2013. https://www.yumpu.com/en/document/view/40314990/tail-docking-animal-welfare-standards; Collective Fashion Justice. "Issues in the Wool Supply Chain." Accessed September 29, 2023. https://www.collectivefashionjustice.org/wool.
22. Pound, Pandora, and Michael B. Bracken. "Is Animal Research Sufficiently Evidence-Based to Be a Cornerstone of Biomedical Research?" *BMJ* (2014). https://doi.org/10.1136/bmj.g3387; Cruelty Free International. "Facts and Figures on Animal Testing," Accessed September 29, 2023. https://crueltyfreeinternational.org/about-animal-testing/facts-and-figures-animal-testing.
23. Lockwood, Alex. "Test Subjects." Vimeo video, 16:47, 2019. https://vimeo.com/359497969.
24. Slusher, Michael. *They All Had Eyes: Confessions of a Vivisectionist.* Danvers, MA: Vegan Publishers, 2016.
25. Hessler, Kathy. "The Role of the Animal Law Clinic." *Journal of Legal Education* 60, no. 2 (November 2010): 263–384. https://www.jstor.org/stable/42894173.
26. Mackay-Sim, Alan, and David G. Laing. "Rats' Responses to Blood and Body Odors of Stressed and Non-Stressed Conspecifics." *Physiology & Behavior* 27, no. 3 (1981): 503–10. https://doi.org/10.1016/00319384(81)90339-5.
27. Inagaki, Hideaki, Yasushi Kiyokawa, Shigeyuki Tamogami, et al. "Identification of a Pheromone that Increases Anxiety in Rats." *PNAS* 111, no. 52 (2014): 18751–756. https://doi.org/10.1073/pnas.1414710112; Oscar's Law. "Ethical Dog Buyer's Guide." Accessed September 29, 2023. https://www.oscarslaw.org/ethical-dog-buyers-guide.htm.
28. Mackay-Sim, Alan, and David G. Laing. "Rats' Responses to Blood and Body Odors of Stressed and Non-Stressed Conspecifics." *Physiology & Behavior* 27, no. 3 (1981): 503–10. https://doi.org/10.1016/00319384(81)90339-5.
29. Maldarelli, Claire. "Although Purebred Dogs Can Be Best in Show, Are They Worst in Health?" *Scientific American*, February 21, 2014. https://www.scientificamerican.com/article/although-purebred-dogs-can-be-best-in-show-are-they-worst-in-health/.
30. Oscar's Law. "Ethical Dog Buyer's Guide." Accessed September 29, 2023. https://www.oscarslaw.org/ethical-dog-buyers-guide.htm; The Humane Society of the United States. "Puppy Mills FAQ." Accessed September 29, 2023. https://www.humanesociety.org/resources/puppy-mills-faq.

31. Coren, Stanley. "Do Adult Dogs Still Recognize Their Mothers?" *Psychology Today*, August 22, 2017. https://www.psychologytoday.com/au/blog/canine-corner/201708/do-adult-dogs-still-recognize-their-mothers.
32. GoodReads. "Lydia Nevzorova's Blog." January 28, 2018. https://www.goodreads.com/author/show/5505714.Lydia_Nevzorova/blog.
33. Hurst, Ren. *Riding on the Power of Others: A Horsewoman's Path to Unconditional Love*. Danvers, MA: Vegan Publishers, 2015.
34. Ibid; McGowan, Catherine, Narelle Stubbs, Paul Hodges, et al. "Back Pain in Horses: Epaxial Musculature." Rural Industries Research and Development Corporation, November 2007. https://agrifutures.com.au/wp-content/uploads/publications/07-118.pdf.
35. Hinchcliff, Kenneth W., Andris Kaneps, and Raymond Geor. *Equine Sports Medicine & Surgery* (2nd Edition). Philadelphia: Saunders, 2014; ABC News In-Depth. "The Dark Side of Australia's Horse Racing Industry." YouTube video, 49:15, October 18, 2019. https://www.youtube.com/watch?v=Zp-ALoBRW20.
36. Barnes, Hannah. "How Many Healthy Animals Do Zoos Put Down?" *BBC News*, February 27, 2014. https://www.bbc.com/news/magazine-26356099; Bekoff, Marc. "'Zoothanasia' Is Not Euthanasia: Words Matter." *Psychology Today*, August 9, 2012. https://www.psychologytoday.com/au/blog/animal-emotions/201208/zoothanasia-is-not-euthanasia-words-matter; Browning, Heather. "No Room at the Zoo: Management Euthanasia and Animal Welfare." *Journal of Agricultural and Environmental Ethics* 31 (2018): 483–98. https://doi.org/10.1007/s10806-018-9741-8.
37. Smith, Laura. "Zoos Drive Animals Crazy." *Slate*, June 20, 2014. https://slate.com/technology/2014/06/animal-madness-zoochosis-stereotypic-behavior-and-problems-with-zoos.html; Morgan, Kathleen M., and Chris T. Tromborg. "Sources of Stress in Captivity." *Applied Animal Behaviour Science* 102, no. 3–4 (2007): 262–302. https://doi.org/10.1016/j.applanim.2006.05.032.
38. Cowperthwaite, Gabriela, director. *Blackfish*. Magnolia Pictures, 2013. https://www.magpictures.com/profile.aspx?id=df6cf88f-28aa-4be9-8293-06213d2e5b50.
39. Barton, Robert A. "Animal Communication: Do Dolphins Have Names?" *Current Biology* 16, no. 15 (2006): R598–R599. https://doi.org/10.1016/j.cub.2006.07.002.
40. Cowperthwaite, Gabriela, director. *Blackfish*. Magnolia Pictures, 2013. https://www.magpictures.com/profile.aspx?id=df6cf88f-28aa-4be9-8293-06213d2e5b50; Williamson, Cathy. "How Long Do Bottlenose Dolphins Survive in Captivity?" Whale & Dolphin Conservation USA, August 23, 2018. https://us.whales.org/2018/08/23/how-long-do-bottlenose-dolphins-survive-in-captivity/.

Chapter 3: This Is What Else We Justify

1. Harari, Yuval Noah. *Sapiens: A Brief History of Humankind*. London: Random House UK, 2015; Taylor, Sunaura. *Beasts of Burden: Animal and Disability Liberation*. New York: The New Press, 2017.

2. Human Rights Watch. "Saudi Arabia: 10 Reasons Why Women Flee." January 30, 2019. https://www.hrw.org/news/2019/01/30/saudi-arabia-10-reasons-why-women-flee.
3. USDA. "Chicken and Eggs: 2017 Summary." National Agricultural Statistics Service, February 2018. https://www.nass.usda.gov/Publications/Todays_Reports/reports/ckegan18.pdf; Romanov, M.N., and S. Weigend. "Analysis of Genetic Relationships Between Various Populations of Domestic and Jungle Fowl Using Microsatellite Markers." *Poultry Science* 80, no. 8 (2001): 1057–63. https://doi.org/10.1093/ps/80.8.1057.
4. Animal Liberation. "Egg Farming Exposed." Accessed September 29, 2023. https://www.al.org.au/egg-campaigns.
5. Compassion in World Farming. "Statistics: Laying Hens." Updated August 28, 2013. https://www.ciwf.org.uk/media/5235021/Statistics-Laying-hens.pdf.
6. Compassion in World Farming. "Statistics: Dairy Cows." Updated July 1, 2012. https://www.ciwf.org.uk/media/5235182/Statistics-Dairy-cows.pdf; Dairy Australia. "You Ask. We Answer. Dairy Matters." Updated June 30, 2023. https://www.dairy.com.au/dairy-matters/you-ask-we-answer/what-is-the-average-age-a-dairy-cow-lives-to; The Cattle Site. "Cow Longevity Economics: Cost Benefits of Keeping a Cow in the Herd." June 10, 2014. https://www.thecattlesite.com/articles/3950/cow-longevity-economics-cost-benefits-of-keeping-a-cow-in-the-herd/.
7. UN Women. "Facts and Figures: Ending Violence Against Women." Updated September 21, 2023.
8. Olson, Lester C. "Anger Among Allies: Audre Lorde's 1981 Keynote Admonishing the National Women's Studies Association." *Quarterly Journal of Speech* 97, no. 3 (2011): 283–308. https://doi.org/10.1080/00335630.2011.585169.
9. Adams, Carol J. *The Sexual Politics of Meat: A Feminist-Vegetarian Critical Theory*. London: Continuum, 1990.
10. Lebwohl, Michael. "A Call to Action: Psychological Harm in Slaughterhouse Workers." *The Yale Global Health Review*, January 25, 2016. https://yaleglobalhealthreview.com/2016/01/25/a-call-to-action-psychological-harm-in-slaughterhouse-workers/; Fitzgerald, Amy J, Linda Kalof, and Thomas Dietz. "Slaughterhouses and Increased Crime Rates: An Empirical Analysis of the Spillover From 'The Jungle' Into the Surrounding Community." *Organization & Environment* 22, no. 2 (2009): 158–84. https://doi.org/10/1177/1086026609338164.
11. Grossman, David. "Trained to Kill." *Christianity Today*, August 10, 1998. https://www.christianitytoday.com/ct/1998/august10/8t9030.html.
12. Dillard, Jennifer. "A Slaughterhouse Nightmare: Psychological Harm Suffered by Slaughterhouse Employees and the Possibility of Redress Through Legal Reform." *Georgetown Journal on Poverty Law & Policy* (2007). https://ssrn.com/abstract=1016401.
13. Sentient. "This Is the Truth About 'Humane' Free-Range Meat." Accessed September 29, 2023.

14. Lebwohl, Michael. "A Call to Action: Psychological Harm in Slaughterhouse Workers." *The Yale Global Health Review*, January 25, 2016. https://yaleglobalhealthreview.com/2016/01/25/a-call-to-action-psychological-harm-in-slaughterhouse-workers/; Dillard, Jennifer. "A Slaughterhouse Nightmare: Psychological Harm Suffered by Slaughterhouse Employees and the Possibility of Redress Through Legal Reform." *Georgetown Journal on Poverty Law & Policy* (2007). https://ssrn.com/abstract=1016401.
15. Slusher, Michael. *They All Had Eyes: Confessions of a Vivisectionist.* Danvers, MA: Vegan Publishers, 2016.
16. Comis, Bob. "Birth, Death, and Money on a Livestock Farm." *HuffPost*, updated June 21, 2014. https://www.huffpost.com/entry/birth-death-and-money-on_b_5186257.
17. SARX: For All God's Creatures. "Jay Wilde: A Story of Human and Animal Liberation." Accessed September 29, 2023. https://sarx.org.uk/articles/art-and-film/jay-wilde/; Capps, Ashley. "'It Was Soul Destroying'—UK Beef & Dairy Farmer Goes Vegan, Grows Vegetables Instead." Free from Harm, December 31, 2018. https://freefromharm.org/animal-farmer-turned-vegan/jay-wilde/; Lockwood, Alex. "73 Cows." Vimeo video, 15:00, 2018. https://vimeo.com/293352305.
18. Thomas, Keith. *Man and the Natural World: A History of the Modern Sensibility.* New York: Pantheon Books, 1983.
19. Concord, Dan. "Global Leather Production Overview." Liberty Leather Goods, accessed September 29, 2023. https://www.libertyleathergoods.com/global-leather-production-overview/; Gallagher, Sean. "India: The Toxic Price of Leather." Pulitzer Center, May 8, 2014. https://pulitzercenter.org/stories/india-toxic-price-leather-0.
20. Rastogi, Subodh Kumar, Amit Pandey, and Sachin Tripathi. "Occupational Health Risks Among the Workers Employed in Leather Tanneries at Kanpur." *Indian Journal of Occupational and Environmental Medicine* 12, no. 3 (2008): 132–5. https://doi.org/10.4103/0019-5278.44695; Hedberg, Yolanda S., Carola Lidén, and Inger Odnevall Wallinder. "Chromium Released from Leather—I: Exposure Conditions that Govern the Release of Chromium (III) and Chromium (VI)." *Contact Dermatitis* 72, no. 4 (2015): 206–15. https://doi.org/10.1111/cod.12329; Junaid, Muhammad, Muhammad Zaffar Hashmi, Yu-Mei Tang, et al. "Potential Health Risk of Heavy Metals in the Leather Manufacturing Industries in Sialkot, Pakistan." *Scientific Reports* 7 (2017). https://doi.org/10.1038/s41598-017-09075-7; Gallagher, Sean. "The Toxic Price of Leather." Vimeo video, 9:06, 2014. https://vimeo.com/88261827; Rastogi, S.K., C. Kesavachandran, Farzana Mahdi, et al. "Occupational Cancers in Leather Tanning Industries: A Short Review." *Indian Journal of Occupational and Environmental Medicine* 11, no. 1 (2007): 3–5. https://doi.org/10.4103/0019-5278.32456.
21. Gallagher, Sean. "The Toxic Price of Leather." Vimeo video, 9:06, 2014. https://vimeo.com/88261827.

22. Rastogi, S.K., C. Kesavachandran, Farzana Mahdi, et al. "Occupational Cancers in Leather Tanning Industries: A Short Review." *Indian Journal of Occupational and Environmental Medicine* 11, no. 1 (2007): 3–5. https://doi.org/10.4103/0019-5278.32456; China Water Risk. "Leather: Time for Business Unusual." February 11, 2014. https://chinawaterrisk.org/resources/analysis-reviews/leather-time-for-business-unusual/.
23. Milmo, Cahal, Alexandra Heal, and Andrew Wasley. "Revealed: Heavy Toll of Injury Suffered by Slaughter Workers in Britain's £8bn Meat Industry." *i News*, updated July 6, 2020. https://inews.co.uk/news/uk/revealed-heavy-toll-of-injury-and-amputations-suffered-by-slaughter-workers-serving-britains-8bn-meat-industry-180819; Newkey-Burden, Chas. "There's a Christmas Crisis Going On: No One Wants to Kill Your Dinner." *The Guardian*, November 19, 2018. https://www.theguardian.com/commentisfree/2018/nov/19/christmas-crisis-kill-dinner-work-abattoir-industry-psychological-physical-damage.
24. British Meat Processors Associations. "Meat Industry Workforce." Accessed September 29, 2023. https://britishmeatindustry.org/industry/workforce/.
25. Engdahl, F. William. "Bird Flu and Chicken Factory Farms: Profit Bonanza for US Agribusiness." Global Research, November 27, 2005. https://www.globalresearch.ca/bird-flu-and-chicken-factory-farms-profit-bonanza-for-us-agribusiness/1333; Philpott, Tom. "Refugees Make Your Dinner. Literally." *Mother Jones*, January 31, 2017. https://www.motherjones.com/environment/2017/01/meat-industry-refugees-trump/; Cook, Israel. "How Fast Is Too Fast? OSHA's Regulation of the Meat Industry's Line Speed and the Price Paid by Humans and Animals." *Sustainable Development Law & Policy* 18, no. 1 (2017). https://digitalcommons.wcl.american.edu/cgi/viewcontent.cgi?article=1606&context=sdlp.
26. Human Rights Watch. "Meatpacking's Human Toll." August 2, 2005. https://www.hrw.org/news/2005/08/02/meatpackings-human-toll.
27. Collective Fashion Justice. "Slaughterhouse Workers' Suffering in Fashion Supply Chains." Accessed September 29, 2023. https://www.collectivefashionjustice.org/slaughterhouse-workers.
28. Bird, Susan. "Slaughterhouse Work Is So Horrible, Canada Can't Find Anyone to Do It." Care2, January 19, 2016. https://web.archive.org/web/20160122081607/http:/www.care2.com/causes/slaughterhouse-work-is-so-horrible-canada-cant-find-anyone-to-do-it.html.
29. Ibid; Canadian Meat Council. "Critical Shortage of Labour in Canada's Largest Food Processing Industry." Accessed September 29, 2023. https://web.archive.org/web/20160127182930/http:/www.cmc-cvc.com/sites/default/files/news-releases/Critical%20Shortage%20of%20Labour.pdf.
30. Amarshall. "Union Investigates Raw Deal for Refugees at Abattoir." *The Courier Mail*, December 1, 2017. https://www.couriermail.com.au/news/queensland/rockhampton/union-investigates-raw-deal-for-refugees-at-abattoir/news-story/f992d7869fc552e0f7ba3abaa108edea.

31. Physicians Committee for Responsible Medicine. "BREAKING: Santa Is Lactose Intolerant." December 22, 2014. https://www.pcrm.org/news/blog/breaking-santa-lactose-intolerant; Morgan, Nancy. "Introduction: Dairy Development in Asia." Bangkok: FAO Regional Office, accessed September 29, 2023. https://www.fao.org/3/i0588e/I0588E02.htm.
32. Physicians Committee for Responsible Medicine. "BREAKING: Santa Is Lactose Intolerant." December 22, 2014. https://www.pcrm.org/news/blog/breaking-santa-lactose-intolerant.
33. Berton, P., N.D. Barnard, and M. Mills. "Racial Bias in Federal Nutrition Policy, Part I: The Public Health Implications of Variations in Lactase Persistence." *Journal of the National Medical Association* 91, no. 3 (1999): 151–7. https://www.ncbi.nlm.nih.gov/pmc/articles/PMC2608451/; Leyva, Kenny, and Jasmine C. Perry, directors. *The Invisible Vegan*. 2019. https://theinvisiblevegan.com/.
34. Leyva, Kenny, and Jasmine C. Perry, directors. *The Invisible Vegan*. 2019. https://theinvisiblevegan.com/.
35. Ko, Aph, and Syl Ko. *Aphro-ism: Essays on Pop Culture, Feminism, and Black Veganism from Two Sisters*. New York: Lantern Publishing & Media, 2017.
36. World Health Organization. "Origins of SARS-CoV-2." March 26, 2020. https://iris.who.int/bitstream/handle/10665/332197/WHO-2019-nCoV-FAQ-Virus_origin-2020.1-eng.pdf.
37. *Aljazeera*. "Trump Defends Calling Coronavirus the 'Chinese Virus.'" March 23, 2020. https://www.aljazeera.com/program/newsfeed/2020/3/23/trump-defends-calling-coronavirus-the-chinese-virus.
38. Kandil, Caitlin Yoshiko. "Asian Americans Report Over 650 Racist Acts Over Last Week, New Data Says." *ABC News*, March 26, 2020. https://www.nbcnews.com/news/asian-america/asian-americans-report-nearly-500-racist-acts-over-last-week-n1169821.
39. Italiano, Laura. "Asian Man Reportedly Attacked in London by Racist Angry About Coronavirus." *New York Post*, updated March 5, 2020. https://nypost.com/2020/03/05/asian-man-reportedly-attacked-in-london-by-racist-angry-about-coronavirus/.
40. Gregory, Andy. "Coronavirus: China Declares Dogs Are Companions and Should Not Be Eaten, Signalling Possible End to Brutal Meat Trade." *The Independent*, April 9, 2020. https://www.independent.co.uk/climate-change/news/china-dog-meat-trade-ban-cats-coronavirus-wuhan-wet-market-wildlife-a9457426.html.
41. Centers for Disease Control and Prevention. "Influenza Planning and Response." Updated November 23, 2021. https://www.cdc.gov/flu/pandemic-resources/1918-commemoration/pandemic-preparedness.htm#:~:text=The%201918%2D19%20flu%20pandemic,may%20not%20be%20readily%20available; Surge. "COVID-19 and Animal Exploitation: Preventing the Next Global Pandemic." Accessed September 29, 2023. https://www.surgeactivism.org/covid19.

42. Leaked Australia. "Leaked CCTV—Melbourne, Australia." YouTube video, 4:11, August 30, 2019. https://www.youtube.com/watch?v=6s08wsaZaro.
43. Roach, John. "Seafood May Be Gone by 2048, Study Says." *National Geographic*, November 2, 2006. https://www.nationalgeographic.com/animals/article/seafood-biodiversity.
44. Willingham, Richard. "Australian Sheep Clubbed, Stabbed, Buried Alive: Pakistan Report." *The Sydney Morning Herald*, September 27, 2012. https://www.smh.com.au/environment/conservation/australian-sheep-clubbed-stabbed-buried-alive--pakistan-report-20120927-26n91.html; Animal Welfare Victoria. "Code of Accepted Farming Practice for the Welfare of Sheep (Victoria) (Revision Number 3)." Accessed September 29, 2023. https://agriculture.vic.gov.au/livestock-and-animals/animal-welfare-victoria/pocta-act-1986/victorian-codes-of-practice-for-animal-welfare/code-of-accepted-farming-practice-for-the-welfare-of-sheep-victoria-revision-number-3; Animal Health Australia. "Australian Animal Welfare Standards and Guidelines for Sheep." January 2016. https://www.integritysystems.com.au/globalassets/isc/pdf-files/sheep-standards-and-guidelines-for-endorsed-jan-2016-061017.pdf.

Chapter 4: This Is How We Got Here

1. Bekoff, Marc. "Disabled Whale Missing Two Fins Cared for by Family." *Psychology Today*, November 5, 2013. https://www.psychologytoday.com/us/blog/animal-emotions/201311/disabled-whale-missing-two-fins-cared-family; Evans Becky. "Disabled Killer Whale with Missing Fins Survives with the Help of Family Who Hunt for Its Food." *Daily Mail*, updated May 19, 2013. https://www.dailymail.co.uk/news/article-2326868/Disabled-killer-whale-missing-fins-survives-help-family-hunt-food.html; Hogenboom, Melissa. "The Wild Chimpanzee Who Cared for Her Child with Disability." *BBC Earth*, 2016. https://www.4apes.com/news/science/item/1542-http-www-bbc-com-earth-story-20151112-a-wild-chimp-cares-for-her-disabled-child-ocid-fbert.
2. Barras, Colin. "Ancient Leftovers Show the Real Paleo Diet Was a Veggie Feast." *New Scientist*, December 5, 2016. https://www.newscientist.com/article/2115127-ancient-leftovers-show-the-real-paleo-diet-was-a-veggie-feast/.
3. Adler, Jerry. "Why Fire Makes Us Human." *Smithsonian Magazine*, June 2013. https://www.smithsonianmag.com/science-nature/why-fire-makes-us-human-72989884/.
4. Harari, Yuval Noah. *Sapiens: A Brief History of Humankind*. London: Random House UK, 2015.
5. Watson, Traci. "Ancient Oat Discovery May Poke Holes in Paleo Diet." *National Geographic*, September 11, 2015. https://www.nationalgeographic.com/culture/food/the-plate/2015/09/11/ancient-oat-discovery-may-poke-more-holes-in-paleo-diet/.
6. Harari, Yuval Noah. "Industrial Farming Is One of the Worst Crimes in History." The Guardian, September 25, 2015. https://www.theguardian.com/books/2015/sep/25/industrial-farming-one-worst-crimes-history-ethical-question; Harari, Yuval Noah. *Sapiens: A Brief History of Humankind*. London: Random House UK, 2015.

7. Hogenboom, Melissa. "We Did Not Invent Clothes Simply to Stay Warm." Awaken, November 18, 2016. https://awaken.com/2016/11/we-did-not-invent-clothes-to-stay-warm/.
8. Britannica. "The History of Jewelry Design." Accessed September 29, 2023. https://www.britannica.com/art/jewelry/The-history-of-jewelry-design.
9. Topsfield, Jewel, and Karuni Rompies. "Prehistoric Jewellery Found in Indonesian Cave Challenges View Early Humans Less Advanced." *The Sydney Morning Herald*, updated April 5, 2017. https://www.smh.com.au/world/prehistoric-jewellery-found-in-indonesian-cave-challenges-view-early-humans-less-advanced-20170405-gvecxi.html.
10. Harari, Yuval Noah. *Sapiens: A Brief History of Humankind.* London: Random House UK, 2015.
11. Ibid.
12. Hemsworth, Lauren, Paul Hemsworth, Rutu Achraya, et al. "Review of the Scientific Literature and the International Pig Welfare Codes and Standards to Underpin the Future Standards and Guidelines for Pigs." Department of Agriculture, Water and the Environment, August 2018. https://www.australianpork.com.au/sites/default/files/2021-07/2017-2217.pdf.
13. Harari, Yuval Noah. *Sapiens: A Brief History of Humankind.* London: Random House UK, 2015.
14. NSW Government. "Weaning Beef Calves." Department of Primary Industries, accessed September 29, 2023. https://www.dpi.nsw.gov.au/animals-and-livestock/beef-cattle/husbandry/general-management/weaning-beef-calves; RSPCA. "What Are the Animal Welfare Issues with Weaning Nose Rings and Other Anti-Suckling Devices for Calves?" Accessed September 29, 2023. https://kb.rspca.org.au/knowledge-base/what-are-the-animal-welfare-issues-with-weaning-nose-rings-and-other-anti-suckling-devices-for-calves/.
15. Harari, Yuval Noah. *Sapiens: A Brief History of Humankind.* London: Random House UK, 2015.
16. Curry, Andrew. "Parents' Emotional Trauma May Change Their Children's Biology. Studies in Mice Show How." *Science*, July 18, 2019. https://www.science.org/content/article/parents-emotional-trauma-may-change-their-children-s-biology-studies-mice-show-how.
17. Daley, Paul. "Colonial Australia's Foundation Is Stained with the Profits of British Slavery." *The Guardian*, September 21, 2018. https://www.theguardian.com/world/2018/sep/21/colonial-australias-foundation-is-stained-with-the-profits-of-british-slavery.
18. Collective Fashion Justice. "Issues in the Kangaroo Skin Leather Supply Chain." Accessed September 29, 2023. https://www.collectivefashionjustice.org/kangaroo-leather.
19. Ibid.
20. Anthis, Kelly, and Jacy Reese Anthis. "Global Farmed & Factory Farmed Animals Estimates." Sentience Institute, updated February 21, 2019. https://www.sentienceinstitute.org/global-animal-farming-estimates.

21. National Chicken Council. "U.S. Chicken Industry History." Accessed September 29, 2023. https://www.nationalchickencouncil.org/about-the-industry/history/.
22. First Broiler House. National Register of Historic Places Inventory—Nomination Form. United States Department of the Interior National Park Service, July 1969. https://npgallery.nps.gov/NRHP/GetAsset/NRHP/74000607_text.
23. Ritchie, Hannah, Pablo Rosado, and Max Roser. "Meat and Dairy Production." Our World in Data, updated November 2019. https://ourworldindata.org/meat-production.
24. Lymbery, Philip, and Isabel Oakeshott. *Farmageddon: The True Cost of Cheap Meat.* New York: Bloomsbury, 2014.
25. Ibid.
26. Andrewbackhouse. "Piggery Expands to Become Second Biggest in Country." *The Courier Mail,* October 4, 2016. https://www.couriermail.com.au/news/piggery-expands-to-become-second-biggest-in-country/news-story/7a2f2b3f99485f5be6160a27100b5779.
27. Canon, Gabrielle. "Secret Footage Exposes Abuse of Calves at Coca-Cola Affiliated Dairy Farm." *The Guardian,* June 6, 2019. https://www.theguardian.com/environment/2019/jun/06/secret-footage-calves-fair-oaks-farms-illinois; Animal Recovery Mission. "Operation Fair Oaks Farms Dairy Adventure." Accessed September 29, 2023. https://animalrecoverymission.org/operations/factory-farm-division/operation-fair-oaks-farms-dairy-adventure/.
28. Roberts, Callum. "Industrial Meat Production Is Killing Our Seas. It's Time to Change Our Diets." *The Guardian,* August 4, 2017. https://www.theguardian.com/commentisfree/2017/aug/04/meat-industry-gulf-mexico-dead-zones-pollution.
29. Yeoman, Barry. "'It Smells Like a Decomposing Body': North Carolina's Polluting Pig Farms." *The Guardian,* August 27, 2019. https://www.theguardian.com/environment/2019/aug/27/it-smells-like-a-decomposing-body-north-carolinas-polluting-pig-farms.
30. Delforce, Chris, director. *Dominion.* Farm Transparency Project, 2018. https://www.dominionmovement.com/.
31. Poultry Hub Australia. "Meat Chicken (Broiler) Industry." Accessed September 29, 2023. https://www.poultryhub.org/production/meat-chicken-broiler-industry.
32. RSPCA. "What Are Some of the Painful Procedures Experienced by Pigs on Farm?" Accessed September 29, 2023. https://kb.rspca.org.au/knowledge-base/what-are-some-of-the-painful-procedures-experienced-by-pigs-on-farm/.
33. Delforce, Chris, director. *Dominion.* Farm Transparency Project, 2018. https://www.dominionmovement.com/.
34. RSPCA. "What Are the Animal Welfare Issues Associated with Turkey Production?" Accessed September 29, 2023. https://kb.rspca.org.au/knowledge-base/what-are-the-animal-welfare-issues-associated-with-turkey-production/; RSPCA. "What Is Beak Trimming and Why Is It Carried Out?" Accessed September 29, 2023. https://kb.rspca.org.au/knowledge-base/what-is-beak-trimming-and-why-is-it-carried-out/.

35. Animals Australia. "Making Sense of Egg Labels." Updated May 2, 2023. https://animalsaustralia.org/our-work/factory-farming/egg-labels/.
36. RSPCA. "What Is the Difference Between Free Range, Outdoor Bred, Organic, Sow-Stall Free, RSPCA Approved?" Accessed September 29, 2023. https://kb.rspca.org.au/knowledge-base/what-is-the-difference-between-free-range-outdoor-bred-organic-sow-stall-free-rspca-approved/.
37. Hardy, Rich. *Not as Nature Intended: An Undercover Journey into the Secret World of Animal Exploitation*. London: Unbound, 2020.
38. FAO. "The State of World Fisheries and Aquaculture." 2018. https://www.fao.org/3/i9540en/I9540EN.pdf.
39. Changing Markets Foundation. "Fishing for Catastrophe." October 2019. http://changingmarkets.org/wp-content/uploads/2019/10/CM-WEB-FINAL-FISHING-FOR-CATASTROPHE-2019.pdf; Meza, Salvador. "Fish in: Fish out (FIFO) Ratios for the Conversion of Wild Feed to Farmed Fish, Including Salmon." *Aquaculture Magazine*, October 25, 2017. https://aquaculturemag.com/2017/10/25/fish-in-fish-out-fifo-ratios-for-the-conversion-of-wild-feed-to-farmed-fish-including-salmon/.
40. RSPCA Australia. "RSPCA Approved Farming Scheme Standard: Farmed Atlantic Salmon." May 2020. https://rspcaapproved.org.au/wp-content/uploads/2022/03/2020-05_FARMEDATLANTICSALMON_Standard.pdf; RSPCA. "How Are Salmon Farmed in Australia?" Accessed September 29, 2023. https://kb.rspca.org.au/knowledge-base/how-are-salmon-farmed-in-australia/; White, Cliff. "Huon Aquaculture Confirms Escape of 120,000 Atlantic Salmon from 'Fortress Pen.'" Seafood Source, September 14, 2018. https://www.seafoodsource.com/news/aquaculture/huon-aquaculture-confirms-escape-of-120-000-atlantic-salmon.
41. Vindas, Marco A., Ida B. Johansen, Ole Folkedal, et al. "Brain Serotonergic Activation in Growth-Stunted Farmed Salmon: Adaption Vs. Pathology." *Royal Society* 3, no. 5 (May 1, 2016). https://doi.org/10.1098/rsos.160030.
42. RSPCA. "How Can Farmed Fish Be Slaughtered Humanely?" Accessed September 29, 2023. https://kb.rspca.org.au/knowledge-base/how-can-farmed-fish-be-slaughtered-humanely/.
43. Northern Territory Government, Australia. "Conservation of Crocodiles." Accessed September 29, 2023. https://nt.gov.au/environment/animals/conservation-of-crocodiles/saltwater-crocodile-conservation.
44. Collective Fashion Justice. "Native Crocodiles Confined and Killed for 'Luxury' Fashion." Accessed September 29, 2023. https://www.collectivefashionjustice.org/drop-croc.
45. Australian Government. "Invasive Bees." Department of Climate Change, Energy, the Environment and Water, accessed September 29, 2023. https://www.dcceew.gov.au/environment/invasive-species/insects-and-other-invertebrates/invasive-bees; Geldmann, Jonas, and Juan P. González-Varo. "Conserving Honey Bees Does Not Help Wildlife." *Science* 359, no. 6374 (January 26, 2018): 392–3. https://doi.org/10.1126/science.aar2269.

Chapter 5: How We Began to Fight the System

1. Buddharakkhita, Acharya. *The Dhammapada: The Buddha's Path of Wisdom.* Kandy, Sri Lanka: Buddhist Publication Society, 1985.
2. Saxena, Anand M. *The Vegetarian Imperative.* Baltimore: The John Hopkins University Press, 2011.
3. Dhammika, Ven. S. *The Edicts of King Asoka: An English Rendering.* Kandy, Sri Lanka: Buddhist Publication Society, 1993; Brittanica. "Ashoka's Edicts." Accessed September 29, 2023. https://www.britannica.com/place/India/Ashokas-edicts.
4. Walli, Koshelya. *The Conception of Ahiṁsā in Indian Thought, According to Sanskrit Sources.* Bharata Manisha, 1974; Maheshwari, Krishna. "Ahimsa in Scriptures." Hindupedia, accessed September 29, 2023. http://www.hindupedia.com/en/Ahimsa_in_Scriptures; The Statutes Project. "1835: 5 & 6 William 4 c.59: Cruelty to Animals Act." Accessed September 29, 2023. https://statutes.org.uk/site/the-statutes/nineteenth-century/1835-5-6-william-4-c-59-cruelty-to-animals-act/.
5. Gregory, Horace. *Ovid: The Metamorphoses.* New York: The Viking Press, 1958.
6. Zaraska, Marta. "The Bizarre Story of One of the World's First Modern Vegetarians—and How His Diet Made Him an Outcast from Society." Business Insider, March 13, 2016. https://www.businessinsider.com/the-story-of-one-of-the-worlds-first-modern-vegetarians-2016-3.
7. Hiroyuki, Ishi. "Human-Animal Ties: Japanese Takes in Both Life and Death. Nippon.com, February 27, 2018. https://www.nippon.com/en/features/c03911/human-animal-ties-japanese-takes-in-both-life-and-death.html.
8. Da Vinci, Leonardo, and Edward McCurdy. *Leonardo Da Vinci's Note-Books Arranged and Rendered into English with Introductions.* New York: Empire State Book Company, 1923.
9. Howell, Bethany. "'Rabbit food': The Romantic Roots of Vegetarianism." Devon & Exeter Institution, April 10, 2020. https://devonandexeterinstitution.org/rabbit-food-the-romantic-roots-of-vegetarianism/.
10. Adams, Carol J. *The Sexual Politics of Meat: A Feminist-Vegetarian Critical Theory.* London: Continuum, 1990.
11. Perkins, David. *Romanticism and Animal Rights.* Cambridge: Cambridge University Press, 2003.
12. George, Kathryn Paxton. "Should Feminists Be Vegetarians?" *Signs* 19, no. 2 (1994): 405–34. https://www.jstor.org/stable/3174804.
13. Katcher, Joshua. *Fashion Animals.* Danvers, MA: Vegan Publishers, 2018.
14. Murray, Lorraine. "The Brown Dog Affair." Saving Earth: Encyclopedia Britannica, accessed September 29, 2023. https://www.britannica.com/explore/savingearth/the-brown-dog-affair; Lind-af-Hageby, Lizzy, and Leisa Katherina Schartau. *The Shambles of Science: Extracts from the Diary of Two Students of Physiology. . . .* New York: Nabu Press, 2012.
15. Ibid.

16. Ibid; Gålmark, Lisa. "Women Antivivisectionists—The Story of Lizzy Lind af Hageby and Leisa Schartau." *Animal Issues* 4, no. 2 (2000): 1–32. https://ro.uow.edu.au/ai/vol4/iss2/1/.
17. Murray, Lorraine. "The Brown Dog Affair." Saving Earth: Encyclopedia Britannica, accessed September 29, 2023. https://www.britannica.com/explore/savingearth/the-brown-dog-affair; Lind-af-Hageby, Lizzy, and Leisa Katherina Schartau. *The Shambles of Science: Extracts from the Diary of Two Students of Physiology. . . .* New York: Nabu Press, 2012; Birke, Lynda. "Supporting the Underdog: Feminism, Animal Rights and Citizenship in the Work of Alice Morgan Wright and Edith Goode." *Women's History Review* 9, no. 4 (2000): 693–719. https://doi.org/10.1080/09612020000200261.
18. Murray, Lorraine. "The Brown Dog Affair." Saving Earth: Encyclopedia Britannica, accessed September 29, 2023. https://www.britannica.com/explore/savingearth/the-brown-dog-affair; Tansey, E.M. "'The Queen Has Been Dreadfully Shocked': Aspects of Teaching Experimental Physiology Using Animals in Britain, 1876–1986." *The American Journal of Physiology* (June 1, 1998). https://doi.org/10.1152/advances.1998.274.6.S18; "Final Report of the Royal Commission on Vivisection." London: His Majesty's Stationery Office, 1912. https://babel.hathitrust.org/cgi/pt?id=uiug.30112089397381&view=1up&seq=7.
19. Van de Weerd, Heleen, and Victoria Sandilands. "Bringing the Issue of Animal Welfare to the Public: A Biography of Ruth Harrison (1920–2000)." *Applied Animal Behaviour Science* 113, no. 4 (2008): 404–10. https://doi.org/10.1016/j.applanim.2008.01.014; Harrison, Ruth. *Animal Machines: The New Factory Farming Industry.* London: Vincent Stuart Publishers, 1964.
20. Harrison, Ruth. *Animal Machines: The New Factory Farming Industry.* London: Vincent Stuart Publishers, 1964.
21. Cronin, Keri. "Ruth Harrison." Unbound Project, August 24, 2017. https://unboundproject.org/ruth-harrison/.
22. Elischer, Melissa. "The Five Freedoms: A History Lesson in Animal Care and Welfare." Michigan State University Extension, September 6, 2019. https://www.canr.msu.edu/news/an_animal_welfare_history_lesson_on_the_five_freedoms.
23. Farm Transparency Project. "Aussie Pigs." Accessed September 29, 2023. https://www.farmtransparency.org/campaigns/aussie-pigs.
24. Singer, Peter. *Practical Ethics.* Cambridge: Cambridge University Press, 1979.
25. Bentham, Jeremy. *An Introduction to the Principals of Morals and Legislation.* Oxford: Clarendon Press, 1907.
26. Singer, Peter. *Practical Ethics.* Cambridge: Cambridge University Press, 1979.
27. Regan, Tom. *The Case for Animal Rights.* Berkeley: University of California Press, 1983.
28. Parry, Tom. "Thousands of Healthy Foxhounds—Including Pups—Are Clubbed to Death or Shot if They're 'Unsuitable.'" Mirror, updated July 14, 2015. https://www.mirror.co.uk/news/uk-news/thousands-healthy-foxhounds---including-6061265.

29. Hunt Saboteurs Association. "1963—Protest to Resistance." September 21, 2009. https://www.huntsabs.org.uk/hsahistorypt1/.
30. Hunt Saboteurs Association. "Two Decades of Hunt Violence." September 21, 2009. https://www.huntsabs.org.uk/2decadesviolence/.
31. Curnutt, Jordan. *Animals and the Law: A Sourcebook.* Santa Barbara, CA: ABC-CLIO, 2001.
32. Ibid.
33. Best, Steven, and Anthony J. Nocella II, editors. *Terrorists or Freedom Fighters?: Reflections on the Liberation of Animals.* New York: Lantern Publishing & Media, 2004.
34. Potter, Will. *Green Is the New Red: An Insider's Account of a Social Movement under Siege.* San Francisco: City Light Books, 2011; VeganKanal. "From Activist to Terrorist—Jake Conroy at IARC 2016." YouTube video, 1:00:30, April 14, 2017. https://www.youtube.com/watch?v=XgARuabK_x0.
35. Suchan, Casey, and Denis Henry Hennelly, directors. *The Animal People.* Jorja Fox, Andy Roth, Mikko Alanne, et al., 2019. https://www.imdb.com/title/tt2337280/.
36. Liddick, Donald R. *Eco-Terrorism: Radical Environmental and Animal Liberation Movements.* Westport, CT: Praeger, 2006.
37. Williams, Yohuru. "'Some Abstract Thing Called Freedom': Civil Rights, Black Power, and the Legacy of the Black Panther Party." *OAH Magazine of History* 22, no. 3 (2008): 16–21. https://www.jstor.org/stable/25162181.
38. Renteria, Yolanda. "'Fight for your rights, but do it peacefully.'" Instagram, May 29, 2020. https://www.instagram.com/p/CAye_85DGnr/?igshid=vt9d6qkdh34i.
39. Young, Peter. *Liberate: Stories & Lessons on Animal Liberation Above the Law.* Warcry Communications: 2019.
40. OpenRescue.org. "About Open Rescue." Accessed September 29, 2023. https://openrescue.org/about/index.html.
41. Associated Press. "Around the Nation: Group Says It 'Rescued' 260 Animals from Lab." April 21, 1985. https://www.nytimes.com/1985/04/21/us/around-the-nation-group-says-it-rescued-260-animals-from-lab.html; Centar Key. "Britches Liberation—1985." YouTube video, 12:12, March 7, 2012. https://www.youtube.com/watch?v=Eth7p7zHqgo.
42. Adam Austin. "ALF Liberate 11 Chickens 9-19-98." Vimeo video, 5:56, 2013. https://vimeo.com/69390339.
43. Agence France-Presse. "France Moves to Ban Mass Live-Shredding of Male Chicks." *The Guardian*, January 28, 2020. https://www.theguardian.com/world/2020/jan/29/france-moves-to-ban-mass-live-shredding-of-male-chicks.
44. Not as Nature Intended. "Deep undercover with fur trappers." Instagram, September 20, 2019. https://www.instagram.com/p/B2oBhgWpXYO/; PETA (People for the Ethical Treatment of Animals). "Trapped Coyote's Last Moments of Life." YouTube video, 0:15, July 13, 2018. https://www.youtube.com/watch?v=-4SqtWJGqW0; Canada Goose. "Sustainability Report 2019." Accessed September 29, 2023. https://investor.canadagoose.com/static-files/4a3298bb-de3c-4d47-9ffd-76d0195eab6e.

45. Animal Equality. "The Brutal Killing of Bluefin Tuna Exposed: Animal Equality Undercover Investigation." YouTube video, 3:07, June 2, 2012. https://www.youtube.com/watch?v=GPlDrCOJUCg.

Chapter 6: How the System Fought Back

1. Suchan, Casey, and Denis Henry Hennelly, directors. *The Animal People.* Jorja Fox, Andy Roth, Mikko Alanne, et al., 2019. https://www.imdb.com/title/tt2337280/; BBC News. "US Banks Cuts Ties with Ailing Lab Firm." January 17, 2001. http://news.bbc.co.uk/2/hi/business/1122453.stm; CrimethInc. "The SHAC Model: A Critical Assessment." September 1, 2008. https://crimethinc.com/2008/09/01/the-shac-model-a-critical-assessment.
2. Rosebraugh, Craig. *Burning Rage of a Dying Planet: Speaking for the Earth Liberation Front.* New York: Lantern Publishing & Media, 2004.
3. CrimethInc. "The SHAC Model: A Critical Assessment." September 1, 2008. https://crimethinc.com/2008/09/01/the-shac-model-a-critical-assessment.
4. Potter, Will. "Sentinel Species: The Criminalization of Animal Rights Activists as Terrorists, and What It Means for the Civil Liberties in Trump's America." *Denver Law Review* 95, no. 4 (2018): 877–907. https://digitalcommons.du.edu/cgi/viewcontent.cgi?article=1032&context=dlr.
5. Brown, Alleen. "The Green Scare: How a Movement that Never Killed Anyone Became the FBI's No. 1 Domestic Terrorism Threat." *The Intercept*, March 23, 2019. https://theintercept.com/2019/03/23/ecoterrorism-fbi-animal-rights/; Federal Bureau of Investigation. "John E. Lewis. Deputy Assistant Director, Counterterrorism Division. Federal Bureau of Investigation. Senate Committee on Environment and Public Works. Washington, DC." May 18, 2005. https://archives.fbi.gov/archives/news/testimony/addressing-the-threat-of-animal-rights-extremism-and-eco-terrorism.
6. Suchan, Casey, and Denis Henry Hennelly, directors. *The Animal People.* Jorja Fox, Andy Roth, Mikko Alanne, et al., 2019. https://www.imdb.com/title/tt2337280/.
7. Federal Bureau of Investigation. "John E. Lewis. Deputy Assistant Director, Counterterrorism Division. Federal Bureau of Investigation. Senate Committee on Environment and Public Works. Washington, DC." May 18, 2005. https://archives.fbi.gov/archives/news/testimony/addressing-the-threat-of-animal-rights-extremism-and-eco-terrorism.
8. Bjelopera, Jerome P. "Domestic Terrorism: An Overview." Congressional Research Service, August 21, 2017. https://fas.org/sgp/crs/terror/R44921.pdf.
9. Khan, Amina. "Getting Killed by Police Is a Leading Cause of Death for Young Black Men in America." *Los Angeles Times*, August 16, 2019. https://www.latimes.com/science/story/2019-08-15/police-shootings-are-a-leading-cause-of-death-for-black-men.
10. Press Association. "Pro-Meat Protesters Fined for Eating Raw Squirrels at Vegan Stall." *The Guardian*, July 23, 2019. https://www.theguardian.com/uk-news/2019/jul/23/pro-meat-protesters-fined-eating-raw-squirrels-vegan-stall.

11. r/vegan. "Reported the event 'punch a vegan day.' Wtf Facebook?!" Reddit, 2016. https://www.reddit.com/r/vegan/comments/529bie/reported_the_event_punch_a_vegan_day_wtf_facebook/.
12. Hakkansson, Emma, Nicholas Carter, Lucy Coen, et al. "Under Their Skin: Leather's Impact on the Planet." Collective Fashion Justice, November 2022. https://static1.squarespace.com/static/5f5f02dd9b510014eef4fc4f/t/6386865fa112a35adea84ccd/1669760650422/CFJ+leather%27s+impact+on+the+planet+%28launch%29.pdf.
13. Truth About Fur. "The Sustainability of Fur." Accessed September 29, 2023. https://www.truthaboutfur.com/sustainability/#:~:text=Fake%20furs%20and%20other%20petroleum,and%20even%20our%20drinking%20water.; Bijleveld, Marijn. "Natural Mink Fur and Faux Fur Products, an Environmental Comparison." Delft, June 2013. https://www.furfreealliance.com/wp-content/uploads/2016/01/CE_Delft_22203_Natural_mink_fur_and_faux_fur_products_DEF-1.pdf.
14. Delforce, Chris, director. *Dominion.* Farm Transparency Project, 2018. https://www.dominionmovement.com/.
15. World Health Organization. "Cancer: Carcinogenicity of the Consumption of Red Meat and Processed Meat." October 26, 2015. https://www.who.int/news-room/questions-and-answers/item/cancer-carcinogenicity-of-the-consumption-of-red-meat-and-processed-meat.
16. Staff and agencies. "Scott Morrison Denounces 'Green Criminals' as Vegan Protests Block Melbourne CBD." *The Guardian*, April 8, 2019. https://www.theguardian.com/world/2019/apr/08/animal-rights-activists-block-melbourne-cbd-amid-protests-at-abattoirs-around-australia.
17. Johnson, Paul. "Australian Charities and Not-for-Profits Commission Strips Aussie Farms of Charity Status." *ABC News*, updated November 20, 2019. https://www.abc.net.au/news/2019-11-19/aussie-farms-hits-back-after-revocation-of-charity-status/11715622.
18. Parliament of Victoria. "Inquiry into the Impact of Animal Rights Activism on Victorian Agriculture." Accessed September 29, 2023. https://new.parliament.vic.gov.au/get-involved/inquiries/inquiry-into-the-impact-of-animal-rights-activism-on-victorian-agriculture/.
19. Dodd, Vikram, and Jamie Grierson. "Greenpeace Included with Neo-Nazis on UK Counter-Terror List." *The Guardian*, January 17, 2020. https://www.theguardian.com/uk-news/2020/jan/17/greenpeace-included-with-neo-nazis-on-uk-counter-terror-list.
20. Global Witness. "Last Line of Defence." September 13, 2021. https://www.globalwitness.org/en/campaigns/environmental-activists/last-line-defence/.
21. Brown, Alleen. "Louisiana Environmental Activists Charged with 'Terrorizing' for Nonviolent Stunt Targeting Plastics Giant." *The Intercept*, June 25, 2020. https://theintercept.com/2020/06/25/environmental-activists-charged-terrorizing-louisiana-formosa/.

22. Workman, Alice. "This Politician Wants Environmental Activists to Be Charged as Terrorists." *BuzzFeed News*, October 16, 2017. https://www.buzzfeed.com/aliceworkman/eco-terrorists; *SBS News*. "'We Want Them Out': Traditional Owners Block Road to Adani Coal Mine in Central Queensland." August 24, 2020. https://www.sbs.com.au/news/article/we-want-them-out-traditional-owners-block-road-to-adani-coal-mine-in-central-queensland/hou7usx2z; Van Extel, Cathy, and Gregg Borschmann. "Dozens More Ancient Heritage Sites Could Be Destroyed by Australian Mining Companies." *ABC News*, updated June 13, 2020. https://www.abc.net.au/news/2020-06-13/letter-traditional-owners-40-sites-that-bhp-planned-to-destroy/12348396.
23. U.S. Government Printing Office. "Animal Enterprise Terrorism Act." Accessed September 29, 2023. https://www.govinfo.gov/content/pkg/PLAW-109publ374/html/PLAW-109publ374.htm; Shalev, Moshe. "Animal Enterprise Terrorism Act Becomes Law." *Lab Animal* 36 (2007): 15. https://doi.org/10.1038/laban0107-15a.
24. Pilkington, Ed. "Animal Rights 'Terrorists'? Legality of Industry-Friendly Law to Be Challenged." *The Guardian*, February 19, 2015. https://www.theguardian.com/us-news/2015/feb/19/animal-rights-activists-challenge-federal-terrorism-charges.
25. Ibid.
26. Green Is the New Red. "SHAC 7." Accessed September 29, 2023. http://www.greenisthenewred.com/blog/tag/shac-7/.
27. Potter, Will. "First 'Ag-Gag' Prosecution: Utah Woman Filmed a Slaughterhouse from the Public Street." Green Is the New Red, April 29, 2013. http://www.greenisthenewred.com/blog/first-ag-gag-arrest-utah-amy-meyer/6948/.
28. Prygoski, Alicia. "Brief Summary of Ag-Gag Laws." Michigan State University College of Law, 2015. https://www.animallaw.info/article/brief-summary-ag-gag-laws; Gibbons, Chip. "Ag-Gag Across America: Corporate-Backed Attacks on Activists and Whistleblowers." Center for Constitutional Rights, Defending Rights & Dissent, 2017. https://ccrjustice.org/sites/default/files/attach/2017/09/Ag-GagAcrossAmerica.pdf.
29. Stop Bill 156. "New Ontario Bill Will Make It Illegal to Expose Cruelty on Farms." Accessed September 29, 2023. https://stopbill156.com/; Hardeman, Ernie. "Bill 156, Security from Trespass and Protecting Food Safety Act, 2020." Legislative Assembly of Ontario, accessed September 29, 2020.
30. Craggs, Samantha. "Pig Trial: Anita Krajnc Found Not Guilty of Mischief Charge for Giving Water to Pigs." *CBC News*, updated May 4, 2017. https://www.cbc.ca/news/canada/hamilton/pig-trial-verdict-1.4098046.
31. Craggs, Samantha. "Man Charged with Careless Driving in Death of Hamilton Animal Rights Activist: Police." *CBC News*, updated July 20, 2020. https://www.cbc.ca/news/canada/hamilton/driver-charged-1.5656070.
32. Hardeman, Ernie. "Bill 156, Security from Trespass and Protecting Food Safety Act, 2020." Legislative Assembly of Ontario, accessed September 29, 2020.

33. Craggs, Samantha. "'My Life Ended' Friday: Regan Russell's Supporters Want Justice, Bill 156 Overturned." *CBC News*, updated June 26, 2020. https://www.cbc.ca/news/canada/hamilton/regan-russell-1.5627216.
34. Bridget McKenzie. "Government Delivers to Protect Farmers." July 4, 2019. https://www.bridgetmckenzie.com.au/media-releases/government-delivers-to-protect-farmers/; Visentin, Lisa. "Lawyers Say Animal Activist Crackdown Is 'Harsh and Disproportionate.'" *The Sydney Morning Herald*, October 3, 2019. https://www.smh.com.au/politics/nsw/lawyers-say-animal-activist-crackdown-is-harsh-and-disproportionate-20191002-p52wxx.html; Becker, Joshua, and Michael Condon. "NSW Government Reveals 'Right to Farm' Laws with Three Year Jail Term for Farm Trespass." *ABC News*, August 20, 2019. https://www.abc.net.au/news/rural/2019-08-20/new-nsw-right-to-farm-laws/11431934.
35. Becker, Joshua, and Michael Condon. "NSW Government Reveals 'Right to Farm' Laws with Three Year Jail Term for Farm Trespass." *ABC News*, August 20, 2019. https://www.abc.net.au/news/rural/2019-08-20/new-nsw-right-to-farm-laws/11431934.
36. National Agricultural Law Center Staff. "States' Right-to-Farm Statutes." The National Agricultural Law Center, accessed September 29, 2023. https://nationalaglawcenter.org/state-compilations/right-to-farm/.
37. Mock, Brentin. "North Carolina's Environmental History Is Littered with Racial Injustice." *Pacific Standard*, updated October 7, 2018. https://psmag.com/social-justice/environmental-racism-in-north-carolina.
38. Forrest, Adam. "Animal Rights Activists Designated 'Domestic Terrorists' in Australia." *The Independent*, July 22, 2019. https://www.independent.co.uk/news/world/australasia/animal-rights-activists-australia-domestic-terrorists-new-south-wales-a9015346.html.
39. Burt, Michael. "Farm Invasions Are a Biosecurity Risk." NSW Farmers, July 22, 2019. https://www.nswfarmers.org.au/NSWFA/Posts/Media_Releases/mr.19.85.aspx; Bettles, Colin. "34 Animal Rights Activists to Face Court over Trespass Claims." *The Advocate*, updated April 17, 2018. https://www.theadvocate.com.au/story/5349458/animal-rights-activists-to-face-court-over-trespass-claims/.
40. Giuffre, Emmanuel. "Case Note: ABC v Lenah Game Meats." Voiceless, accessed September 29, 2023. https://voiceless.org.au/case-note-abc-v-lenah-game-meats/.
41. Animal Liberation. "Egg Farming Exposed." Accessed September 29, 2023. https://www.al.org.au/egg-campaigns; Dalton, Jane. "Goats Punched, Hit, Kicked and 'Left Lame' at Farm Supplying Milk to Tesco, Sainsbury, Waitrose and Ocado, Video Shows." *The Independent*, July 27, 2020. https://www.independent.co.uk/climate-change/news/goats-milk-st-helens-farm-yoghurt-hit-kick-animal-cruelty-video-a9639021.html.

42. Animal Welfare Institute. "Legal Protections for Animals on Farms." Accessed September 29, 2023. https://awionline.org/sites/default/files/uploads/documents/FA-AWI-LegalProtections-AnimalsonFarms-110714.pdf; Victorian Current Acts. "Prevention of Cruelty to Animals Act 1986—Sect 6." Accessed September 29, 2023. http://www5.austlii.edu.au/au/legis/vic/consol_act/poctaa1986360/s6.html.
43. Reppy Jr., William A. "Broad Exemptions in Animal-Cruelty Statutes Unconstitutionally Deny Equal Protection of the Law." *Law and Contemporary Problems* (2007): 255–324. https://scholarship.law.duke.edu/faculty_scholarship/2192.
44. Government UK. "Guidance: Animal Welfare." Updated August 16, 2023." https://www.gov.uk/guidance/animal-welfare; Hurnik, Frank, and Hugh Lehman. "Unnecessary Suffering: Definition and Evidence." *International Journal for the Study of Animal Problems* 3, no. 2 (1982): 131–7. https://www.wellbeingintlstudiesrepository.org/cgi/viewcontent.cgi?article=1008&context=acwp_sata.
45. RSPCA. "Man Breaches Court Order and Obtains Two Dogs." July 11, 2019. https://www.rspcaqld.org.au/news-and-events/news/man-breaches-animal-prohibition-order-2019.
46. Parliament of Victoria Economy and Infrastructure Committee. "Inquiry into the Impact of Animal Rights Activism on Victorian Agriculture." February 2020. https://www.parliament.vic.gov.au/file_uploads/LCEIC_59-02_Impact_of_animal_activisim_on_Victorian_agriculture_n8Zx02Bz.pdf.
47. Graham, Vernon. "Mulesing Ban Would Risk Millions of Sheep, Says NSW Farmers." Farm Online National, updated October 1, 2019. https://www.farmonline.com.au/story/6415557/farmers-say-mulesing-ban-in-nsw-would-put-millions-of-sheep-at-risk/.
48. Allbirds. "Superfine Merino Wool: Our Materials." Accessed September 29, 2023. https://www.allbirds.com/pages/our-materials-wool.
49. Hurnik, Frank, and Hugh Lehman. "Unnecessary Suffering: Definition and Evidence." *International Journal for the Study of Animal Problems* 3, no. 2 (1982): 131–7. https://www.wellbeingintlstudiesrepository.org/cgi/viewcontent.cgi?article=1008&context=acwp_sata.
50. Jenkins, Simon. "Votes for Dogs Appeals, but Giving Animals Rights Is Moral Chaos." *The Guardian*, March 18, 2010. https://www.theguardian.com/commentisfree/2010/mar/18/animal-rights-moral-chaos.
51. Canadian Trapper. "Canadian Trapper Talk Forum." Accessed September 29, 2023. http://www.trapper.ca/cnta/viewtopic.php?f=1&t=13913&start=15.
52. Footie. "Economic Value of Manure." TFF Farming Forum, November 29, 2018. https://thefarmingforum.co.uk/index.php?threads/economic-value-of-manure.261114/.

53. Coughlan, Matt, and Marnie Banger. "Agriculture Minister David Littleproud Fires Up over Aussie Farms Map." Perth Now, January 22, 2019. https://www.perthnow.com.au/business/agriculture/agriculture-minister-david-littleproud-fires-up-over-aussie-farms-map-ng-b881081920z.

Chapter 7: Fighting with a "Terrorist" Label

1. O'Sullivan, Siobhan. "'Ag-Gag' Laws: The Battle for Animal Welfare Is a Battle over Information." *The Guardian*, May 4, 2014. https://www.theguardian.com/commentisfree/2014/may/05/ag-gag-laws-the-battle-for-animal-welfare-is-a-battle-over-information.
2. Farm Transparency Project. "Ban Gas Chambers." Accessed September 29, 2023. https://www.farmtransparency.org/campaigns.php?article=gas-chambers.
3. Humane Society International. "Breaking: France Announces Ban on Mink Fur Farming One Month After Shocking Cruelty Investigation." September 29, 2020. https://www.hsi.org/news-media/france-bans-mink-fur-farming/; Kość, Wojciech. "Film Showing Mink 'Cannibalism' Prompts Probable Ban on Fur Farms in Poland." *The Guardian*, September 29, 2020. https://www.theguardian.com/environment/2020/sep/29/film-showing-cannibalism-prompts-probable-ban-on-fur-farms-in-poland; Collective Fashion Justice. "1.7 Million of You Have Signed the Fur Free Europe Petition!" Accessed September 29, 2023. https://www.collectivefashionjustice.org/fur-free-europe.
4. MEAA. "Whistleblower Protection." Medium, Truth versus Disinformation—The Challenge for Public Interest Journalism, May 4, 2016. https://pressfreedom.org.au/whistleblower-protection-f14e75b174d0.
5. Australian Securities & Investments Commission. "Whistleblower Protections." Accessed September 29, 2023. https://asic.gov.au/about-asic/contact-us/reporting-misconduct-to-asic/whistleblower-protections/#whistleblower; United States Consumer Product Safety Commission. "Whistleblower Protections." Accessed September 29, 2023. https://www.cpsc.gov/About-CPSC/Inspector-General/Whistleblower-Protection-Act-WPA; Collins, Erika, and Marjorie Culver. "Rights and Protections for Whistleblowers." Thomson Reuters Practical Law, accessed September 29, 2023. https://uk.practicallaw.thomsonreuters.com/2-203-2258?transitionType=Default&contextData=(sc.Default)&firstPage=true.
6. ABC News In-depth. "The Dark Side of Australia's Horse Racing Industry." YouTube video, 49:15, October 18, 2019. https://www.youtube.com/watch?v=Zp-ALoBRW20.
7. Bridget McKenzie. "Government Delivers to Protect Farmers." July 4, 2019. https://www.bridgetmckenzie.com.au/media-releases/government-delivers-to-protect-farmers/; Visentin, Lisa. "Lawyers Say Animal Activist Crackdown Is 'Harsh and Disproportionate.'" *The Sydney Morning Herald*, October 3, 2019. https://www.smh.com.au/politics/nsw/

lawyers-say-animal-activist-crackdown-is-harsh-and-disproportionate-20191002-p52wxx.html; Parliament of Victoria. "Inquiry into Animal Rights Activism on Victorian Agriculture." February 5, 2020. https://www.parliament.vic.gov.au/eic-lc/inquiries/inquiry/965.

8. Animal Liberation ORG. "Dairy Is Scary: Australia." YouTube video, 4:32, August 6, 2019. https://www.youtube.com/watch?v=LhPn2qTnT1g.
9. Henriques-Gomes, Luke. "Melbourne Cup Attendance Falls as Animal Rights Activists Take up Positions." *The Guardian*, November 5, 2019. https://www.theguardian.com/sport/2019/nov/05/melbourne-cup-attendance-falls-as-animal-rights-activists-take-up-position.
10. The Cranky Vegan. "Start Pressure Campaigning / S03 E02 / Are We Winning." YouTube video, 12:35, April 13, 2020. https://www.youtube.com/watch?v=3ngZa21Buc8.
11. Sharpley, A. "Agricultural Phosphorus, Water Quality, and Poultry Production: Are They Compatible?" *Poultry Science* 78, no. 5 (1999): 660–73. https://doi.org/10.1093/ps/78.5.660.
12. Robson, David. "The '3.5% Rule': How a Small Minority Can Change the World." *BBC*, May 13, 2019. https://www.bbc.com/future/article/20190513-it-only-takes-35-of-people-to-change-the-world.
13. Ibid.
14. Ibid.

Chapter 8: Metaphorical Fences to Be Broken

1. APE: Animal Protection Education. "Legal Personhood." Accessed September 29, 2023. https://voiceless.org.au/schools/legal-personhood/; Stein, Elizabeth. "Legal Persons Capable of 'Rights or Duties,' Not 'Rights and Duties.'" Nonhuman Rights Project, April 6, 2017. https://www.nonhumanrights.org/blog/rights-or-duties/.
2. Linder, Douglas O. "Animal Rights on Trial." Famous Trials, accessed September 29, 2023. https://famous-trials.com/animalrights/; Nonhuman Rights Project. "Tommy: The NhRP's First Client." Accessed September 29, 2023. https://www.nonhumanrights.org/client-tommy/.
3. Ibid.
4. Warne, Kennedy. "This River in New Zealand Is a Legal Person. How Will It Use Its Voice?" *National Geographic*, April 22, 2019. https://www.nationalgeographic.com/culture/2019/04/maori-river-in-new-zealand-is-a-legal-person/.
5. APE: Animal Protection Education. "Legal Personhood." Accessed September 29, 2023. https://voiceless.org.au/schools/legal-personhood/; Stein, Elizabeth. "Legal Persons Capable of 'Rights or Duties,' Not 'Rights and Duties.'" Nonhuman Rights Project, April 6, 2017. https://www.nonhumanrights.org/blog/rights-or-duties/.

6. Fieldstadt, Elisha, and Tim Stelloh. "Outrage Grows After Gorilla Harambe Shot Dead at Cincinnati Zoo to Save Tot." *NBC News*, updated May 31, 2016. https://www.nbcnews.com/news/us-news/outrage-grows-after-gorilla-harambe-shot-dead-cincinnati-zoo-save-n582706.
7. Linder, Douglas O. "Animal Rights on Trial." Famous Trials, accessed September 29, 2023. https://famous-trials.com/animalrights/.
8. Choplin, Lauren. "Chimpanzee Recognized as Legal Person." Nonhuman Rights Project, December 5, 2016. https://www.nonhumanrights.org/blog/cecilia-chimpanzee-legal-person/.
9. Hedges, Chris. "'What Every Person Should Know About War.'" *The New York Times*, July 6, 2003. https://www.nytimes.com/2003/07/06/books/chapters/what-every-person-should-know-about-war.html; FAO. "Food and Agriculture Data." Accessed September 29, 2023. https://www.fao.org/faostat/en/#home.
10. JBS. "Annual and Sustainability Report." 2019. https://apicatalog.mziq.com/filemanager/v2/d/043a77c1-0127-4502-bc5b-21427b991b22/41de5cc6-19dd-a604-4cc3-89450a520625?origin=1.
11. Mongabay. "Investigation Links Meat Giant JBS to Amazon Deforestation." July 27, 2020. https://news.mongabay.com/2020/07/investigation-links-meat-giant-jbs-to-amazon-deforestation/.
12. JBS USA. "Who We Are: About Our Company." Accessed September 29, 2023. https://sustainability.jbsfoodsgroup.com/chapters/who-we-are/about-our-company/.
13. Earthsight. "Bad Beef: UK Retailers Feed Illegal Deforestation Fears as JBS Corned Beef Imports Persist." May 5, 2019. https://www.earthsight.org.uk/news/idm/brazil-corned-beef-jbs-uk-supermarkets-deforestation-amazon; Phillips, Dom, Daniel Camargos, Andre Campos, et al. "Revealed: Rampant Deforestation of Amazon Driven by Global Greed for Meat." *The Guardian*, July 2, 2019. https://www.theguardian.com/environment/2019/jul/02/revealed-amazon-deforestation-driven-global-greed-meat-brazil; PETA Investigates. "Calves Dragged and Face-Branded for Leather Car Interiors." Accessed September 29, 2023. https://investigations.peta.org/calves-face-branded-leather-car-interiors/.
14. Greger, Michael. "Peeks Behind the Egg Industry Curtain." Nutrition Facts, updated December 22, 2020. https://nutritionfacts.org/blog/peeks-behind-the-egg-industry-curtain/.
15. American Egg Boards. "Luci, Luke, the Importance of Awards in Advertising." Ads of the World, February 2009. https://www.adsoftheworld.com/campaigns/luci.
16. World Health Organization. "Cancer: Carcinogenicity of the Consumption of Red Meat and Processed Meat." October 26, 2015. https://www.who.int/news-room/questions-and-answers/item/cancer-carcinogenicity-of-the-consumption-of-red-meat-and-processed-meat; Harvard Health Publishing.

"What's the Beef with Red Meat?" February 1, 2020. https://www.health.harvard.edu/staying-healthy/whats-the-beef-with-red-meat.

17. Meat & Livestock Australia. "New MLA Ads Show Australian Women 'You're Better on Beef.'" April 1, 2016. https://www.mla.com.au/news-and-events/industry-news/archived/2016/new-mla-ads-show-australian-women-youre-better-on-beef-/#.
18. Lilydale Free Range Chicken. "Dedication You Can Taste, Lilydale Free Range Chicken." YouTube video, 0:30, July 19, 2020. https://www.youtube.com/watch?v=i4DjJm1pUgY.
19. Lilydale Free Range Chicken. "FAQ." Accessed September 29, 2023. https://lilydalefreerange.com.au/faq.
20. Free Range Egg and Poultry Australia. "FREPA Chicken Meat Standard." September 10, 2020. https://frepa.com.au/wp-content/uploads/2020/09/FREPA-Chicken-Meat-Standard-Sept-2020.pdf.
21. Francis, C. "Victoria Plans $900K Campaign to Counter Activists' Message." *The Weekly Times*, 2019. https://www.weeklytimesnow.com.au/subscribe/news/1/?sourceCode=WTWEB_WRE170_a&dest=https%3A%2F%2Fwww.weeklytimesnow.com.au%2Fnews%2Fvictoria%2Fvictoria-plans-900k-campaign-to-counter-animal-activists-message%2Fnews-story%2F416736ecb187880523966d840203a1c1&memtype=anonymous&mode=premium.
22. Australian Government Department of Agriculture, Fisheries and Forestry. "Leviable Commodities." Accessed September 29, 2023. https://www.agriculture.gov.au/agriculture-land/farm-food-drought/levies/commodities#horticulture; Australian Government Department of Agriculture, Fisheries and Forestry. "Levies and Charges." Accessed September 29, 2023. https://www.agriculture.gov.au/agriculture-land/farm-food-drought/levies.
23. Meat and Livestock Australia. "Financial Report." 2019. https://www.mla.com.au/globalassets/mla-corporate/about-mla/documents/ar-2018-19/financial-report-mla-annual-report-2018-19.pdf.
24. Australian Government Department of Agriculture and Water Resources, Meat & Livestock Australia. "Funding Agreement 2016–2020." October 13, 2016. https://www.mla.com.au/globalassets/mla-corporate/about-mla/documents/planning--reporting/2016-2020-sfa-signed-13-october-2016.pdf; Australian Government Department of Agriculture, Water and the Environment, Australian Pork Limited. Funding Agreement, 2013; Dairy Australia. Strategic Plan, 2017; Australian Government Department of Agriculture, Water and the Environment, Dairy Australia. Statutory Funding Contract, 2013; Australian Government Department of Agriculture, Water and the Environment, Australian Wool Innovation. Statutory Funding Agreement, 2016; Australian Government Department of Agriculture, Water and the Environment, Australian Live Export Corporation. Funding Agreement, 2017.
25. Orden, David, and Carl Zulauf. "Political Economy of the 2014 Farm Bill." *American Journal of Agricultural Economics* 97, no. 5 (2015): 1298–311. https://www.jstor.org/stable/24477205.

26. Sheingate, Adam, Allysan Scatterday, Bob Martin, et al. "Post-Exceptionalism and Corporate Interests in US Agricultural Policy." *Journal of European Public Policy* 24, no. 11 (2017): 1641–657. https://doi.org/10.1080/13501763.2017.1334082.
27. Sainato, Michael. "'I Can't Get Above Water': How America's Chicken Giant Perdue Controls Farmers." *The Guardian*, March 14, 2020. https://www.theguardian.com/environment/2020/mar/14/i-cant-get-above-water-how-americas-chicken-giant-perdue-controls-farmers; Leggate, James. "American Farms Are Billions in Debt. The Numbers Are Eye-Popping." *Fox Business*, August 14, 2019. https://www.foxbusiness.com/economy/american-farms-billions-debt; Mock, Sarah. "From Farm to Factory: The Unstoppable Rise of American Chicken." *The Guardian*, August 17, 2020. https://www.theguardian.com/environment/2020/aug/17/from-farm-to-factory-the-unstoppable-rise-of-american-chicken.
28. Stein, Jeff. "President Trump Signs $867 Billion Farm Bill into Law." *The Washington Post*, December 20, 2018. https://www.washingtonpost.com/business/2018/12/20/president-trump-signs-billion-farm-bill-into-law/; LaFraniere, Sharon. "Farmers Get Billions in Virus Aid, and Democrats Are Wary." *New York Times*, updated June 9, 2020. https://www.nytimes.com/2020/06/07/us/politics/virus-trump-aid-farmers.html.
29. Moon, Wanki, and Gabriel Pino. "Do U.S. Citizens Support Government Intervention in Agriculture? Implications for the Political Economy of Agricultural Protection." *Agricultural Economics* 49 (2017): 119–29. https://doi.org/10.1111/agec.12400.
30. Dohms-Harter, E. "Animal Rights Activist's New Purpose Is Helping Factory Farmers." Wisconsin Public Radio, 2020.
31. Bellemare, Marc F., and Nicholas Carnes. "Why Do Members of Congress Support Agricultural Protection?" *Food Policy* (2015): 20–34. https://people.duke.edu/~nwc8/Bellemare_Carnes.pdf.
32. *Forbes*. "Perdue Family: $3.2B." 2015 America's Richest Families Net Worth, July 1, 2015. https://www.forbes.com/profile/perdue/?sh=3656d12145aa.
33. Farm Aid. "What's In the 2018 Farm Bill? The Good, the Bad and the Offal. . . ." December 20, 2018. https://www.farmaid.org/issues/farm-policy/whats-in-the-2018-farm-bill-the-good-the-bad-and-the-offal/.
34. Bellemare, Marc F., and Nicholas Carnes. "Why Do Members of Congress Support Agricultural Protection?" *Food Policy* (2015): 20–34. https://people.duke.edu/~nwc8/Bellemare_Carnes.pdf.
35. Badger, Emily. "As American as Apple Pie? The Rural Vote's Disproportionate Slice of Power." *New York Times*, November 20, 2016. https://www.nytimes.com/2016/11/21/upshot/as-american-as-apple-pie-the-rural-votes-disproportionate-slice-of-power.html.
36. Marshall, Andrew. "NFF and Agribusiness Lobby Target $100b Ag Production Agenda." Farm Online National, updated August 5, 2018. https://www.farmonline.com.au/story/5568463/nff-and-agribusiness-target-100b-ag-production-agenda/.

37. Levitt, Tom. "Nearly a Fifth of the EU's Budget Goes on Livestock Farming, Says Greenpeace." *The Guardian*, February 12, 2019. https://www.theguardian.com/environment/2019/feb/12/nearly-a-fifth-of-eu-budget-goes-on-livestock-farming-greenpeace; Eurostat. "EU Key Indicators." Accessed September 29, 2023. https://ec.europa.eu/eurostat/.
38. Vegan Society of Canada. "Show Me the Money: Following the Money Trail of Animal Agriculture." Updated August 16, 2022. https://www.vegancanada.org/news/article/2020/01/04/animal-agriculture-money-trail.html.
39. Futureye. "Australia's Shifting Mindset on Farm Animal Welfare." 2018.
40. Lake Research Partners. "Results from a Recent Survey of American Consumers." June 29, 2016. https://www.aspca.org/sites/default/files/aspca-2016_labeling_survey.pdf.
41. European Commission. "Animal Welfare Labelling." Accessed September 29, 2023. https://food.ec.europa.eu/animals/animal-welfare/other-aspects-animal-welfare/animal-welfare-labelling_en.
42. Thompson, E. "How the USDA Allows Producers to Use 'Humane' and 'Sustainable' Claims on Meat Packages and Deceive Consumers." Animal Welfare Institute, 2019; Lake Research Partners. "Results from a Recent Survey of American Consumers." June 29, 2016. https://www.aspca.org/sites/default/files/aspca-2016_labeling_survey.pdf.
43. Garcés, Leah. *Grilled: Turning Adversaries into Allies to Change the Chicken Industry*. London: Bloomsbury Sigma, 2019.
44. Federal Register of Legislation. "Australian Consumer Law (Free Range Egg Labelling) Information Standard 2017." Accessed September 29, 2023. https://www.legislation.gov.au/Details/F2017L00474/Explanatory%20Statement/Text.
45. RSPCA Approved Farming. "Why Choose RSPCA Approved." Accessed September 29, 2023. https://rspcaapproved.org.au/why-choose/#intro.
46. Smith, Alexandra. "Consumers Duped by RSPCA, Farmers Claim." *The Sydney Morning Herald*, January 9, 2012. https://www.smh.com.au/environment/conservation/consumers-duped-by-rspca-farmers-claim-20120108-1pq77.html.
47. Animal Rights. "Pig Truth." Vimeo video, 5:00, 2015. https://vimeo.com/147914620; Hamblin, Andrea. "Animal Liberation Victoria Claims Pigs Suffer Horrific Deaths When Killed Using Carbon Dioxide." *Herald Sun*, December 7, 2015. https://www.heraldsun.com.au/news/animal-liberation-victoria-claims-pigs-suffer-horrific-deaths-when-killed-using-carbon-dioxide/news-story/c3194210f834052c9bc3b017a6304e8b.
48. Aussie Farms. Submission—Inquiry into the Impact of Animal Rights Activism on Victorian Agriculture. Parliament Victoria, 2019; RSPCA Approved Farming. "RSPCA Approved Farming Scheme Standards: Pigs." November 2018. https://rspcaapproved.org.au/wp-content/uploads/2022/03/2018-11_PIGS_Standards.pdf.

49. Diamond Valley Pork. Submission—Inquiry into the Impact of Animal Rights Activism on Victorian Agriculture." July 31, 2019. https://www.parliament.vic.gov.au/images/stories/committees/SCEI/Animal_rights_activism/Submissions/S251_-_Diamond_Valley_Pork_Redacted.pdf.
50. RSPCA Approved Farming. "RSPCA Approved Farming Scheme Standards: Pigs." November 2018. https://rspcaapproved.org.au/wp-content/uploads/2022/03/2018-11_PIGS_Standards.pdf.
51. RSPCA Approved Farming. "RSPCA Approved Farming Scheme Standard: Meat Chickens." August 2020. https://rspcaapproved.org.au/wp-content/uploads/2022/03/2020_08_MEATCHICKENS_Standard_v1.1.pdf.
52. RSPCA Approved Farming. "RSPCA Approved Farming Scheme Standards: Layer Hens." September 2015. https://rspcaapproved.org.au/wp-content/uploads/2022/03/RSPCALayerhensStandards.pdf; RSPCA. "What Is Beak TrimmingandWhyIsItCarriedOut?"AccessedSeptember29,2023.https://kb.rspca.org.au/knowledge-base/what-is-beak-trimming-and-why-is-it-carried-out/.
53. Machin, Karen L. "Avian Pain: Physiology and Evaluation." *Compendium* 27, no. 2 (2005): 98–109. https://vetfolio-vetstreet.s3.amazonaws.com/mmah/63/dfdc71c01717f0a2ee3674ebd81438/filePV_27_02_98.pdf.
54. Sheep Inc. Accessed September 29, 2023. https://us.sheepinc.com/.
55. Sheep Inc, @sheepinc. "Professor Fluffykins." Instagram, 2020; Sheep Inc, @sheepinc. "Bruce." Instagram, 2020; Sheep Inc, @sheepinc. "Big boy." Instagram, 2020; ZQ Natural Fibre. "Animal Welfare." Accessed September 29, 2023. https://www.discoverzq.com/animal-welfare.
56. Textile Exchange. "The Responsible Down Standard Aims to Protect Ducks and Geese Used for Down." Accessed September 29, 2023. https://textileexchange.org/responsible-down-standard/.
57. Boffey, Daniel. "'Veggie Discs' to Replace Veggie Burgers in EU Crackdown on Food Labels." *The Guardian*, April 4, 2019. https://www.theguardian.com/food/2019/apr/04/eu-to-ban-non-meat-product-labels-veggie-burgers-and-vegan-steaks; Irfan, Umair. "'Fake Milk': Why the Dairy Industry Is Boiling over Plant-Based Milks." *Vox*, updated December 21, 2018. https://www.vox.com/2018/8/31/17760738/almond-milk-dairy-soy-oat-labeling-fda; Barbour, Lucy. "Nationals Push for Ban on Plant-Based, Alternative Products Being Called 'Milk,' 'Meat,' 'Seafood.'" *ABC News*, updated September 14, 2019. https://www.abc.net.au/news/2019-09-15/push-to-ban-milk-meat-seafood-labels-on-plant-based-produce/11513754; Leather International. "German Leather Federation in Bid to Ban Terms Like 'Vegan Leather.'" August 20, 2019. http://www.leathermag.com/news/newsgerman-leather-federation-in-bid-to-ban-terms-like-vegan-leather-7374920.
58. Jasper, Clint. "Dairy Farmers Seek Public Support over Push to Stop Plant-Based Alternatives Being Called 'Milk.'" *ABC News*,

August 9, 2017. https://www.abc.net.au/news/rural/2017-08-10/dairy-farmers-push-to-tighten-use-of-milk-food-labelling/8790294.

59. Sustainable Apparel Coalition. "The Higg Index." Accessed September 29, 2023. https://apparelcoalition.org/the-higg-index/; Bijleveld, Marijn. "Natural Mink Fur and Faux Fur Products, an Environmental Comparison." Delft, June 2013. https://www.furfreealliance.com/wp-content/uploads/2016/01/CE_Delft_22203_Natural_mink_fur_and_faux_fur_products_DEF-1.pdf; Fur Free NYC. "Fur Industry Lies." January 1, 2020. https://www.furfreenyc.com/blog/fur-industry-lies.
60. Debeer, Lies. "High Solids Anaerobic Biodegradation and Disintegration Test of Undyed Mink Fur, Undyed Fox Fur, Dyed Mink Fur and Fake Fur." Fur Europe, May 25, 2018. https://www.sustainablefur.com/wp-content/uploads/2018/12/Biodragadation_and_Disintegration_test_of_fur.pdf.
61. The Humane Society of the United States. "Toxic Fur. The Impacts of Fur Production on the Environment and the Risks to Human Health." January 29, 2009. https://www.furfreealliance.com/wp-content/uploads/2019/09/HSUS_EN_Toxic-fur-Report-2009.pdf.
62. Mythical Mia, @mythical.mia. "Today 16 lives were rescued. . . . ' Instagram, 2019.
63. Studio 10. "Hot Topic: Vegan Claims She Was Chased & Shot At.." Facebook video, 2:06, September 5, 2019. https://www.facebook.com/watch/?v=2376601722668144.
64. Parliament of Victoria. "Parliamentary Debates (Hansard): Legislative Council, Fifty-Ninth Parliament, First Session." May 1, 2019. https://www.parliament.vic.gov.au/images/stories/daily-hansard/Council_2019/Legislative_Council_2019-05-01.pdf; Hope, Zach. "'You're a Walking Talking Corpse': Vile Threats Toward Vegan Activist." *The Age*, April 13, 2019. https://www.theage.com.au/national/victoria/you-re-a-walking-talking-corpse-vile-threats-toward-vegan-activist-20190411-p51d2z.html.
65. Contemptor. "Seb Gorka Warns That Democrats 'Want to Take Away Your Hamburgers': Stalin Dreamed About This!" YouTube video, 3:05, February 28, 2019. https://www.youtube.com/watch?v=Pm62gg8A1VU; Blum, Jeremy. "Mike Pence Says He'll Keep Kamala Harris From Meddling with America's Meat." *HuffPost*, August 14, 2020. https://www.huffpost.com/entry/mike-pence-kamala-harris-meat_n_5f3614dbc5b69fa9e2f938fc.
66. Gorvett, Zaria. "The Mystery of Why There Are More Women Vegans." *BBC*, February 18, 2020. https://www.bbc.com/future/article/20200214-the-mystery-of-why-there-are-more-women-vegans; Henderson, Alex. "Inside the 'Soy Boy' Conspiracy Theory: It Combines Misogyny and the Warped World of Pseudoscience." *Salon*, November 14, 2018. https://www.salon.com/2018/11/14/the-soy-boy-conspiracy-theory-alt-right-thinks-left-wing-has-it-out-for-them-with-soybeans_partner/.
67. Reiley, Laura. "The Fastest-Growing Vegan Demographic Is African Americans. Wu-Tang Clan and Other Hip-Hop Acts Paved the Way." *The Washington Post*,

January 24, 2020. https://www.washingtonpost.com/business/2020/01/24/fastest-growing-vegan-demographic-is-african-americans-wu-tang-clan-other-hip-hop-acts-paved-way/; Laws, Rita. "History of Vegetarianism: Native Americans and Vegetarianism." International Vegetarian Union, accessed September 29, 2023. https://ivu.org/history/native_americans.html; Sarambi. "Deconstructing Myths Surrounding Veganism & People of Color." The Anarchist Library, accessed September 29, 2023. https://theanarchistlibrary.org/library/sarambi-deconstructing-myths-surrounding-veganism-people-of-color.

Chapter 9: The Movement in the Mainstream

1. Yaser, Jessica. "The Environmental Impact of Meat Consumption: Meatless Monday Can Do More Good Than You Think." School of Public Health, University of Michigan, January 2, 2019. https://sph.umich.edu/pursuit/2019posts/meatless-monday-010219.html.
2. Chang, Ha-Joon. *23 Things They Don't Tell You About Capitalism.* London: Penguin, 2010.
3. Gay, Roxane. "Where Are the Serious Movies About Non-Suffering Black People?" *Vulture*, November 6, 2013. https://www.vulture.com/2013/11/12-years-a-slave-black-oscar-bait-essay.html.
4. Erastova, Anastasia. "Woman Adopts a 10-Year-Old Goldfish and Completely Transforms Him." *The Dodo*, August 21, 2020. https://www.thedodo.com/videos/our-shows/woman-adopts-a-10-year-old-goldfish-and-completely-transforms-him.
5. The Dodo, @thedodo. "10-year-old goldfish turned bright red after he got adopted—and found a girlfriend!" Instagram, August 30, 2020. https://www.instagram.com/p/CEhWO93FW-3/.
6. VeganForVendetta. "Huntingdon Life Sciences—Pure Evil!" YouTube video, 6:17, June 12, 2017, https://www.youtube.com/watch?v=dPIHFQoH29k
7. Beagle Freedom Project. Accessed September 29, 2023. https://bfp.org.
8. Suchan, Casey, and Denis Henry Hennelly, directors. *The Animal People.* Jorja Fox, Andy Roth, Mikko Alanne, et al., 2019. https://www.imdb.com/title/tt2337280/.
9. International Council of Tanners. "Statistics & Sources of Information." Accessed September 29, 2023. https://leather-council.org/information/statistics-sources-of-information/.
10. The Vegan View. "Collective Liberation!" YouTube video, 0:58, August 3, 2020. https://www.youtube.com/watch?v=hTd1H3EU5W8.
11. Food and Agricultural Organization of the United Nations. "Food and Agricultural Data." Accessed September 29, 2023. http://www.fao.org/faostat/en/#home.
12. Edgar's Mission. "Edgar's Mission Passport: Clarabelle & Valentine." Updated November 28, 2014. https://edgarsmission.org.au/animal/clarabelle-and-valentine/; Nielsen, Ole Bødtker, and Percy W. Hawkes. "Fetal Bovine Serum and the Slaughter of Pregnant Cows: Animal Welfare and Ethics."

BioProcessing Journal (January 2019). https://www.serumindustry.org/uploads/cms/nav-42-5c3a30db2162f.pdf; Ladds, P.W., P.M. Summers, and J.D. Humphrey. "Pregnancy in Slaughtered Cows in North-Eastern Australia: Incidence and Relationship to Pregnancy Diagnosis, Season, Age and Carcase Weight." *Australian Veterinary Journal* 51, no. 10 (1975): 472–7. https://doi.org/10.1111/j.1751-0813.1975.tb02383.x.

13. Edgar's Mission. "Edgar's Mission Passport: Clarabelle & Valentine." Updated November 28, 2014. https://edgarsmission.org.au/animal/clarabelle-and-valentine/; Grandin, Temple. "Thinking the Way Animals Do: Unique Insights from a Person with a Singular Understanding." *Western Horseman* (November 1997): 140–5, updated January 2015. https://www.grandin.com/references/thinking.animals.html.
14. Edgar's Mission. "Kind Christmas." Accessed September 29, 2023. https://edgarsmission.org.au/campaign/kindchristmas/.

Chapter 10: The Time Is Now

1. Barrett, Mike, Alan Belward, Sarah Bladen, et al. "Living Planet Report 2018: Aiming Higher." World Wildlife Fund, 2018. https://www.worldwildlife.org/pages/living-planet-report-2018.
2. Werner, Joel, and Suzannah Lyons. "The Size of Australia's Bushfire Crisis Captured in Five Big Numbers." *ABC News*, March 4, 2020. https://www.abc.net.au/news/science/2020-03-05/bushfire-crisis-five-big-numbers/12007716; The University of Sydney. "3 Billion Animals Impacted by Fires Including 60,000 Koalas: Report." December 7, 2020. https://www.sydney.edu.au/news-opinion/news/2020/12/07/3-billion-animals-impacted-by-fires-including-60000-koalas-repor.html.
3. Revkin, A. "Climate Change First Became News 30 Years Ago. Why Haven't We Fixed It?" *National Geographic*, 2018. https://www.nationalgeographic.com/magazine/2018/07/embark-essay-climate-change-pollution-revkin/.
4. Bond, Chelsea. "Starting at Strengths . . . An Indigenous Early Years Intervention." *Medical Journal of Australia* 191, no. 3 (2009): 175–7. https://doi.org/10.5694/j.1326-5377.2009.tb02733.x.
5. Thornton, Alex. "This Is How Many Animals We Eat Each Year." World Economic Forum, February 8, 2019. https://www.weforum.org/agenda/2019/02/chart-of-the-day-this-is-how-many-animals-we-eat-each-year/.
6. United Nations Climate Change. "The Paris Agreement." Accessed September 29, 2023. https://unfccc.int/process-and-meetings/the-paris-agreement/the-paris-agreement.
7. Food and Agricultural Organization of the United Nations. "Livestock's Long Shadow: Environmental Issues and Options." 2006. http://www.fao.org/3/a-a0701e.pdf.
8. Ibid; Hickman, Leo. "Do Critics of UN Meat Report Have a Beef with Transparency?" *The Guardian*, March 24, 2010. https://www.theguardian.com/environment/blog/2010/mar/24/un-meat-report-climate-change.

9. The Good Food Institute. "IPCC: Plant-Based and Cultivated Meat Can Play a Critical Role in Halving Global Emissions by 2030." Accessed September 29, 2023. https://gfi.org/press/ipcc-plant-based-and-cultivated-meat-critical-in-halving-global-emissions-by-2030/#:~:text=WASHINGTON%20%E2%80%94%20The%20Intergovernmental%20Panel%20on,halve%20global%20emissions%20by%202030.
10. Carrington, Damian. "Avoiding Meat and Dairy Is 'Single Biggest Way' to Reduce Your Impact on Earth." *The Guardian*, May 31, 2018. https://www.theguardian.com/environment/2018/may/31/avoiding-meat-and-dairy-is-single-biggest-way-to-reduce-your-impact-on-earth; Hakansson, Emma. "The IPCC's Mitigation of Climate Change Report Explained, and What It Means for the Fashion Industry." Collective Fashion Justice, accessed September 29, 2023. https://www.collectivefashionjustice.org/articles/the-ipccs-mitigation-of-climate-change-report-explained-and-what-it-means-for-the-fashion-industry.
11. Poore, J, and T. Nemecek. "Reducing Food's Environmental Impacts Through Producers and Consumers." *Science* 360, no. 6392 (June 2018): 987–92. https://doi.org/10.1126/science.aaq021.
12. Hakansson, Emma. "The Carbon Cost of Our Leather Goods, Calculated." Collective Fashion Justice, accessed September 29, 2023. https://www.collectivefashionjustice.org/articles/carbon-cost-leather-goods.
13. Poore, J, and T. Nemecek. "Reducing Food's Environmental Impacts Through Producers and Consumers." *Science* 360, no. 6392 (June 2018): 987–92. https://doi.org/10.1126/science.aaq021.
14. John Hopkins Center for a Livable Future. "A Response to Dr. Franklin Mitloehner's White Paper, 'Livestock's Contributions to Climate Change: Facts and Fiction.'" Accessed September 29, 2023. https://clf.jhsph.edu/sites/default/files/2019-04/frank-mitloehner-white-paper-letter.pdf.
15. Pearce, Fred. "As Climate Change Worsens, A Cascade of Tipping Points Looms." Yale Environment 360, December 5, 2019. https://e360.yale.edu/features/as-climate-changes-worsens-a-cascade-of-tipping-points-looms.
16. Weisse, Mikaela, and Elizabeth Goldman. "We Lost a Football Pitch of Primary Rainforest Every 6 Seconds in 2019." World Resources Institute, June 2, 2020. https://www.wri.org/blog/2020/06/global-tree-cover-loss-data-2019.
17. A Well-Fed World. "Deforestation." Updated June 1, 2020. https://awellfedworld.org/deforestation/.
18. Ibid.
19. Zia, Mustafa, James Hansen, Kim Hjort, et al. "Brazil Once Again Becomes the World's Largest Beef Exporter." USDA Economic Research Service, July 1, 2019. https://www.ers.usda.gov/amber-waves/2019/july/brazil-once-again-becomes-the-world-s-largest-beef-exporter/; International Council of Tanners. "Statistics & Sources of Information." Accessed September 29, 2023. https://leather-council.org/information/statistics-sources-of-information/.
20. Australian Collaborative Land Use and Management Program. "Land Use in Australia—At a Glance." Accessed September 29, 2023. https://www.

agriculture.gov.au/sites/default/files/abares/aclump/documents/Land%20use%20in%20Australia%20at%20a%20glance%202016.pdf.

21. Greenpeace European Unit. "Feeding the Problem: The Dangerous Intensification of Animal Farming in Europe." December 2, 2019. https://www.greenpeace.org/eu-unit/issues/nature-food/1803/feeding-problem-dangerous-intensification-animal-farming/.
22. De Ruiter, Henri, Jennie I. Macdiarmid, Robin B., Matthews, et al. "Total Global Agricultural Land Footprint Associated with UK Food Supply 1986–2011." *Global Environmental Change* 43 (March 2017): 72–81. https://doi.org/10.1016/j.gloenvcha.2017.01.007.
23. Merrill, Dave, and Lauren Leatherby. "Here's How America Uses Its Land." *Bloomberg*, July 31, 2018. https://www.bloomberg.com/graphics/2018-us-land-use/.
24. Ritchie, Hannah, and Max Roser. "Land Use." Our World in Data, September 2019. https://ourworldindata.org/land-use#citation.
25. Poore, J., and T. Nemecek. "Reducing Food's Environmental Impacts Through Producers and Consumers." *Science* 360, no. 6392 (June 2018): 987–92. https://doi.org/10.1126/science.aaq021.
26. Carrington, Damian. "Avoiding Meat and Dairy Is 'Single Biggest Way' to Reduce Your Impact on Earth." *The Guardian*, May 31, 2018. https://www.theguardian.com/environment/2018/may/31/avoiding-meat-and-dairy-is-single-biggest-way-to-reduce-your-impact-on-earth.
27. United Nation Convention to Combat Desertification. "Data and Facts About Recent Assessments of Land Degradation." Accessed September 29, 2023. https://www.unccd.int/sites/default/files/relevant-links/2019-06/Summary_Assessement_Land_Degradation.pdf.
28. McLaughlin, Kathleen. "Exploding Demand for Cashmere Wool Is Ruining Mongolia's Grasslands." *Science*, January 30, 2019. https://www.science.org/content/article/exploding-demand-cashmere-wool-ruining-mongolia-s-grasslands.
29. Franklin, Jonathan. "Can the World's Most Ambitious Rewilding Project Restore Patagonia's Beauty?" *The Guardian*, May 30, 2018. https://www.theguardian.com/environment/2018/may/30/can-the-worlds-largest-rewilding-project-restore-patagonias-beauty.
30. Environment Agency. "Phosphorus and Freshwater Eutrophication Pressure Narrative." October 2019. https://consult.environment-agency.gov.uk/environment-and-business/challenges-and-choices/user_uploads/phosphorus-pressure-rbmp-2021.pdf; Weaver, David, and Robert Summers. "Soil Factors Influencing Eutrophication. In Soilguide. A Handbook for Understanding and Managing Agricultural Soils." Government of Western Australia: Department of Primary Industries and Regional Development, 2001. https://library.dpird.wa.gov.au/cgi/viewcontent.cgi?article=1060&context=bulletins.

31. Amirkolaie, Abdolsamad K. "Reduction in the Environmental Impact of Waste Discharged by Fish Farms Through Feed and Feeding." *Reviews in Aquaculture* 3, no. 1 (2011): 19–26. https://doi.org/10.1111/j.1753-5131.2010.01040.x.
32. Zielinski, Sarah. "Ocean Dead Zones Are Getting Worse Globally Due to Climate Change." *Smithsonian Magazine*, November 10, 2014. https://www.smithsonianmag.com/science-nature/ocean-dead-zones-are-getting-worse-globally-due-climate-change-180953282/.
33. Bagley, Carley Anderson. "Potential Risk Factors of Amoebic Gill Disease in Tasmanian Atlantic Salmon." Thesis, University of Tasmania, 2006. https://eprints.utas.edu.au/19226/; Boison, Solomon Antwi, Bjarne Gjerde, Borghild Hillestad, et al. "Genomic and Transcriptomic Analysis of Amoebic Gill Disease Resistance in Atlantic Salmon (*Salmo salar* L.)." *Frontiers in Genetics* 10 (2019). https://doi.org/10.3389/fgene.2019.00068.
34. Adams, Lucy. "Is There a Problem with Salmon Farming?" *BBC News*, May 20, 2019. https://www.bbc.com/news/uk-scotland-48266480; Edwards, Rob. "Horror Photos of Farmed Salmon Spark Legal Threat." The Ferret, June 27, 2018. https://theferret.scot/pictures-diseases-farmed-fish/.
35. Peeler, E.J, and A.G. Murray. "Disease Interaction Between Farmed and Wild Fish Populations." *Journal of Fish Biology* 65 (2004): 321–2. https://doi.org/10.1111/j.0022-1112.2004.0559s.x.
36. Thorstad, Eva B., Ian A. Fleming, Philip McGinnity, et al. "Incidence and Impacts of Escaped Farmed Atlantic Salmon *Salmo salar* in Nature." NINA Special Report 36, 2008. http://www.fao.org/3/a-aj272e.pdf.
37. Adams, Lucy. "Is There a Problem with Salmon Farming?" *BBC News*, May 20, 2019. https://www.bbc.com/news/uk-scotland-48266480.
38. Yong, Ed. "Farmed Salmon Decimate Wild Populations by Exposing Them to Parasites." National Geographic, August 2, 2008. https://www.nationalgeographic.com/science/phenomena/2008/08/02/farmed-salmon-decimate-wild-populations-by-exposing-them-to-parasites/.
39. Animal Equality News. "Argentina Makes History with Salmon Farming Ban." July 8, 2021. https://animalequality.org/news/argentina-ban-salmon-farming/.
40. Chilcott, Lesley, director. *Watson.* Participant Media, 2019. https://www.imdb.com/title/tt10011252/.
41. IUCN Red List. "Tuna." Accessed September 29, 2023. https://www.iucnredlist.org/search?query=tuna&searchType=species.
42. Lindsay, Greg. "Bluefinger: The Race to Freeze or Breed Bluefin Tuna Before Extinction." Fast Company, August 9, 2011. https://www.fastcompany.com/1772179/bluefinger-race-freeze-or-breed-bluefin-tuna-extinction.
43. Chilcott, Lesley, director. *Watson.* Participant Media, 2019. https://www.imdb.com/title/tt10011252/; Paris, Francesca. "Threatened Bluefin Tuna Sells for $3 Million in Tokyo Market." NPR Environment, January 5, 2019. https://www.npr.org/2019/01/05/682526465/threatened-bluefin-tuna-sells-for-5-000-per-pound-in-tokyo-market.

44. Novogratz, Amy, and Mike Velings. "The End of Fish." *The Washington Post*, June 3, 2014. https://www.washingtonpost.com/posteverything/wp/2014/06/03/the-end-of-fish/.
45. Mukhisa, Kituyi. "90% of Fish Stocks Are Used Up—Fisheries Subsidies Must Stop." UNCTAD, July 13, 2018. https://unctad.org/news/90-fish-stocks-are-used-fisheries-subsidies-must-stop.
46. NOAA Fisheries. "Fishing Gear: Purse Seines." Accessed September 29, 2023. https://www.fisheries.noaa.gov/national/bycatch/fishing-gear-purse-seines; NOAA Fisheries. "Fishing Gear: Pelagic Longlines." Accessed September 29, 2023. https://www.fisheries.noaa.gov/national/bycatch/fishing-gear-pelagic-longlines.
47. Mukhisa, Kituyi. "90% of Fish Stocks Are Used Up—Fisheries Subsidies Must Stop." UNCTAD, July 13, 2018. https://unctad.org/news/90-fish-stocks-are-used-fisheries-subsidies-must-stop.
48. Roach, John. "Seafood May Be Gone by 2048, Study Says." *National Geographic*, November 2, 2006. https://www.nationalgeographic.com/animals/article/seafood-biodiversity; Pearl, Mike. "This Is Exactly What Will Happen After the Last Fish in the Ocean Dies." *Vice*, September 20, 2019. https://www.vice.com/en/article/qvg3zm/this-is-exactly-what-will-happen-after-the-last-fish-in-the-ocean-dies.
49. National Ocean Service. "How Much Oxygen Comes from the Ocean?" Accessed September 29, 2023. https://oceanservice.noaa.gov/facts/ocean-oxygen.html.
50. Collective Fashion Justice. "Native Crocodiles Confined and Killed for 'Luxury' Fashion." Accessed September 29, 2023. https://www.collectivefashionjustice.org/drop-croc.
51. Dell'Amore, Christine. "Species Extinction Happening 1,000 Times Faster Because of Humans?" *National Geographic*, May 30, 2014. https://www.nationalgeographic.com/adventure/article/140529-conservation-science-animals-species-endangered-extinction.
52. IUCN Red List. "Extinct." Accessed September 29, 2023. https://www.iucnredlist.org/search?redListCategory=ex.
53. UN Sustainable Development Goals. "UN Report: Nature's Dangerous Decline 'Unprecedented'; Species Extinction Rates 'Accelerating.'" May 6, 2019. https://www.un.org/sustainabledevelopment/blog/2019/05/nature-decline-unprecedented-report/.
54. Su, Yvonne. "UN Ruling Could Be a Game-Changer for Climate Refugees and Climate Action." *The Conversation*, January 28, 2020. https://theconversation.com/un-ruling-could-be-a-game-changer-for-climate-refugees-and-climate-action-130532.
55. Judd, Bridget, and Catherine Taylor. "Smoke and Bushfires Are the New Norm, So How Do We Beat the 'Airpocalypse'?" *ABC News*, updated December 9, 2019. https://www.abc.net.au/news/2019-12-07/nsw-fire-smoke-air-pollution-how-our-lives-will-need-to-change/11761098; Dick, Samantha. "Scientists

Say Australia's Worst-Ever Bushfire Season 'Not the New Normal.'" *The New Daily*, updated October 1, 2023. https://thenewdaily.com.au/news/national/2020/02/25/bushfires-not-new-normal/.

56. Podesta, John. "The Climate Crisis, Migration, and Refugees." Brookings, July 25, 2019. https://www.brookings.edu/research/the-climate-crisis-migration-and-refugees/#footnote-3.
57. Rigaud, Kanta Kumari, Alex de Sherbinin, Bryan Jones, et al. *Groundswell: Preparing for Internal Climate Migration.* World Bank, March 19, 2018. http://hdl.handle.net/10986/29461.
58. Rothkopf, David, and Claire Casey. "Impacts of Climate Change, Resource Scarcity and Foreign Policy." World Wildlife Fund, 2018. https://www.worldwildlife.org/magazine/issues/winter-2014/articles/impacts-of-climate-change-resource-scarcity-and-foreign-policy.
59. Foley, Jonathan. "A Five-Step Plan to Feed the World." *National Geographic Magazine*, accessed September 29, 2023. https://www.nationalgeographic.com/foodfeatures/feeding-9-billion/.
60. Berners-Lee, M., C. Kennelly, R. Watson, et al. "Current Global Food Production Is Sufficient to Meet Human Nutritional Needs in 2050 Provided There Is a Radical Societal Adaptation." *Elementa: Science of the Anthropocene* 6 (2018): 52. https://doi.org/10.1525/elementa.310.
61. World Health Organization. "World Hunger Is Still Not Going Down After Three Years and Obesity Is Still Growing—UN Report." July 15, 2019. https://www.who.int/news/item/15-07-2019-world-hunger-is-still-not-going-down-after-three-years-and-obesity-is-still-growing-un-report.
62. Mills, Nicole. "Bird Flu Outbreak Confirmed on Second Golden Plains Shire Free-Range Egg Farm, Prompting Warning for Producers." *ABC News*, August 7, 2020. https://www.abc.net.au/news/2020-08-07/bird-flu-avian-influenza-confirmed-on-egg-farm-golden-plains-vic/12529704.
63. Xinhua Net. "Philippines Culls Nearly 39,000 Chicken to Contain Bird Flu Outbreak." July 29, 2020. http://www.xinhuanet.com/english/2020-07/29/c_139248893.htm.
64. Agence France-Presse. "New Swine Flu with Pandemic Potential Identified by China Researchers." *The Guardian*, June 29, 2020. https://www.theguardian.com/world/2020/jun/30/new-swine-flu-with-pandemic-potential-identified-by-china-researchers.
65. Kesslen, Ben. "Here's Why Denmark Culled 17 Million Minks and Now Plans to Dig Up Their Buried Bodies. The Covid Mink Crisis, Explained." *NBC News*, December 1, 2020. https://www.nbcnews.com/news/animal-news/here-s-why-denmark-culled-17-million-minks-now-plans-n1249610.
66. Can, Özgün Emre, Neil D'Cruze, and David W. Macdonald. "Dealing in Deadly Pathogens: Taking Stock of the Legal Trade in Live Wildlife and Potential Risks to Human Health." *Global Ecology and Conservation* 17 (2019). https://doi.org/10.1016/j.gecco.2018.e00515.

67. Goug, A. "COVID-19 & Animal Exploitation: Preventing the Next Global Pandemic." Surge, 2020. https://www.surgeactivism.org/covid19.
68. World Health Organization. "Antibiotic Resistance." July 31, 2020. https://www.who.int/news-room/fact-sheets/detail/antibiotic-resistance.
69. *Science Daily*. "Antibiotic Resistance in Food Animals Nearly Tripled Since 2000." Princeton University, October 9, 2019. https://www.sciencedaily.com/releases/2019/10/191009132321.htm.
70. World Health Organization. "Antimicrobial Resistance: The Food Chain." November 1, 2017. https://www.who.int/news-room/questions-and-answers/item/antimicrobial-resistance-in-the-food-chain.
71. Martin, Michael J., Sapna E. Thottathil, and Thomas B. Newman. "Antibiotics Overuse in Animal Agriculture: A Call to Action for Health Care Providers." *American Journal of Public Health* 105, no. 12 (2015): 2409–10. https://doi.org/10.2105/AJPH.2015.302870.
72. *Science Daily*. "Antibiotic Resistance in Food Animals Nearly Tripled Since 2000." Princeton University, October 9, 2019. https://www.sciencedaily.com/releases/2019/10/191009132321.htm.
73. World Health Organization. "Antimicrobial Resistance: The Food Chain." November 1, 2017. https://www.who.int/news-room/questions-and-answers/item/antimicrobial-resistance-in-the-food-chain.
74. Torok, Simon. "Maker of the Miracle Mould." *ABC News*, accessed September 29, 2023. https://www.abc.net.au/science/slab/florey/story.htm.
75. Gupta, Mehr. "Diet and Disease." Kindness Project. Accessed March 25, 2023. https://web.archive.org/web/20230325082503/https://www.kindnessproject.org.au/issues/health/diet-and-disease/.
76. World Health Organization. "The Top 10 Causes of Death." December 9, 2020. https://www.who.int/news-room/fact-sheets/detail/the-top-10-causes-of-death.

Chapter 11: Systemic Change

1. Meadows, Donella H., Dennis L. Meadows, Jørgen Randers, et al. *The Limits to Growth*. New York: Universe Books, 1972.
2. Turner, Graham, and Cathy Alexander. "Limits to Growth Was Right. New Research Shows We're Nearing Collapse." *The Guardian*, September 1, 2014. https://www.theguardian.com/commentisfree/2014/sep/02/limits-to-growth-was-right-new-research-shows-were-nearing-collapse.
3. Meadows, Donella H., Dennis L. Meadows, Jørgen Randers, et al. *The Limits to Growth*. New York: Universe Books, 1972.
4. Animals Australia. "Koalas Are Being Bulldozed for Quarries & Cattle Farms." September 21, 2017. https://www.animalsaustralia.org/features/koalas-queensland-bulldozed-tree-land-clearing-beef.php.
5. Semuels, Alana. "Does the Economy Really Need to Keep Growing Quite So Much?" *The Atlantic*, November 4, 2016. https://www.theatlantic.com/business/archive/2016/11/economic-growth/506423/.

6. Ellsmoor, James. "New Zealand Ditches GDP for Happiness and Wellbeing." *Forbes*, July 11, 2019. https://www.forbes.com/sites/jamesellsmoor/2019/07/11/new-zealand-ditches-gdp-for-happiness-and-wellbeing/#3c9bad181942.
7. Kate Raworth: Exploring Doughnut Economics. "What on Earth Is the Doughnut?" Accessed September 29, 2023. https://www.kateraworth.com/doughnut/; Monbiot, George. "Is Protecting the Environment Incompatible with Social Justice?" *The Guardian*, February 13, 2012. https://www.theguardian.com/environment/georgemonbiot/2012/feb/13/protecting-environment-social-justice?.
8. Ellsmoor, James. "New Zealand Ditches GDP for Happiness and Wellbeing." *Forbes*, July 11, 2019. https://www.forbes.com/sites/jamesellsmoor/2019/07/11/new-zealand-ditches-gdp-for-happiness-and-wellbeing/#3c9bad181942.
9. Worm, Boris, and Robert T. Paine. "Humans as a Hyperkeystone Species." *Trends in Ecology & Evolution* 31, no. 8 (2016): 600–7. https://doi.org/10.1016/j.tree.2016.05.008.
10. Yong, Ed. "Humans: The Hyperkeystone Species." *The Atlantic*, June 21, 2016. https://www.theatlantic.com/science/archive/2016/06/humans-the-hyperkeystone-species/487985/.
11. Party for the Animals. "International Movement." Accessed September 29, 2023. https://www.partyfortheanimals.com/en/international-movement.
12. Ibid.
13. Emma Hurst MP: Animal Justice Party. "About the Animal Justice Party." Accessed September 29, 2023. https://www.emmahurstmp.com/ajp; Hurst, Emma. "City of Sydney Moves to Ban Fur in Australian First: Animal Justice Party MP Says Council Is Leading the Way for Change." Emma Hurst MP: Animal Justice Party, March 11, 2020. https://www.emmahurstmp.com/city_of_sydney_moves_to_ban_fur_in_australian_first; Hurst, Emma. "MP Response to New Report: Up to 3 in 5 Domestic Violence Victims Report Animal Abuse." Emma Hurst MP: Animal Justice Party, August 27, 2020. https://www.emmahurstmp.com/mp_response_to_new_report_domestic_violence.
14. We Are Union OHS Reps. "Industrial Manslaughter Laws." July 2020. https://www.ohsrep.org.au/industrial_manslaughter_laws.
15. Richings, Nadine. "Inquiry into Ecosystem Decline in Victoria." enRICHed Pursuits, September 25, 2020. https://new.parliament.vic.gov.au/4a4ce9/contentassets/477d3185890b4e988d1341b646f246fd/submission-documents/s925---enriched-pursuits_redacted.pdf; Dick, Samantha. "Wombats Now Protected All Over Victoria After Outrage Over Hunting Lodge." *The New Daily*, February 6, 2020. https://thenewdaily.com.au/news/national/2020/02/06/wombat-killing-laws-fixed/; We Are Union OHS Reps. "SafetyNet." Accessed 29, 2023. https://www.ohsrep.org.au/safetynet; Party for the Animals. "Australian Animal Justice Party Stops Draconian Laws that Attack Whistle-Blowers Who Expose Animal Cruelty." October 22, 2019. https://www.partyfortheanimals.com/en/australian-animal-justice-party-stops-draconian-laws-that-attack-whistle-blowers-who-expose-animal-cruelty; Price, Kimberly. "Western Victoria's Andy

Meddick, Transgender Eden Thrilled Birth Certificate Bill Passes. *The Standard*, updated September 1, 2019. https://www.standard.net.au/story/6355718/legislation-more-accepting-of-trans-and-gender-diverse-victorians/; Animal Justice Party. "Our Achievements Across Australia." Accessed September 29, 2023. https://www.animaljusticeparty.org/our_achievements.

16. The Greens. "Dr. Mehreen Faruqi." Accessed September 29, 2023. https://greens.org.au/nsw/person/mehreen-faruqi.
17. Ibid.
18. Animal Welfare Party. "Our Policies." Accessed September 29, 2023. https://www.animalwelfareparty.org/.
19. Mansoor, Sanya. "Environmental Injustice Is Another Form of 'Assault on Black Bodies,' Says Sen. Cory Booker." *Time*, July 9, 2020. https://time.com/5863757/cory-booker-environmental-injustice-race/; Miller, D. Lee, and Gregory Muren. "CAFOS: What We Don't Know Is Hurting Us." NRDC, September 2019. https://www.nrdc.org/sites/default/files/cafos-dont-know-hurting-us-report.pdf.
20. Farm Sanctuary. "The Farm System Reform Act." March 1, 2023. https://www.farmsanctuary.org/news-stories/fsra-good-news/.
21. Klein, Ezra. "Farmers and Animal Rights Activists Are Coming Together to Fight Big Factory Farms." *Vox*, July 8, 2020. https://www.vox.com/future-perfect/2020/7/8/21311327/farmers-factory-farms-cafos-animal-rights-booker-warren-khanna.
22. Cigna Healthcare. "African American/Black Health Disparities." Accessed September 29, 2023. https://www.cigna.com/health-care-providers/resources/african-american-black-health-disparities; Percival, Amy. "Brooklyn's Borough President Just Shut Down the Meat Industry." Live Kindly, accessed September 29, 2023. https://www.livekindly.com/politician-just-put-meat-industry-on-notice/; The New York City Council. File #Res 0238-2018. March 22, 2018. https://legistar.council.nyc.gov/LegislationDetail.aspx?ID=3458218&GUID=E2D39627-1649-42BB-AF90-A7E364FE5329; Physicians Committee for Responsible Medicine. "New York City Schools Ban Processed Meat!" September 26, 2019. https://www.pcrm.org/news/blog/new-york-city-schools-ban-processed-meat.
23. Brooklyn Borough President Antonio Reynoso. "One Brooklyn—PSA: 42 Doctors of Color: Keepin' It Real." YouTube video, May 7, 2020. https://www.youtube.com/watch?v=VenMeA-EJ2I&feature=youtu.be; NYC Health + Hospitals. "NYC Health + Hospitals/Bellevue and Brooklyn Borough President Eric L. Adams Announce January Launch of Plant-Based Diet Program." December 18, 2018. https://www.nychealthandhospitals.org/pressrelease/plant-based-lifestyle-medicine-program-launches-on-january-16/#:~:text=NYC%20Health%20%2B%20Hospitals%2FBellevue%20announced,with%20more%20enrollees%20every%20day.
24. Oscar's Law. Accessed September 29, 2023. https://www.oscarslaw.org/.

25. Government of Western Australia: Department of Local Government, Sport and Cultural Industries. "Landmark Stop Puppy Farming Legislation Passes WA Parliament." December 16, 2021. https://www.dlgsc.wa.gov.au/department/news/news-article/2021/12/16/landmark-stop-puppy-farming-legislation-passes-wa-parliament.
26. Mays, Jeffery C., and Amelia Nierenberg. "Foie Gras, Served in 1,000 Restaurants in New York City, Banned." *The New York Times*, updated July 17, 2021. https://www.nytimes.com/2019/10/30/nyregion/foie-gras-ban-nyc.html.
27. Verley, Angus, Lydia Burton, Lara Webster, et al. "Mandatory Pain Relief for Mulesing in Victoria Looks Set to Become a Reality." *ABC News*, July 15, 2019. https://www.abc.net.au/news/rural/2019-07-16/mandatory-mulesing-pain-relief-in-victoria/11312596.
28. The Humane Society of the United States. "Cosmetics Animal Testing FAQ." Accessed September 29, 2023. https://www.humanesociety.org/resources/cosmetics-animal-testing-faq.
29. The Humane Society of the United States. "Timeline: Cosmetics Testing on Animals." Accessed September 29, 2023. https://www.humanesociety.org/resources/timeline-cosmetics-testing-animals.
30. Kotzmann, Jane. "ACT's New Animal Sentience Law Recognises an Animal's Psychological Pain and Pleasure, and May Lead to Better Protections." *The Conversation*, October 3, 2019. https://theconversation.com/acts-new-animal-sentience-law-recognises-an-animals-psychological-pain-and-pleasure-and-may-lead-to-better-protections-124577.
31. Australian Capital Territory. "Animal Welfare Act 1992." February 22, 2023. https://www.legislation.act.gov.au/View/a/1992-45/current/PDF/1992-45.PDF.
32. Animal Legal & Historical Center. "Animal Welfare Act." October 2010. https://www.animallaw.info/statute/germany-cruelty-german-animal-welfare-act; Stephens, Thomas. "Fact Check: Lonely Guinea Pigs and Other Quirky Swiss Rumors." Swissinfo, July 4, 2019. https://www.swissinfo.ch/eng/loo-flushing-- explosives---gold_fact-check--lonely-guinea-pigs-and-other-quirky-swiss-rumours/45067078; Swiss Federal Council. "Animal Welfare Act of 16 December 2005 (AniWA)." Accessed September 29, 2023. https://www.fedlex.admin.ch/eli/cc/2008/414/en.
33. International Whaling Commission. "Commercial Whaling." Accessed September 29, 2023. https://iwc.int/commercial.
34. Garnett, Tara, Cécile Godde, Adrian Muller, et al. "Grazed and Confused?" Food Climate Research Network, 2017. https://www.oxfordmartin.ox.ac.uk/downloads/reports/fcrn_gnc_report.pdf; Ketcham, Christopher. "Allan Savory's Holistic Management Theory Falls Short on Science." *Sierra*, February 23, 2017. https://www.sierraclub.org/sierra/2017-2-march-april/feature/allan-savory-says-more-cows-land-will-reverse-climate-change; Nordborg, Maria. "Holistic Management—A Critical Review of Allan Savory's Grazing Method." SLU/EPOK—Centre for Organic Food & Farming &

Chalmers, 2016. https://publications.lib.chalmers.se/records/fulltext/244566/local_244566.pdf; Roberts, Spencer. "How Big Ag Bankrolled Regenerative Ranching." *Jacobin*, March 5, 2022. https://jacobin.com/2022/03/big-agriculture-funding-regenerative-ranching-amp-grazing-soil-carbon/.

35. Hayek, Matthew N., Helen Harwatt, William J. Ripple, et al. "The Carbon Opportunity Cost of Animal-Sourced Food Production on Land." *Nature Sustainability* 4 (2021): 21–4. https://doi.org/10.1038/s41893-020-00603-4.
36. Ritchie, Hannah. "If the World Adopted a Plant-Based Diet We Would Reduce Global Agricultural Land Use From 4 to 1 Billion Hectares." Our World in Data, March 4, 2021. https://ourworldindata.org/land-use-diets.
37. Schirmer, Jacki, and Melinda R. Mylek. "People and Communities: The 2014 Regional Wellbeing Survey." University of Canberra, June 2015. https://www.researchgate.net/publication/304541310_People_and_Communities_The_2014_Regional_Wellbeing_Survey_University_of_Canberra_Canberra.
38. *ABC News*. "Video: Breaking New Ground." Updated January 12, 2022. https://www.abc.net.au/austory/breaking-new-ground/12697330.
39. Humane Society International. "EU Must Help Animal Farmers Transition to Plant-Crop Farming to Benefit from Plant-Based Boom, Experts Tell MEPs." March 6, 2019. https://www.hsi.org/news-media/eu-plant-crop-farming-031119/; Carrington, Damian. "Nearly All Global Farm Subsidies Harm People and Planet—UN." *The Guardian*, September 14, 2021. https://www.theguardian.com/environment/2021/sep/14/global-farm-subsidies-damage-people-planet-un-climate-crisis-nature-inequality; Springmann, M., and F. Freund. "Options for Reforming Agricultural Subsidies from Health, Climate, and Economic Perspectives." *Nature Communications* 13 (2022). https://doi.org/10.1038/s41467-021-27645-2.
40. Parliament of Victoria. "Inquiry into the Impact of Animal Rights Activism on Victorian Agriculture." February 2020. https://new.parliament.vic.gov.au/4a49cb/contentassets/184245b7cfef487b9e24cfd01302f172/inquiry-into-the-impact-of-animal-activisim-on-victorian-agriculture.pdf.
41. Agriculture Fairness Alliance. "AFA Legislation." Accessed September 29, 2023. https://agriculturefairnessalliance.org/legislation/.
42. Plumer, Brad, and Nadja Popovich. "These Countries Have Prices on Carbon. Are They Working?" *The New York Times*, April 2, 2019. https://www.nytimes.com/interactive/2019/04/02/climate/pricing-carbon-emissions.html.
43. Carrington, Damian. "$1m a Minute: The Farming Subsidies Destroying the World—Report." *The Guardian*, September 16, 2019. https://www.theguardian.com/environment/2019/sep/16/1m-a-minute-the-farming-subsidies-destroying-the-world.
44. Springmann, Marco, H. Charles J. Godfray, Mike Rayner, et al. "Analysis and Valuation of the Health and Climate Change Cobenefits of Dietary Change." *PNAS* 113, no. 15 (2016): 4146–51. https://doi.org/10.1073/pnas.1523119113.

45. Harwatt, Helen, and Matthew N. Hayek. "Eating Away at Climate Change with Negative Emissions." Harvard Law School, April 11, 2019. https://animal.law.harvard.edu/wp-content/uploads/Eating-Away-at-Climate-Change-with-Negative-Emissions%E2%80%93%E2%80%93Harwatt-Hayek.pdf.
46. Pascoe, Bruce. *Dark Emu.* Broome, Australia: Magabala Books Aboriginal Corporation, 2014.
47. Deadly Story. "Food and Agriculture." Accessed September 29, 2023. https://deadlystory.com/page/culture/Life_Lore/Food.
48. Humane Society International. "EU Must Help Animal Farmers Transition to Plant-Crop Farming to Benefit from Plant-Based Boom, Experts Tell MEPs." March 6, 2019. https://www.hsi.org/news-media/eu-plant-crop-farming-031119/.

Chapter 12: Innovative, Organizational, and Grassroots Change

1. Nagesh, Ashitha. "Confessions of a Slaughterhouse Worker." *BBC News*, January 6, 2020. https://www.bbc.com/news/stories-50986683.
2. Runkle, Nathan, and Gene Stone. *Mercy For Animals.* New York: Avery, 2017.
3. Chuck, Elizabeth. "Poultry Workers, Denied Bathroom Breaks, Wear Diapers: Oxfam Report." *NBC News*, May 12, 2016. https://www.nbcnews.com/business/business-news/poultry-workers-denied-bathroom-breaks-wear-diapers-oxfam-report-n572806.
4. Garcés, Leah. *Grilled: Turning Adversaries into Allies to Change the Chicken Meat Industry.* London: Bloomsbury Sigma, 2019.
5. Ibid; Food Integrity Campaign. "Whistleblower Profile: Craig Watts." Accessed September 29, 2023. https://foodwhistleblower.org/profile/craig-watts/.
6. Reynolds, Matt. "The Clean Meat Industry Is Racing to Ditch Its Reliance on Foetal Blood." *Wired*, March 20, 2018. https://www.wired.co.uk/article/scaling-clean-meat-serum-just-finless-foods-mosa-meat.
7. Juntti, Melaina. "Miyoko's Kitchen Chef Creates Cheese That's Better for People and the Planet." New Hope Network, August 27, 2018. https://www.newhope.com/people-and-company-profiles/miyoko-s-kitchen-chef-creates-cheese-s-better-people-and-planet.
8. Ibid.
9. Ibid.
10. Levitt, Tom. "Why Some Farmers Are Ditching Livestock and Growing Plants Instead." *HuffPost*, updated August 20, 2020. https://www.huffingtonpost.com.au/entry/why-farmers-ditching-livestock-growing-plants_n_5e9620b8c5b6a4470cb77646?ri18n=true.
11. Hijosa, Carmen. "The Story of How I Reinvented a Material and the Fruit That Changed My Life." TED: Ideas Worth Spreading, September 2017. https://www.ted.com/talks/carmen_hijosa_la_historia_de_como_reinvente_un_material_y_la_fruta_que_cambio_mi_vida?language=en.

12. Ibid; Motlagh, Jason. "Hell for Leather: Bangladesh's Toxic Tanneries Ravage Lives and Environment." *Time*, updated November 13, 2013. https://world.time.com/2013/09/03/hell-for-leather-bangladeshs-toxic-tanneries-ravage-lives-and-environment/.
13. Hijosa, Carmen. "The Story of How I Reinvented a Material and the Fruit That Changed My Life." TED: Ideas Worth Spreading, September 2017. https://www.ted.com/talks/carmen_hijosa_la_historia_de_como_reinvente_un_material_y_la_fruta_que_cambio_mi_vida?language=en.
14. Blodgett, Sequoia. "22-Year-Old Builds Affordable Vegan Spot in Brooklyn." Black Enterprise, November 5, 2018. https://www.blackenterprise.com/meet-the-22-year-old-girl-boss-behind-sol-sips-an-affordable-vegan-spot-in-brooklyn/; "Bushwick BK04." NYU Furman Center. Accessed September 29, 2023. https://furmancenter.org/neighborhoods/view/bushwick.
15. Meyersohn, Nathaniel. "How the Rise of Supermarkets Left Out Black America." *CNN Business*, updated June 16, 2020. https://edition.cnn.com/2020/06/16/business/grocery-stores-access-race-inequality/index.html; Teaching Tolerance. "Food Desert Statistics." Accessed September 29, 2023. https://www.learningforjustice.org/sites/default/files/general/desert%20stats.pdf; Food Empowerment Project. "Access to Healthy Food." Accessed September 29, 2023. https://foodispower.org/access-to-healthy-food/.
16. Davy, Deanna. "Australia's Efforts to Improve Food Security for Aboriginal and Torres Strait Islander Peoples." *Health and Human Rights Journal* 18, no. 2 (2016): 209–18. https://www.ncbi.nlm.nih.gov/pmc/articles/PMC5394999/.
17. Hungry For Justice Productions. "They're Trying to Kill Us Official Trailer." YouTube video, 2:34, June 18, 2020. https://www.youtube.com/watch?v=BSrUnhxUazA.
18. Food Empowerment Project. "Our Work." Accessed September 29, 2023. https://foodispower.org/our-work/.
19. White, Monica M. "Sisters of the Soil: Urban Gardening as Resistance in Detroit." *Race/Ethnicity: Multidisciplinary Global Contexts* 5, no. 1 (2011): 13–28. http://www.jstor.org/stable/10.2979/racethmulglocon.5.1.13; Paynter, Kevon. "Black Farmers Reviving Their African Roots: 'We Are Feeding Our Liberation.'" Civil Eats, April 5, 2018. https://civileats.com/2018/04/05/black-farmers-reviving-their-african-roots-we-are-feeding-our-liberation/.
20. Woke Foods. Accessed September 29, 2023. https://wokefoods.coop/.
21. Democracy Now! "Glenn Greenwald Unveils New Project to Build Animal Shelter in Brazil Staffed by Homeless People." YouTube video, 7:46, May 10, 2017. https://www.youtube.com/watch?v=QSDdYcWquiA.
22. Ko, Aph, and Syl Ko. *Aphro-ism: Essays on Pop Culture, Feminism, and Black Veganism from Two Sisters.* New York: Lantern Publishing & Media, 2017.
23. Krantz, Rachel. "Advocating for Food Justice During a Pandemic: Lauren Ornelas Speaks Out." *Sentient Media*, June 3, 2020. https://sentientmedia.org/advocating-for-food-justice-during-a-pandemic-lauren-ornelas-speaks-out/.
24. Frerie, Paulo. *Pedagogy of the Oppressed.* New York: Continuum, 2005.

25. Outman, Nicole. "Women Portrayed as Animals/Beasts." Ferris State University, 2014. https://www.ferris.edu/moso/objectification/womenasanimals/index.htm.
26. Frerie, Paulo. *Pedagogy of the Oppressed.* New York: Continuum, 2005.
27. Agents of Liberation, @agents_of_liberation. "25th June 2020, Switzerland." Instagram, June 28, 2020. https://www.instagram.com/p/CB_VjvTJv6U/.
28. Frerie, Paulo. *Pedagogy of the Oppressed.* New York: Continuum, 2005.

Epilogue: Individual Change, A Call to Arms

1. Morales, Aurora Levins. *Medicine Stories: Essays for Radicals.* London: Duke University Press, 2019.
2. Adams, Carol J. *The Sexual Politics of Meat: A Feminist-Vegetarian Critical Theory.* London: Continuum, 1990.
3. Reilly, Katie. "Read Elie Wiesel's Nobel Peace Prize Acceptance Speech." *Time,* July 2, 2016. https://time.com/4392267/elie-wiesel-dead-nobel-peace-prize-speech/.

About the Author

Emma Hakansson is a dedicated advocate working to upheave oppression facing our fellow animals, children, women, and working people. As the author of *How Veganism Can Save Us*, Hakansson has lectured internationally on ethics and sustainability, and her work and words have been featured in *The Guardian*, *Forbes*, *Earth Island Journal*, *Sentient Media*, and many other publications.

About the Publisher

Lantern Publishing & Media was founded in 2020 to follow and expand on the legacy of Lantern Books—a publishing company started in 1999 on the principles of living with a greater depth and commitment to the preservation of the natural world. Like its predecessor, Lantern Publishing & Media produces books on animal advocacy, veganism, religion, social justice, humane education, psychology, family therapy, and recovery. Lantern is dedicated to printing in the United States on recycled paper and saving resources in our day-to-day operations. Our titles are also available as ebooks and audiobooks.

To catch up on Lantern's publishing program, visit us at www.lanternpm.org.

facebook.com/lanternpm
twitter.com/lanternpm
instagram.com/lanternpm